An Elfin Book of Trees for the Elven Druid

The Ogham of the Elves
Using Elvish Wizard Script

The Silver Elves

Copyright © 2019 The Silver Elves, Michael J Love and Martha C. Love
All rights reserved.

ISBN: 9781710655704

Printed in the United States of America by AmazonKindle Direct

Without limiting the rights under the copyright reserved above, no part of this publication may be reproduced, stored in or introduced into a retrieval system, or transmitted in any form or by any means (electronic, mechanical, by photocopying, recording or otherwise) without the prior written permission of the copyright owner and the publisher of the book.

DEDICATION

This book is dedicated to our cousins, the trees, whom we elves so dearly love.

"Elfin is like the morning mist nestled among the trees arousing an atavistic sense of mystery and wonder."
—The Silver Elves. . . . .

Group 1 of the Wizard Myne: Letters used in Arvyndase

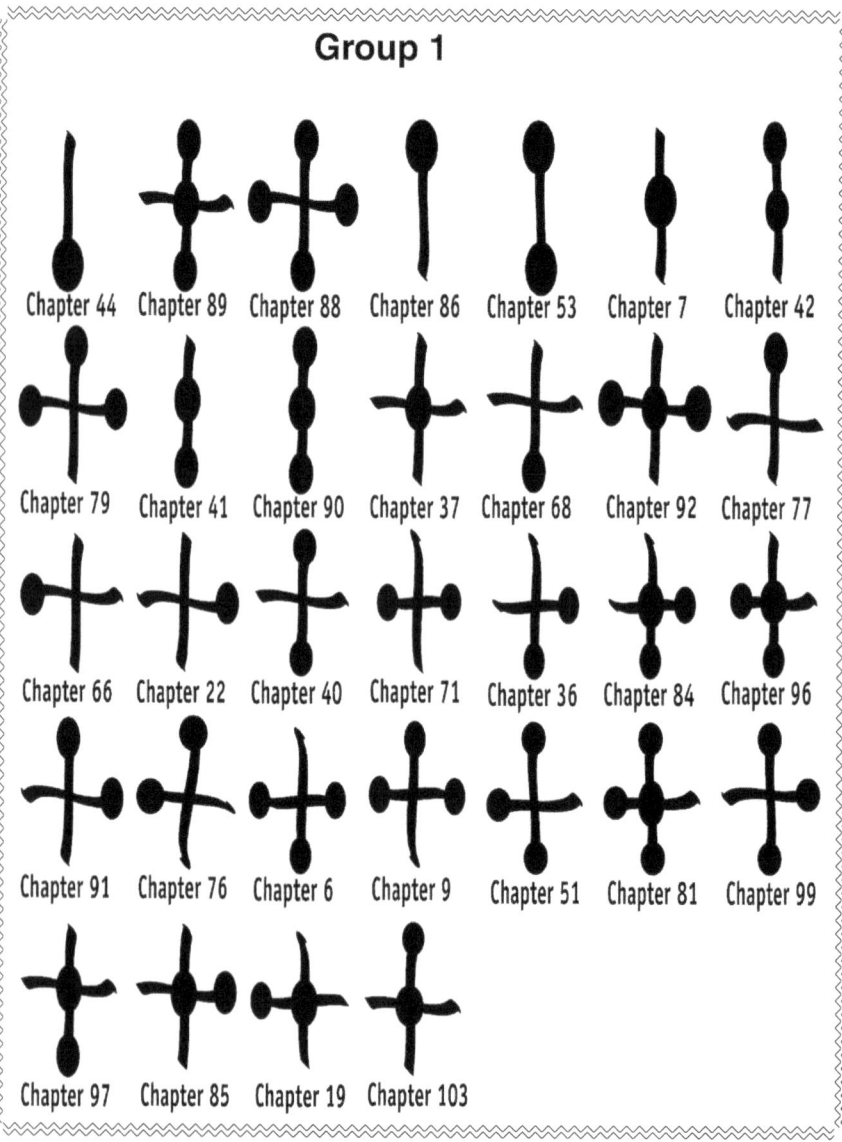

Group 2 of the Wizard Myne: Numbers

Group 2

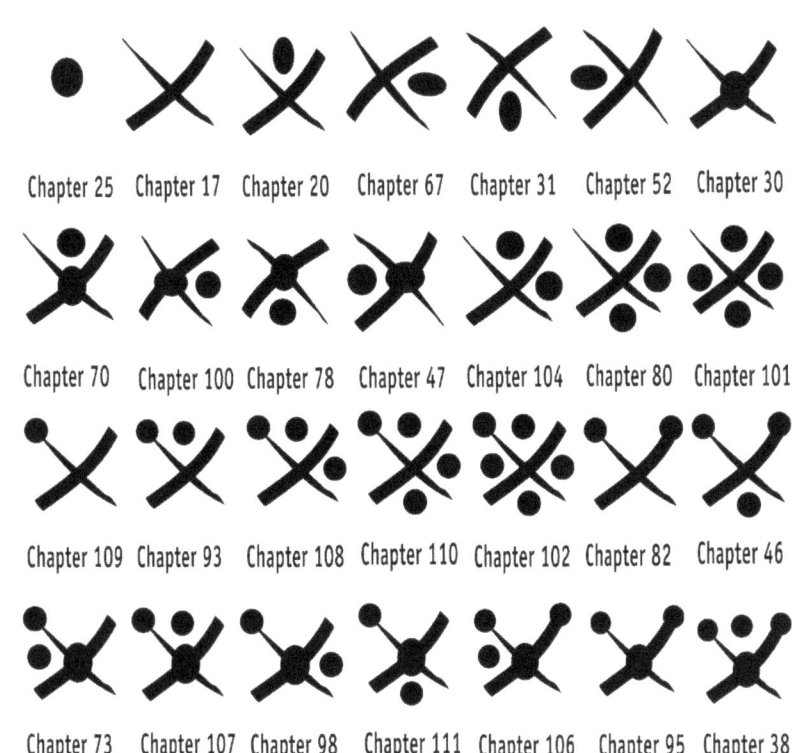

Group 3 of the Wizard Myne:
Elfae Types

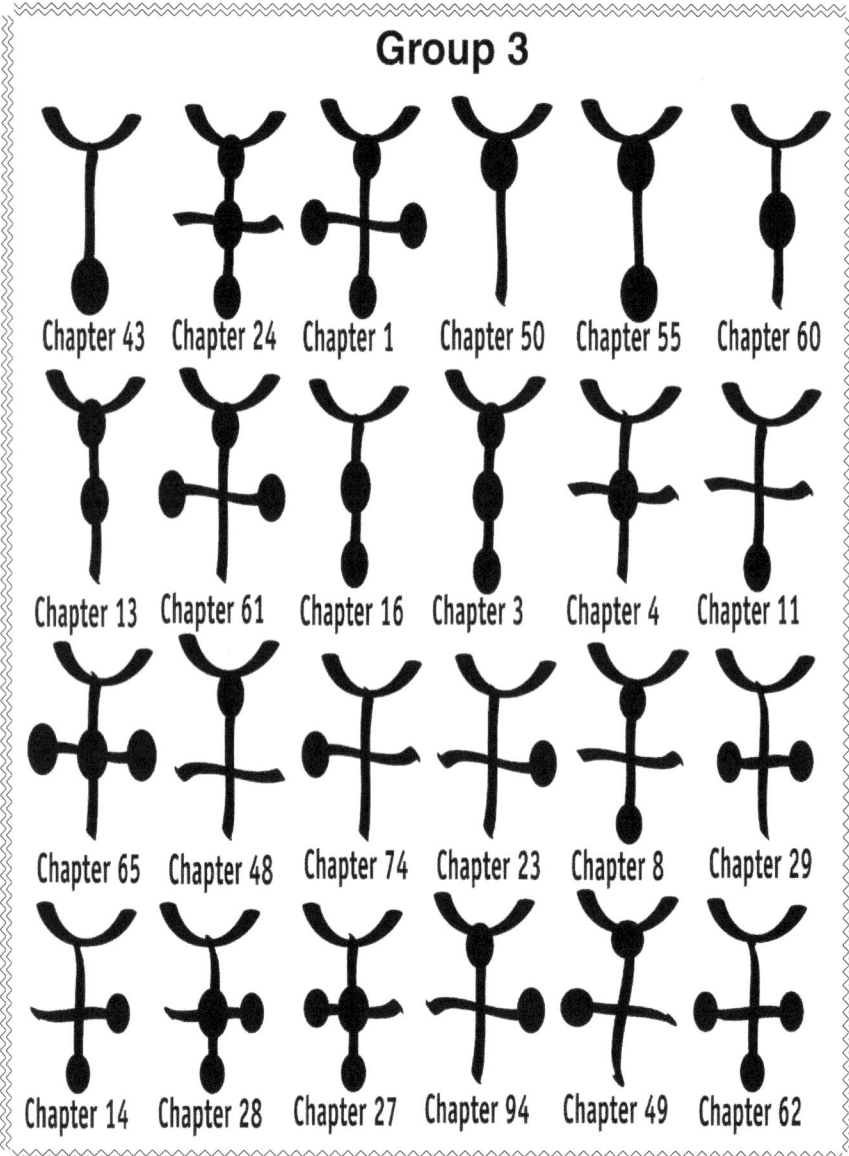

Group 4 of the Wizard Myne: Miscelaneous Magics

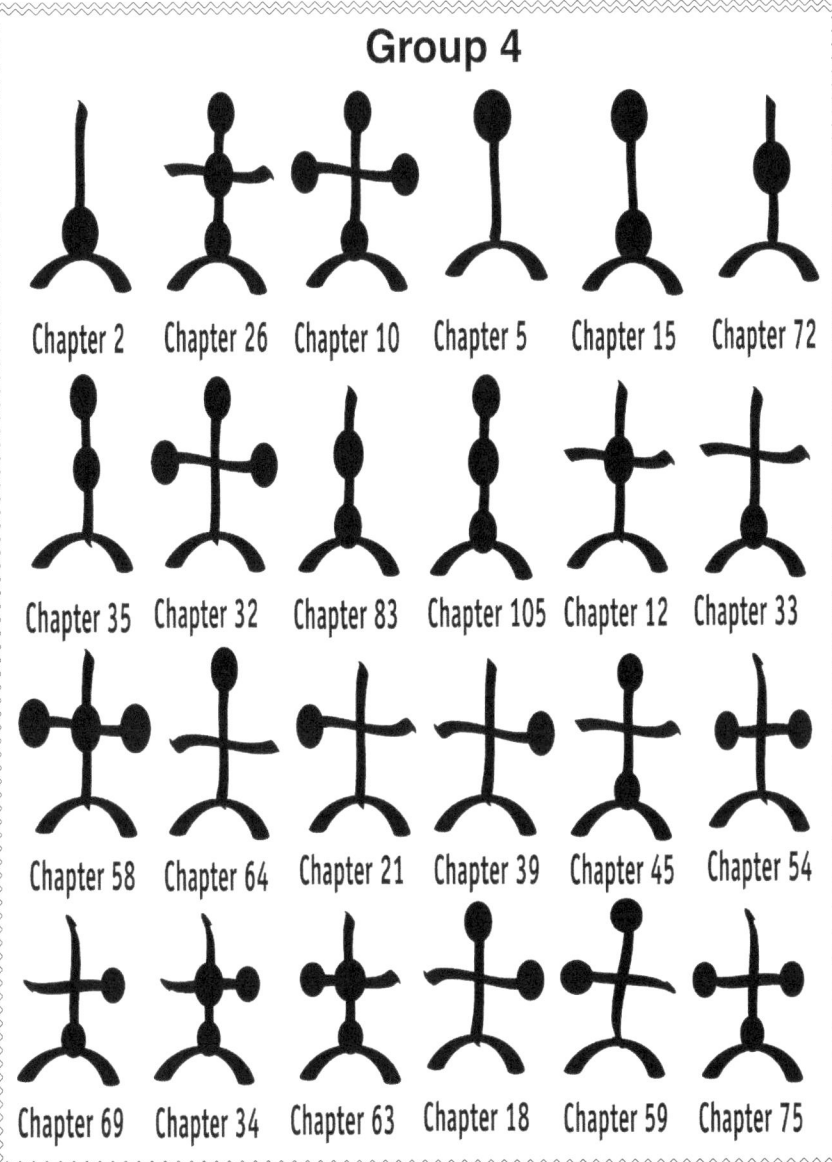

"To enter Elfin, one must bare one's soul and run naked in the light of the elven stars and under the steady gaze of the trees eternal."

—The Wisdom of the Eldars

Table of Contents

Introduction 21
   An Elven Book of Trees 21
   Wizard Script and the Ogham 23
   Elven Druids 23
   Divination 25
   Keywords 27

Chapter 1:
Elderberry 28
Chapter 2:
   Sweetgum 30
Chapter 3:
   Cashew 33
Chapter 4:
   Mango 35
Chapter 5:
   Pistachio 37
Chapter 6:
   Sumac 40
Chapter 7:
   Lacquer tree 42

Chapter 8:
> **Dogbane family** 45

Chapter 9:
> **Holly family** 48

Chapter 10:
> **Kalopanax** 51

Chapter 11:
> **Schefflera** 53

Chapter 12:
> **Alder** 56

Chapter 13:
> **Birch** 59

Chapter 14:
> **Hornbeam** 62

Chapter 15:
> **Hazel** 64

Chapter 16:
> **Tabebuia** 67

Chapter 17:
> **Saguaro** 70

Chapter 18:
> **Hackberry** 73

Chapter 19:
> **Dogwood family** 76

Chapter 20:
> **Dipterocarpaceae Family** 79

Chapter 21:
 Persimmon family 82

Chapter 22:
 Heath family 85

Chapter 23:
 Eucommia family 88

Chapter 24:
 Acacia 91

Chapter 25:
 Orchid tree 94

Chapter 26:
 Brazilwood 97

Chapter 27:
 Honey locust 99

Chapter 28:
 Laburnum 102

Chapter 29:
 Black Locust 105

Chapter 30:
 Chestnut 108

Chapter 31:
 Beech 111

Chapter 32:
 Tanoak 113

Chapter 33:
 Oak 115

Chapter 34:
   Boojum family 118
Chapter 35:
   Persian Ironwood 121
Chapter 36:
   Hickory 123
Chapter 37:
   Walnut 126
Chapter 38:
   Wingnut 128
Chapter 39:
   Brazil Nut 131
Chapter 40:
   Crapemyrtle 133
Chapter 41:
   Mallow family 136
Chapter 42:
   Mahogany family 138
Chapter 43:
   Fig and Banyan 141
Chapter 44:
   Mulberry 143
Chapter 45:
   Eucalyptus 146
Chapter 46:
   Myrtle 148

Chapter 47:
> **Guava** **151**

Chapter 48:
> **Southern Beech family** **153**

Chapter 49:
> **Tupelo family** **156**

Chapter 50:
> **Ash** **158**

Chapter 51:
> **Olive** **161**

Chapter 52:
> **Foxglove** **163**

Chapter 53:
> **Plane** **166**

Chapter 54:
> **Mangrove family** **168**

Chapter 55:
> **Hawthorn** **171**

PHOTOS:

*Some Photos of The Silver Elves with
Our Favorite Tree and Plant Cousins* 174

    Heliconia mariae in Caines Botanical Gardens;
    Caines, Australia... 174

    Metrosideros excelsa in Davenport, New Zealand,
    a coastal everygreen tree in the myrtle family. 175

    Banyan Tree (just one tree),
    related to the Ficus benghalensis... 176

    Waimea Botanical Gardens
    on the North Shore, Oahu, Hawaii.. 177

    Zardoa attuning to the energy of the forest at 9 Oak Farm,
    Monroe, Georgia. 178

    At 9 Oak Farm, Silver Flame finds a special magical oak
    friend! 179

Chapter 56:
    Apple 180

Chapter 57:
    Prunus: Almond, Peach, Apricot, Plums, Cherries 182

Chapter 58:
    Pear 185

Chapter 59:
    Sorbus: Rowans, Whitebeams 187

Chapter 60:
    Bedstraw family or Coffea 190

Chapter 61:
>   **Rue family** 192

Chapter 62:
>   **Willow family** 195

Chapter 63:
>   **Maple** 197

Chapter 64:
>   **Aesculus: Buckeye, Horse-chestnut** 199

Chapter 65:
>   **Golden rain tree** 202

Chapter 66:
>   **Lychee** 204

Chapter 67:
>   **Mexican Buckeye** 207

Chapter 68:
>   **Sapodilla family** 209

Chapter 69:
>   **Tree of heaven** 211

Chapter 70:
>   **Camellia family** 213

Chapter 71:
>   **Thymelaea family** 216

Chapter 72:
>   **Elm family** 218

Chapter 73:
>   **Cabbage tree** 221

Chapter 74:
> Dragon tree 223

Chapter 75:
> Joshua tree 226

Chapter 76:
> Palm family 228

Chapter 77:
> Bamboo family 231

Chapter 78:
> Annona family 233

Chapter 79:
> American Pawpaw 236

Chapter 80:
> Cinnamon 238

Chapter 81:
> Bay Laurel 240

Chapter 82:
> Avocado 243

Chapter 83:
> Sassafras 245

Chapter 84:
> Tulip tree 247

Chapter 85:
> Magnolia 249

Chapter 86:
> Nutmeg family 252

Chapter 87:
> **Araucaria family** 254

Chapter 88:
> **Chamaecyparis** 256

Chapter 89:
> **Cryptomeria japonica, Sugi** 258

Chapter 90:
> **Cupressus** 261

Chapter 91:
> **Fitzroya cupressoides** 263

Chapter 92:
> **Juniper** 265

Chapter 93:
> **Dawn Redwood** 267

Chapter 94:
> **Coast Redwood** 270

Chapter 95:
> **Giant Sequoia** 272

Chapter 96:
> **Bald Cypress** 274

Chapter 97:
> **Western Red cedar** 276

Chapter 98:
> **Fir** 278

Chapter 99:
> **Cedar** 280

Chapter 100:
- Larch 283

Chapter 101:
- Spruce 285

Chapter 102:
- Pine 287

Chapter 103:
- Douglas-fir 289

Chapter 104:
- Yellowwood family 292

Chapter 105:
- Yew family 294

Chapter 106:
- Ginkgo family 296

Chapter 107:
- Cycad family 298

Chapter 108:
- Zamia family 300

Chapter 109:
- Fern trees 303

Chapter 110:
- Kusamaki 305

Chapter 111:
- Wattieza, fossil tree, the earliest known tree 307

About the Authors *311*

THE WIZARD MYNES (Group Images):

Group 1 of the Wizard Myne: 316

Letters used in Arvyndase 316

Group 2 of the Wizard Myne: 317

Numbers 317

Group 3 of the Wizard Myne: 318

Elfae Types 318

Group 4 of the Wizard Myne: 319

Miscelaneous Magics 319

"If you have never been to Elfin, it is hard to understand, the magic that abides there and permeates the land, that from the trees does radiate like star light from within, enchantment woven from true love vast wonders to portent."

—Ancient Elven Knowledge

Introduction

An Elven Book of Trees

We have always loved, from the first moment we encountered them, the trees and therefore admired, from first we heard of it, the relationship of the Druids to the trees. Being Silver Elves — Elves of Starlight, Moonlight and the Radiance of the Trees — we naturally feel an affinity for nearly anyone else who also loves trees. And the Druids, being seers, bards and magic wielders, especially found a place in our hearts, minds and souls for their deep love and connection to the trees and to the spirit world.

We are also genuinely fond of Liz and Colin Murray's *The Celtic Tree Oracle* and even though some people find Robert Graves's book *The White Goddess* and its interpretation of the Language or Alphabet of the Trees to be spurious, we found great insight in it, although we accepted from the beginning that it was a theoretical interpretation and not necessarily a factual representation of the Druids and their Ogham Script and their Alphabet (Ælfabet) of the Trees. After all, the Druids had an oral tradition. They didn't write anything down as far as their teachings, beliefs, tales, myths and history until they became Christianized (those that survived the Romans), and almost everything we know about them comes, for the most part, from their contemporaries, the Romans, and from the archeologists of today who, for their own part, are doing a bit of educated theorizing about the Druids just as the Romans did (although, hopefully, with less bias).

There are only twenty-five letters in the Druid tree alphabet, associated with letters of the English language, but obviously connected previously with various Celtic dialects and languages. That has always seemed too few trees to us. We realized that the Druids, surely, were dealing with the major types of trees in their vicinity, the British Isles, parts of France and Spain and mostly Southern Europe, where they lived and this is certainly understandable. We each tend to speak of and deal with the world that we know.

We, being elves, however, see the whole world as our ancestral lands, and quite frankly there are certain types of trees, which we love and adore, that just weren't represented in the Tree world of the Druids, but which are decidedly part of our own Elven understanding of the world of the trees. The Banyan tree is one of these, one that we truly adore, although there are others. You could say that we woodland elves are tree worshipers; however, this is surely not the case in a religious sense but in the sense of pure absolute love and adoration for the wonder of the trees who have a power of enchantment that is all their own. Some trees are wise beyond our understanding and provide enlightenment and illumination to those who are open to their wisdom.

At the same time, there are over 60,000 species of trees in the world, so dealing with every species seemed a bit more than we wished to take on. Although, we wouldn't mind doing so in a future lifetime. It would be rather like when we created, channeled, remembered, whatever you will, our Silver Elf language of Arvyndase (see *Arvyndase (SilverSpeech): A Short Course in the Magical Language of the Silver Elves* and *The Complete Dictionary of Arvyndase*), which took us over a decade to complete. So, we decided instead to deal with the basic types and families of trees, which gave us 111 possibilities overall and this seemed perfect and doable to our elven minds. In some cases, we picked a whole tree family to be represented by a Wizard Myne (we decided we should call these runes as Wizard Many-s [spelled Mynes in Arvyndase] instead of Ogham Fews) and at other times we selected individual trees. And so, in this way, we have created, channeled, remembered *The Elven Book of Trees* and expanded our Wizard Script to go with it.

Also, please note that the system we used for tree families and their associations is one of a number of possibilities and not all scientists agree about what tree is in what tree family or is related to what other trees, or even how trees should be categorized in the first place. Additionally, scientists often just change their minds about these things. We simply picked the system that worked best for us.

Wizard Script and the Ogham

We Silver Elves love scripts, magical scripts especially, but all sorts of scripts. We are particularly fond of the Tibetan alphabet and also Arabian script, both of which look a bit like tribal tattoos to us. We also love The Alphabet of the Magi, Angelic, also known as Celestial, Enochian, Malachim, Passing the River, Theban and the Ogham Fews (letters) of the Celtic tribes and their Druids. We have even made up our own elven scripts for Arvyndase that can be found in our book of that title and Wizard script, which is our version of the Ogham, the script of the Elven Wizards and Elven Druids.

We had originally created Wizard Script as letters associated, along with the Arvyn and Sylvyn scripts, with our own elven language and the twenty-five letters of the Arvyndase language (there is no X in Arvyndase, the sound X makes is either a Z sound at the beginning of a word or a KS sound within a word or at its end). However, in creating *The Elven Book of Trees*, we realized that we needed a lot more Wizard Script letters than we had originally created, but thankfully found that Wizard Script lent itself easily and naturally to their creation.

Further, we very much admire the look of the Ogham Fews that we have seen in photos of ancient carved stones and in modern times on sticks of wood, short branches that have had a side shaved off with a word spelled using Ogham upon it. We hope that our elven kindred will find Elven Wizard script Mynes as magical as the Ogham Fews and that they will delight in it as we delight in almost every script.

By the way, we still play with new scripts and letters from time to time, and hope to make up more in the future. But for now, let's proceed with the Elven script of the Wizards and of the Elven Druids.

Elven Druids

Some people seem to think that Druids and Elves are mutually exclusive. That notion, to us elves, is like thinking that being a doctor and being an artist is a contradiction. We elves are many things and we do, practice and study magic in nearly every form that we find it. There are elven witches, sorcerers, wizards, magicians and certainly elven druids. Also, surely, elven scientists, also elfae auto-mechanics and computer technicians, although probably more of the latter than the former, but none of these practices are actually incompatible. And we elves are not inclined to limit ours'elves or others, for the most part, but to expand our understanding of things and the possibilities of existence as much as we can possibly do so.

Surely, the Druids of olde knew and associated with the Sidhe, the Elfae, Elfin, Faerie folk of that time and we expect if you could ask them, or even inquire of Druid folk of the present day, if they know of and have learned anything from the Fair Folk, the vast majority would say that indeed they do, have and did. In fact, there are some folks that think that the Druids were originally elven folk who taught their mystical and magic knowledge to men. However, it should be taken into consideration that we elven folk are not primarily teachers of any sort or any particular discipline, although we've done a bit of teaching here and there, now and again, but rather we are, for the most part, as our contemporaries have observed from time to time, perpetual students and learners.

Were the original Druids actually Elfae folk? Possibly. Did they learn from the Elven folk? Surely, yes. But it is certainly also true that we Elven folk learned from the non-Elfae Druids as well, perhaps even more than they learned from us, for that truly is our way. We learn from everyone, as best we may, from the foolish as well as the wise, although the lessons the foolish teach are mostly about what to avoid. However, we elves and elfae folk seek inspiration everywhere.

Still, we are especially fond of those who meet in groves and love the trees and the wisdom of the trees as much as we do, as did and do the Druids, elven and otherkin, man and woman and others but probably not the normal folk in any sense of the word. They don't seem to regard the trees as anything more than property to dispose of as they will.

And we have no doubt that really, the knowledge of the Druids, both Elfae and other, and the knowledge of we Elven Wood Folk concerning the trees and much else, came from the same original source, which is to say from the Trees themselves. For surely, they are the great teachers, ancient, wise and often deep in meditation.

Divination

This book can be used as an oracle. Perhaps, that is its chief purpose. That is up to you, really. For our own part in writing it, we learned a great deal about the tree families of the world and for us that was wonderful. We love trees. Not that we'll remember it all or even most of it. But a passing acquaintance is nice. This book is a way, in a sense, of listening to the trees. It is not the same as being out in the trees and feeling their radiant and wondrous presence, nor ingesting some of the herbs that plants and trees use to enlighten us. However, not all of us, in the modern world, can be among the trees regularly or as much as we would like and this tome is, in that sense, designed to express their voice in the form of an oracle for those of us who are unable at present to spend a great deal of time among them. Although, in our hearts and imaginations, we are ever surrounded by the forest. And in that sense, this book is a forest, an elven woodland, an elvish glade, a living book of tree lore.

At the same time, we Silver Elves are not a mainstream production. You are not going to find a box set containing this book and a Wizard Mynes (plural) set for divination anytime soon, if ever. Rather, if you wish to use this as an oracle of the trees, other than by bibliomancy, which is the process of opening a book to a random page to see what it says for you, you will have to create your own set of Wizard Mynes, (unless you can get someone else to do it for you). But really, in a magical sense, making your own is the best way to create your Mynes for this oracle, for the Mynes will then be filled with your personal energy, power and enchantment, which will make your divination that much stronger and much more attuned to you, your magic and your psyche as well as to the trees.

It occurs to us that there are three basic ways to create your own Wizard Mynes (pronounced men - knees or many-s). The first two involve using either popsicle-like sticks (which, if you don't wish to eat at least 111 popsicles, you can get in bunches from craft stores) or you can gather twigs or small branches of the same girth and cut them to a similar length, shave off one side or cut them into two and put the Wizards Mynes upon them. Just go through the book and on one side of each stick, draw the Wizards Myne that corresponds to each particular tree group and on the other side, write the corresponding chapter number for that tree group and the tree group name. For instance, for the first stick, "chapter one — Elderberry" would be written on one side and the symbol or Wizards Myne would be drawn on the other side. The second stick would be: "chapter two — Sweetgum" on one side and the corresponding Wizards Myne on the other.

The nice thing about using popsicle sticks is their uniformity, so you can reach into a bag, or wherever you will keep them, and not be able to tell by feel which stick is which, so that your choice is truly random. On the other hand, the twigs and branches with the Wizard Mynes on them are just cool to look at. Style and beauty go a long way with we who are elven. The Mynes on branches feel magical in a way that popsicle sticks usually do not. And while there surely will be some variations in their size and feel, there are so many Wizard Mynes that this may not be a significant issue.

The third way to make these Wizard Mynes for oracular use is to do what we Silver Elves often do with many of our oracles (see *The Book of Elven Runes*, *The Elven Book of Dreams* and *The Elven Star Oracle*), which is to paint them upon small tiles about an inch square. The sort of tiles that are frequently used in bathrooms and kitchens and which you can get from a hardware store (they usually come on a sheet of about 100) and paint the Wizard Mynes upon them and then, so they will last, seal the paint upon them. By the way, we also use stones or tiles most often for selecting spirits at random in response to a particular need or task from our book *An Elfin Book of Spirits*. You can also gather small stones that are about equal in size and that are essentially flat on two sides. You may also be able to find these at hardware stores in the garden department, but if you are near a creek or a stony beach, you may collect some there.

Of course, you may have another, perhaps better way, to do the oracle or create the Wizard Mynes, and that would be great. Personal inspiration is nearly always magical. Trust your own sense of the magic and if things don't work out, try it another way. That's the scientific approach and we elves are really quite scientific even while being a mystical and magical folk. We experiment and if something doesn't quite work out as we thought it would, we try again another way or try implementing whatever improvements we think necessary.

You can, naturally, just ask a single question and pick a Myne (singular, pronounced many) or two at random, but you could also use them like tarot cards and pull them out and place them upon a tarot like spread using the Celtic Cross or some other arrangement you may prefer. Use your imagination. You are, after all, one of the Elfae folk and using our imaginations and trusting our instincts is one of the things we do best.

Keywords

In each of the Chapters, associated with a particular Wizard Myne and tree, you will find a Keyword that is related to a letter of the alphabet, a number or a keyword that is associated with Elfin, Faerie or Magic in some way. This is so you can use the Wizard Mynes as a Wizard Script for communication.

Further, we will give you the Arvyndase name for the tree group and the Arvyndase name for a specific Myne as well as the symbol of the Myne at the beginning of each chapter.

We will also give you a, more or less, quick meaning that you can consult if you use *The Elven Book of Trees* as an oracle.

In addition, there will be an Elven Spell for enchantment and spell casting associated with each tree group and Wizard Myne, in English and in Arvyndase, as this book is not only an oracle but also a method for magic, enchantment and spell casting in which you can randomly choose a spell for any particular need, circumstance, desire, aspiration or situation.

So, let us begin.

Chapter 1:

Elderberry

KEYWORD: **ELVES**

TREE NAME IN ARVYNDASE: **ELPANPYNA** (PRONOUNCED: EEL - PAIN - PIN - NAH)

ARVYNDASE NAME OF THE WIZARD MYNE: **ALFAR** (PRONOUNCED: ALE - FAIR)

THIS TREE AND ITS MAGIC:

In some mythologies, the Elder tree is associated with and said to contain within itself the Elder Mother, who protects the Elder tree from harm. We elves associate this tree with our own s'elves, especially since we are noted as the Elder or Eldar race, the first people to manifest in or descend into the material realms.

This tree is thought to be especially lucky and it is thought to bring magic and blessings into one's life and environment if one has this tree growing near one's home or eald, as we elves often call our sphere of influence. If one collects the fallen leaves and creates wreathes with them, or otherwise positions them around one's home or demesne, it helps to bring protection, good health and prosperity to the home and its inhabitants and even to elf friends who come to visit. For we elves share our blessings with all whom we love.

The Elder tree and its berries have been used to treat various and numerous diseases and afflictions and this emphasizes its health giving and longevity providing benefits. The Elderberry tree is also much beloved by various animals, especially the birds who eat the berries and loved also by the honey bees. In traditional Ogham, this tree is associated with the Ogham Ruis and with the Thirteenth and last Month of the Year. The ancient elves also calculated the year into thirteen lunar months instead of the solar year that is currently used in much of the world. We Silver Elves, however, end the year not with Halloween as the Druids and Celts did but at Winter Solstice.

The Elderberry tree regrows damaged parts easily and thus it is associated with rebirth and regeneration and the power to heal. Being that these trees were associated with the last lunar month in Celtic thought, they represent the end that is the new beginning, especially on the spiral of evolution, where each circle around takes us higher, like the Elven Circle itself, wherein our togetherness uplifts us all.

And remember that elderberries are used to make Elderberry wine, an intoxicant and thus, if used wisely, a way to relax one from the cares of the world as well as to provide a glimpse beyond the veil of life into the more subtle realms of being. However, note that the elderberries are toxic if not ripe and cooked.

What This Oracle Means:

If you draw this Wizard Myne, then you should note that the blessing of the elves is upon you and yours. Those who seek to harm you will come to a bad end. Those who seek to interfere with your progress will stumble upon their own feet. However, know also that the magic is in process. Seeking to change things quickly is not advised. We are near the end of a cycle; however, a new cycle has not quite begun. It is best to let things develop naturally. Circumstances will guide you and the time to act, when it does come, will be clear. If you are in doubt, then wait. The elderberries need to cook, so to speak. This wine is best aged and there is no hurry really for your elven kin on the higher planes are looking out for you. Mother Nature is on your side. The Elder Mother smiles upon you. Hang lovely ribbons filled with your wishes and with blessings from tree limbs and be patient and content, all will be fulfilled in due time. Elf magic rises.

ENCHANTMENT SPELL:
We're secure within our Eald
Safe, protected by magic held

This Spell in Arvyndase:
Eli'da yader enåver eli'na Ald
Del, kafäin la êldon gospïn

Pronunciation:
E - lie'dah yeah - deer e - nah - veer e - lie'nah Ale-d
Deal, kay - fah - in lah l - doan go-sp – in

Chapter 2:

Sweetgum

KEYWORD: **MAGIC**

TREE NAME IN ARVYNDASE: **NEMBET** (PRONOUNCED: NEEM - BEET)

ARVYNDASE NAME OF THE WIZARD MYNE: **ÛMBÅR** (PRONOUNCED: UM - BAR)

THIS TREE AND ITS MAGIC:

There are fifteen species of Sweetgum trees that can be found around the world in places as far flung as China, Korea, Thailand, Taiwan, Laos, Vietnam, Turkey, Greece (on the island of Rhodes), North America and Mexico. It exudes a resin that is essentially liquid amber and thus denotes magic in action, as opposed to old or ancient magics, as fossilized amber stone does. Some of the species are best known for their gum balls, or seedpods, which look a bit like caltrops and act like them to one's bare feet. These, however, are ancient trees going back to the Cretaceous period approximately 99 million years ago, although their market share grew in the Tertiary Period around 66 million to 2.6 million years ago, give or take a few million years here and there.

These trees have some medicinal properties and the sap of the American variety can be used as chewing gum. Today, however, it is mostly used as an ornamental tree but it is also utilized at times for making baskets and furniture.

To we Silver Elves, this tree is associated with magic in motion. Not magic that has been done in the past and has already made its mark on the world, nor magics that while they were created in the past are still in the process of developing into realization, but rather magics that are relatively new and, much like various waters from creeks and streams flowing together to form a river, these magics are still very fluid and are becoming, merging and affecting each other and thus finding their place in the world. They are not yet 'set in stone' as solidified amber would seem to be.

WHAT THIS ORACLE MEANS:

If you receive this in answer to a question posed to the oracle, then realize that the magic is in motion. However, your magic is not, by a long shot, the only magic that is striving to fulfill itself. Fit yours'elf into the general scheme of things, but don't try to force anything. Work within Nature and the natural order. Blend your magic with those that are already going on. The simple fact is that whether you agree with the way the world is or not, you will still have to deal with it and, in this case, it is best to do that as easily as you possibly can. Choose the path of least resistance.

At the same time, the spikey nature of the Sweetgum's seed pod indicates that you have every right to protect yours'elf and your kindred from invasive energies from the outside. Still, it is best to pursue your own magic, without being aggressive or attempting to override other people's endeavors. Do your best to find balance, for amber is a wonderful substance for helping to create balance on the etheric and astral planes of being, bringing the Yin and Yang energies into harmony and from this, peace, prosperity and success will come. Also, try to make things better for everyone. Be healing and, in as much as possible, make yours'elf useful for the general good and wellbeing. This will bring positive results and increase the power of your magic and help you find allies whose magic will harmonize with your own.

ENCHANTMENT SPELL:

Into the current I now merge
To see my magic greater surge

This Spell in Arvyndase:
Verva tae zalvas El mat vons
Va ten el'na êldon raltfa posh

Pronunciation:
Veer - vah tay zale - vace Eel mate vones [rhymes with phones]
Vah teen eel'nah l - doan rail-t - fah poe-sh

Chapter 3:

Cashew

KEYWORD: **DWARVES**

TREE NAME IN ARVYNDASE: **ACAJO** (PRONOUNCED: A - CAH - JOE)

ARVYNDASE NAME OF THE WIZARD MYNE: **DWARFYN** (PRONOUNCED: DWARE - FIN)

THIS TREE AND ITS MAGIC:

Who doesn't love Cashews? And despite what Tolkien and other writers have said about there being a natural conflict between elves and dwarves, like the conflict that is supposed to exist between cats and dogs, we elves can't but help love and admire our often more diminutive cousins, who the ancient Scandinavian folk referred to as dark elves. So, this Wizard Myne is connected to the Dwarf folk, whom we love.

The Cashew tree can grow up to 40+ feet, although its smaller, dwarf variety, about 20 feet tall, is found to be more economically productive. The Cashew tree not only produces the nut, which can be used for a variety of purposes, but also the Cashew apple, that is attached to the nut and can also be eaten.

Its generic name Anacardium, which comes from the Greek, means 'heart outside' or 'outside the heart', because the cashew nut or seed grows outside of the fruit, or apple. We elves relate this to the dwarven tendency to 'wear their hearts on their sleeves', so to speak, to be very open and expressive emotionally and less subtle in that way than we

The Silver Elves. . . .   33

elves tend to be. Most of them cannot help being out front and emotionally demonstrative. In other words, they don't tend to hide their feelings and for the most part in dealing with Dwarves, what you see is truly what you get.

WHAT THIS ORACLE MEANS:

If you receive this oracle, it means that it is a good time for doing magic, however, it also means that even if you have very little to start with you can produce a great effect with your spells and that the results will be much more and better than you had expected or even hoped. You don't need to be fancy or extravagant, small means will do just as well. What matters most is sincerity and industrious effort.

At the same time, be careful of people who would use your feelings to manipulate you. It is good to be open as a person, but some individuals would take advantage of that openness for their own benefit and your detriment. Channel your powerful feelings into your magic and into your magical creations. Don't let yours'elf be used and no matter where you are on the Path, whether you seem far along or are just a beginner, feel good about yours'elf and your workings. Dwarves, though small usually, have no lack of confidence. In the vastness of the Universe, we are all on the same level anyway, or very close, otherwise it is unlikely that we would be in this world together.

ENCHANTMENT SPELL:

Small means, vast reward
Accumulates the dwarven hoard
Hard work, magic sure
What I create will long endure

This Spell in Arvyndase:
Tin roth, sud bono
Wyldadoralu tae dwarrynta dråk
Tarl grymbi, êldon vem

Wu El talys yon tiso talos

Pronunciation:
Tine rowth, sued bo - no
Will - day - doe - ray - lou tay dwar - ren - tah drahk
Tayrl grim - by, l - doan veem
Woo Eel tay - liss yone tie - so tay – lowce.

Chapter 4:

Mango

Keyword: **Seelie**

Tree Name in Arvyndase: **Paro** (pronounced: pair - row)

Arvyndase Name of the Wizard Myne: **Hileyn** (pronounced: high - lee - in)

This Tree and its Magic:

The Mango is much beloved by us Silver Elves and we remember when we first encountered it and ate our first one in our early thirties and thought we had finally found the fruit of heaven. We couldn't believe we had never heard of it before. It was a revelation of the sort some folks associate with certain drugs. Paradise made real.

However, be aware, this fruit and tree are related to poison ivy, poison oak and poison sumac and some folks experience an allergic reaction to it (particularly if the fruit touches ones lips). So while we relate this tree and its family to the Seelie folk, the Good Folk, the People of Peace, the Fair Folk, it is good to remember that the Seelie Elves can be harsh if need be and while our disposition and attitude toward the world is somewhat different than that of our Unseelie Cousins, we are still related to the Unseelie Folk and we are closer to the various kinds of Elfae and Otherkin and Otherworldly folk of all sorts than we are to Mankind, and to the normal folk in particular.

This tree can grow up to 100 feet tall. These are the tall folk, much in the way that Tolkien portrays us. Interestingly, besides being used as food and for its antibiotic properties in medicine, its wood is sometimes used for making Ukuleles (actually pronounced by the Hawaiians as ou - coo - lay - lays not as you - coo - lay - lees), a Portuguese instrument beloved of the people of the Elfin Islands of Paradise in the Uttermost West.

Mangos have recalcitrant seeds, which means that they cannot survive freezing or drying. Avocado, cacao, coconut, jackfruit, lychee, mango, rubber and other trees also have recalcitrant seeds.

WHAT THIS ORACLE MEANS:

The name Mango comes from the Dravidian-Tamil words meaning 'highest fruit,' and surely the Seelie Elves are very high elven and in getting this as an oracle it indicates that you will be best served by taking the high road and pursuing the issue you are asking about from the viewpoint of your highest s'elf. Rise above the situation.

At the same time, because the Mango has recalcitrant seeds, it means that reading books of the ancient lore in and of itself is not enough for you to progress further upon the path. Much of the Elven Way (see our book *The Elven Way*) is an oral tradition, one might say, but perhaps even more accurately, we could say it is a symbiotic osmotic tradition. Its deepest magics and tenets are learned by being around others of one's kindred and particularly those who are living the Elven Way and have been for some time.

Thus, the advice here is to seek your kindred, especially to find those who have long been upon the path and interact with them and be around them in order to absorb their energy and their mystical technologies of enchantment as much as you can. This is the place of learning by example and while finding those examples can be difficult in this world, it is very important that you attempt to do so. This will bring you great blessings upon your path and increase your magical abilities, enchantments and adeptship greatly. For these fair folk will instill you with confidence in yours'elf and if they don't do so, they are not whom they claim to be. We elves ever seek to strive to leave people feeling better about thems'elves and more confident in their personal being.

ENCHANTMENT SPELL:
You call to me and I draw near
The Path to Elfin becomes so clear

This Spell in Arvyndase:
Le koar va el nar El omhyr kol
Tae Tâl va Êldat casalu re vyrn

Pronunciation:
Lee co - air vah eel nair Eel ohm - her coal
Tay Tahl vah L - date cah - say - lou ree vern

Chapter 5:

Pistachio

KEYWORD: **PYROMAGERY**

TREE NAME IN ARVYNDASE: **RENO** (PRONOUNCED: REE - KNOW)

ARVYNDASE NAME OF THE WIZARD MYNE: **FURFYN** (PRONOUNCED: FEW-R - FIN)

THIS TREE AND ITS MAGIC:

The Pistachio tree, which is a small tree, originally hales from Central Asia, Iran, Syria and Western Asia. The seeds need to be fully developed and prepared properly. Aflatoxin can be found in poorly harvested pistachios or ones that haven't been processed correctly. Aflatoxins create powerful carcinogenic chemicals that can be caused by molds such as Aspergillus flavus and Aspergillus parasiticus. So, caution is required.

Because of this fact, and the fact that it is mostly a desert tree and also the reality that improper storage can lead to fires, in fact the Pistachios and pistachio products can spontaneously combust, have led these elves to associate these trees and this Wizard Myne with Pyromagery and with the fire djinn of the desert. Also, like the mango and other members of the Cashew family, this tree is related to poison ivy, poison sumac and poison oak. So again, caution is advised as it can cause allergic reactions in some people. So, like fire, the pistachio must be handled carefully and properly. It is clearly magical in its way, but it can be a dangerous magic if it isn't handled with knowledge, understanding and awareness.

However, besides being delicious, pistachios have been noted for lowering systolic and diastolic blood pressure somewhat in individuals who consume them, except for those with diabetes mellitus. It is also said that the ingestion of this nut, along with others, may lower the risk of heart disease. Like fire, it has its dangers and its uses.

WHAT THIS ORACLE MEANS:

This oracle indicates that there is powerful magic in motion but it must be handled with great care or things could go very wrong, could blow up, combust, or sour terribly and turn out in ways that you do not wish and perhaps didn't expect. This is not a magic that you can do and then forget about. This is a magic you must watch constantly or at least check on regularly. You may summon or be dealing with various individuals, spirits or djinn, but know that these may be dangerous spirits. Useful, but not necessarily to be trusted. You need to keep a watch on what is going on. This magic requires oversight and proper care in its conception and production until it is well and truly done and completed. Set up your magical wards and seals and charge them thoroughly. Put salt around your circle of protection and perhaps along the bottom of your doors, entranceways and windows.

At the same time, if you handle this situation properly and with due care, the results may prove to be very beneficial to you. There is a tremendous amount of power involved here. Are you ready to handle such power? Do you have the awareness, concentration and dedication that dealing with such powerful forces demand? Ask yours'elf that before you proceed any further. And if it turns out that this just isn't right for you, don't be afraid to back away cautiously. This sort of magic isn't the magic for everyone and there is nothing wrong in admitting that this may be the case for you. Know and acknowledge your limitations.

ENCHANTMENT SPELL:

Careful, careful, fire bright
This magic that will bring the light
In deepest, darkest time of night
So long as it is handled right

This Spell in Arvyndase:

Synthfel, synthfel, fur ilu
Wyr êldon dij yon cura tae lun
Ver dorador, dasdor mern u sol

Re tiso tat ter da rodaïn mard

Pronunciation:

Sinth - feel, sinth - feel, few-r eye - lou

Were l - doan dye-j yone cur - rah tay loon

Veer doe - ray - door, dace - door mere-n you soul

Ree tie - so tate tier dah row - dah - in mare-d.

Chapter 6:

Sumac

KEYWORD: **THE LETTER S**

TREE NAME IN ARVYNDASE: **POROK** (PRONOUNCED: POUR - ROKE)

ARVYNDASE NAME OF THE WIZARD MYNE: **SARÅN** (PRONOUNCED: SAIR - RAHN)

THIS TREE AND ITS MAGIC:

Sumac trees and shrubs grow to a height of 3 feet for the shrubs and about 33 feet for the trees. Their reddish fruit or drupes, which are called Sumac bobs, can be ground to create a tangy spice but have also been used for a reddish dye. Thus, we Silver Elves relate this tree to the Letter S, since the word for red in Arvyndase is Sara. Additionally, we associate this tree with the Red Caps who are often portrayed as a cross between goblins and brownies or goblins and pixies, thus hob-goblins of a hostile Unseelie nature, who dye their caps red with the blood of their victims. Here, however, we are speaking of the little known, almost never mentioned, Seelie Red Caps, who are daring and adventurous, but not wicked folk, who use Sumac bobs to dye their caps red, which actually lasts longer than blood, for blood will turn brown in the course of time.

Of course, unlike mango, pistachio, and other members of the Cashew family of trees, Sumac is more obviously related to poison oak, poison ivy and poison sumac. So, it should be remembered that these Red Caps, though of a Seelie variety, are related to their more infamous Unseelie cousins.

Also, its fruits when soaked in water produce a vitamin C rich beverage and are the source of the original pink lemonade. The inner stems of the sumac are soft and have been used for pipe making (thus you might see these red caps smoking pipes as leprechauns are often portrayed doing). And the wood of the sumac, when dried, fluoresces under long-wave ultraviolet radiation, which suggests a hidden magic to this tree that manifests long after the tree itself has gone or a branch has parted from its source. This is to say that after such magic has been fulfilled it radiates energy into the future like sound waves that can no longer be heard by the human ear but are still vibrating outwardly into the world.

What This Oracle Means:

Red is generally thought to be a color of action, leadership and activity. Even when it is used in stoplights, it is an indication of a powerful directive. It says STOP emphatically and it means it. Red is a 'take charge' energy. Thus, when you receive this as an oracle, it means you should take charge of the situation. It is also good for starting new things, new relationships, new magics, new endeavors or a new direction in your life.

And because of the tangy, spicy nature of the ground sumac bobs, it further speaks to the possibility of excitement or risk spicing things up a bit for you. However, as indicated, there are dangers here, so proceed into this risky situation with caution. Let it be a calculated risk. Take as many precautions as is possible.

This magic is rather like skateboarding, skiing, racecar driving or other activities that are fun and exciting but inherently dangerous. So, this oracle says, take the risk, but also enact the necessary precautions that will reduce the danger in as much as you can. And remember, these red caps are related to the other more dangerous sort, so be sure you can trust those with whom you are sharing this new magic, this possible exploration into the unknown and possibly into new uncharted territory.

ENCHANTMENT SPELL:
Stepping forth into the dark
I'll light it now with my own spark

This Spell in Arvyndase:
Ciddas soch verva tae das
El'yon lun ter mat ena el'na os naja

Pronunciation:
Sid - dace sow-th veer - vah tay dace
Eel'yone loon tier mate e - nah eel'na ohss nay – jah

Chapter 7:

Lacquer tree

KEYWORD: **THE LETTER D**

TREE NAME IN ARVYNDASE: **CERKO** (PRONOUNCED: SIR - CO)

ARVYNDASE NAME OF THE WIZARD MYNE: **DABAN** (PRONOUNCED: DAY - BANE)

THIS TREE AND ITS MAGIC:

This tree is commonly called the Chinese lacquer tree. It is native to China and the Indian subcontinent, and has been cultivated in China, Korea and Japan. Sometimes it is called the Japanese Lacquer tree or Japanese Sumac, while others know it as the Varnish tree. For these trees are grown for their toxic sap that, like maple syrup, is tapped from the tree, and is utilized as a highly durable lacquer. The sap of these trees and the fumes they produce are very toxic for they contain the allergenic oil urushiol, which is also in poison ivy and leads to the rash for which that plant is known. Note, however, that the term 'Japanning', as a process of lacquering, actually refers to a European imitation of this process that uses different chemicals in its creation.

This process of lacquering, or 'sealing,' one might say, requires repetitive application and drying of the sap in successive layers upon the object to be sealed. Once the lacquer has dried, the possibly of allergic reaction, while still possible, is far less common. Thus, we elves relate this tree to the Letter D and to the magical seal. For the name for seal (not the animal) in Arvyndase is Daba (day - bah). However, this isn't a seal of protection in so much as a seal of transformation. This is a magical sigil for sealing in the good and positive, although the process can be difficult or strewn with danger and requires care, it is not always easy to deal with those who are striving to give up wicked or harmful ways and live in the good, illuminated and positive.

One might compare this process to that of giving up cigarettes, alcohol or drugs. Swearing off these addictive substances forever and sealing one's fate and destiny in a positive direction thereafter is an important step in one's life. One moves into the light and determines ones'elf, seals ones'elf, through will power and dedication and pledges to never return to the dark or to the self or other destructive habits of one's previous life. In a certain sense, it is a sealing of the darkness so it may never hold sway again. This is the theme, in fact, of numerous stories and tales, only its manifestation in reality is usually **more individual than worldwide in effect**, as the tales would usually have it.

WHAT THIS ORACLE MEANS:

In receiving this oracle, it indicates that the time has come to orient yours'elf toward the good, one way or another. If you have been uncertain about your magic, about whether magic is real or not, or wondering if you are really an elfae or other of some sort or whether you are just delusional, it is time to take the leap of faith or to get out entirely. Go for it or not, but get off the fence and once you have decided one way or the other, do your best to commit yours'elf and don't turn back.

Of course, like giving up alcohol or cigarettes or drugs, or even old habits of behavior, this is often easier said than done, especially in the beginning. It requires layers of work over time. One must face the toxic issues of one's soul and spirit and rededicate ones'elf over and over again, until doing what is right and good is not just an accidental aspect of one's being but a permanent and consistent part of one's behavior. Having kindred upon the same path can be very helpful in this regard, that's why recovering addicts hold regular meetings to encourage each other to stay focused on the path toward the good.

So, make up your mind. Are you in or out? With us or not? Is the life of magic for you or will you return to the world of the mundane, reassured that magic doesn't really exist? It's up to you but the time to decide is now.

ENCHANTMENT SPELL:

I step upon this path, for sure
I'll tread it now forevermore

This Spell in Arvyndase:

El cid repton wyr tål, fro vem

El'yon pa ter mat varigostu

Pronunciation:

Eel sid reap - tone were tahl, fro veem

Eel'yone pah tier mate vair - rye - go-ss - two

Chapter 8:

Dogbane family

KEYWORD: **ORC**

TREE GROUP NAME IN ARVYNDASE: **RUZURNELPA** (PRONOUNCED: RUE - ZOOR-N - EEL - PAH)

ARVYNDASE NAME OF THE WIZARD MYNE: **ORCKYN** (PRONOUNCED: ORC - KIN)

THIS TREE AND ITS MAGIC:

The Pachypodium is group of succulent spine-bearing trees and shrubs, native to Madagascar and Africa. They are members of the dogbane family, some of whose related plants and shrubs produce a toxic substance that has been used through the ages to poison dogs, thus the name Dogbane. We Silver Elves associate this tree and its family with Orcs, not only because of its hearty succulent nature but because of its spines and thus prickly outer aspect and the fact that some of them would not hesitate to poison dogs. What sort of being would poison a dog? Bad, bad orcs, bad.

This is not to say that all orcs are bad. We wouldn't want to overly stereotype and profile any people to the point where they couldn't change toward the good, for transformation and enlightenment are the destiny for all of us. Yet, in traditional lore and in our own life experience we have noted that Orcs can be prone toward violence, can be very prickly about being treated with "respect," And even when they don't poison dogs, which we expect most of them don't, they often treat them somewhat brutally, frequently breeding them to fight to the death in pits in violent and bloody matches against other dogs, who were also bred to do the same. We consider this behavior to be cruel and ignorant and they, in turn, think that we elves are wussies who should mind our own business and go play with our elf toys or whatever. In their minds, their dogs, and their children for that matter, are theirs to raise and treat however they desire. And it is none of our business what they choose to do with or to them. They think roughing up dogs and children is good for them and prepares them for life within a harsh, often cruel and predatory world.

Also, these types of trees tend to have few branches, which is to say, these orcs keep to thems'elves and their own kind, and don't tend to branch out and make alliances, unless necessary, with others. They are very clannish, even, sometimes particularly, concerning other orc tribes. Also, unlike many members of the Dogbane family, which often create a milky colored latex, the sap of the Pachypodium species is always clear, which indicates that while these individuals are orcs, they can blend easily into the world of Men and its macho orientation when they choose to do so. Thus, according to our elf sight, many of those who are perceived to be men in the modern world are really orcs, goblins, grimlins and other Unseelie folk (again we would like to point out that we are not saying that all Unseelie folk are of this harsh nature).

WHAT THIS ORACLE MEANS:

In receiving this Wizard Myne as an oracle, you are cautioned concerning the way you deal with people. There are individuals around you or involved in this situation that while they may seem thick-skinned, who may even pretend to be impervious to insult, will take every slight very seriously. Not only that, they themselves are prone to be rude and cutting to others and thus act as though this is just a game for them, but believe us when we tell you, that you'd best be cautious with your words and it is wisest not be get involved in a game of verbal one-upmanship with them. This is not because you might lose that game but because, being the clever elfae that you surely are, you are bound to cut them more deeply than you realize or that they can truly bear. They don't really stand a chance against your superior wit and they will not forget the fact that you out did them at their own game but rather they will hold your superior intelligence against you forever. If, in fact, they are not immediately violent in response to what you have said.

They will bully you if they think they can get away with it, if they are physically bigger and stronger, and the social environment permits. But if they can't get at you in this way, they will work behind your back and most likely they will not attack you directly but will 'poison your dog,' which is to say they will attempt to turn your most loyal friends against you with slander, false rumor and innuendo. So, caution, beloved. Only deal with these types of folks if you have no choice. But, if you have to do so, understand they are very sensitive, whether they show it or not. In fact, the less they show it, the more sensitive and prickly they are likely to be.

ENCHANTMENT SPELL:

I give you respect
That you haven't earned
So, the lesson of courtesy
Will be by you learned

This Spell in Arvyndase:

Eel luth le hodro
Dij le tir'kon orfin

Re, tae lardin u eldava
Yon te la le aduïn

Pronunciation:
Eel lou-th lee hoe - drow
Dye-j lee tire'cone orf - in
Ree, tay lair - dine you eel - day - vah
Yone tea lah lee a - due - in

Chapter 9:

Holly family

KEYWORD: **THE LETTER T.**

TREE GROUP NAME IN ARVYNDASE: **IFOL** (PRONOUNCED: EYE - FOAL)

ARVYNDASE NAME OF THE WIZARD MYNE: **TAVYN** (PRONOUNCED: TAY - VIN)

THIS TREE AND ITS MAGIC:

The Holly family of trees and shrubs are associated by the Druids with protection from evil forces, thus they are said to have worn holly in their hair at times to ward off wicked magic. It is linked to the Ogham Tinne and the month of June. We Silver Elves associated it with the letter T and the Wizard Myne called Tavyn, which is based upon the Arvyndase word Tav (tay-v) which is our elven word for Ward,

48 .... The Elfin Book of Trees for the Elven Druid

meaning both a protected place, a seal or a person that one is protecting or who is under one's care.

The holly grows nearly all over the world from the tropics to temperate zones. Its leaves often have spines, however, these spines are usually soft in the summer and grow harder in the winter time, when food is scarce and predators more likely to seek its leaves for sustenance. They often have berries, or drupes, that range in color from red to brown to black, and occasionally will be green or yellow and these may contain as many as ten seeds each. These drupes, while an important food source for birds and other animals, are slightly toxic to humans, often provoking vomiting or diarrhea. However, some holly species provide the leaves for making Yerba Mate tea. The Holly is a tree that often thrives in shade and moist weather and is seen as an invasive species in some areas for it can be quite hardy and will endure where others have a more difficult time doing so.

In heraldry, holly is often used to symbolize truth and perhaps it is best known in the West as the tree whose leaves are used at and associated with Christmas. Yule time wreaths are often made of its leaves and berries. Thus, there is a celebratory aspect to the holly, especially associated with one's family gathering together in love and harmony for the Yule season celebration, a declaration of union before the potentially long, hard winter.

WHAT THIS ORACLE MEANS:

In drawing this Wizard Myne, one is called to have some caution in regards to one's own cautious nature. It is all good and well to protect ones'elf and one's elf friends and elfae kindred from those who would bring harm to us, but sometimes we can be overly protective and keep to our own and act abruptly or insensitively to others, rebuking and rejecting them when, in fact, they mean us no harm and, on the other hand, might prove useful in some way in the future. The point here is one of discretion and developing the ability to discern between those who are potentially harmful to us and ours or who intend us no good and distinguish them from those who are really quite harmless and are no danger to us at all and may even have good intentions toward us and merely desire our friendship. We may keep some of them at a distance, but it is wisest to do so politely, if such is necessary, and not harshly. Look beyond the stereotypes and really take a look at the individuals who are involved in this situation and are, more than likely, seeking your time and attention.

It is true, there are some folks who are so obnoxious in certain ways that they may make one feel like one wants to vomit. Their company, behaviors and habits seem so crude, disgusting and beneath us that we wish nothing to do with them. However, they may not actually be up to no good, they may simply be no good at being around people. Treat these with some kindness and compassion and perhaps they will learn to be less prickly thems'elves and, while you may not wish to spend much time with them, they may very well prove to be useful in some ways, if you haven't rejected them utterly. The true adept finds value in nearly everyone and in recognizing each one's talents puts them to the best use possible.

And it is a simple truth that if you are consistently truthful yours'elf, you will perceive the truth of others hearts and intentions. But even then, while you may encounter some who wish to prey upon you, be subtle in your dealings with them. Most often, it is best to not let them know that you know until the moment comes when you must act with force and even then, do so with as much restraint as you can. Be of good cheer, and remember the Yule spirit.

ENCHANTMENT SPELL:

You approach, I see you clear
I know your heart and know no fear.

This Spell in Arvyndase:

Le geko, El ten le vyrn
El ken le'na bom nar ken kon mak

Pronunciation:

Lee gee - co, Eel teen lee vern
Eel keen lee'nah bowm nair keen cone make

Chapter 10:

Kalopanax

KEYWORD: **HEALING**

TREE GROUP NAME IN ARVYNDASE: **SAVTHERARA** (PRONOUNCED: SAVE - THEER - VAYR - RAH)

ARVYNDASE NAME OF THE WIZARD MYNE: **HYRNYN** (PRONOUNCED: HER - NIN)

THIS TREE AND ITS MAGIC:

This tree is a member of the Ivy family and thus would be associated with the Ogham of Gort and the month of September. We Silver Elves call this Wizard Myne Hyrnyn, from the Arvyndase word Hyrn (herne) that means Heal. This tree can grow up to nearly 100 feet tall. It is commonly called the Prickly Castor Oil tree, which reminds us of a tale Zardoa (one of us Silver Elves) tells of his boyhood. He spent six years, from the third to eighth grade, at a military school run by nuns. Whenever one of the boys (or pixies as he would call them) would get sick, the first thing the nuns would do, besides stick a thermometer up their butt was to give the boy a large heaping serving spoonful of thick castor oil. We don't know if they did this because they thought it actually had healing value or they just wanted to make sure the boys were really sick and not faking it. But it was awful. The first time Zardoa was forced to take this substance, he

The Silver Elves. . . .   51

threw it right back up. However, that didn't stop the nun from giving him another heaping spoonful.

These trees grow quickly at first and then slow down their rate of growth at about age forty. In Korea, the young shoots are eaten as a blanched dish but mostly the tree, which is native to Asia, is grown as an ornamental tree. This tree produces small white flowers and has tiny black drupes that bear two seeds.

In Korean folk tradition, basic Korean Hedgewitchery, these trees, because of their thorny branches were said to scare off evil spirits and thus to ward off disease and illness. They would hang their prickly branches over gates, doors and entry ways at the time of the Lunar New Year, which these days, in the West, is commonly called the Chinese New Year. Sometimes, malaria patients were taken into forests and magical rituals were performed among the Prickly Castor Oil Trees to invoke healing.

WHAT THIS ORACLE MEANS:

In receiving this tree as an oracle, one is facing a potential problem that has either already manifested or is about to manifest. However, just as all diseases are not ultimately due to germs or viruses, and in fact, come about because someone has low energy, or is exhausted or stressed, and in that way open to disease, so this problem involves issues that may not be directly seen on the surface. There are underlying emotional or psychological issues that are prompting this situation. It is best to look deeper into what is going on but it is also possible that one can only do that on the intuitive and astral planes of being.

Therefore, while evoking healing for this situation, also put up your wards to repel intrusive energies and don't let the whispering demons and dark spirits of doubt and unrest (the restless ghosts) wear you down. Be strong in your magic and keep yours'elf and your loved ones safe from harm and should a problem arise, deal with it not only on the material plane but through the shamanic planes as well.

Also, because this tree grows rapidly at first, it may indicate that you are dealing with someone who had to grow up too quickly or who never really had a chance to fully be a child, or who simply stopped changing and learning at some early time in their life. Some consideration is due, for you don't wish to harm them further, but neither can you let them run all over you. Be true to yours'elf and your kin, but in a basically non-offensive way, as best you can. Simply stand your ground, cast your spells and wait and the situation should right itself in time.

ENCHANTMENT SPELL:

Beneath the surface I do see
The spirit that is ailing thee

This Spell in Arvyndase:

Usco tae shurfa El ba ten
Tae tari dij da sukdas vele

Pronunciation:

Youse - co tay sure - fah Eel bah teen
Tay tay - ray dye-j dah suke - dace vee – lee

Chapter 11:

Schefflera

KEYWORD: **DRYAD**

TREE GROUP NAME IN ARVYNDASE: **ALMAPELA** (PRONOUNCED ALE - MAY - PEE - LAH)

Arvyndase Name of the Wizard Myne: **Aldarys** (pronounced ale - dare - riss)

This tree and its magic:

This tree, like the previous one, is part of the Ivy family and thus also linked to the Ogham Gort. We Silver Elves associated it with the Wizard Myne Aldarys, which is based on the Arvyndase word Aldar, or Forest. We also see this tree as associated with the Dryads and the various other tree nymphs, nyms and forest tree spirits and this would include Tolkien's Ents.

In Greek mythology, these beings come in various types according to the particular tree species. There were the Daphnaie, the nymphs of the Laurel trees and the Maliades, Meliades or Epimelides of apple and fruit trees in general. Hesperides were nymph beings of the golden apple trees. There were also Hamadryad who were so intimately related to their tree that if the tree was harmed or died, they would die as well and there were the Caryatids who were linked to the walnut trees. And surely there are nymph and nyms for every species of tree. But here we are referring to the Dryads overall as the guardians of the woods and forests and thus of the forest itself as a biological vibrancy of related being, like a city of people, only a city that is itself alive not simply an empty shell meant to house life.

We make this association with the forest because this tree is sometimes called the Umbrella tree, and the forest shelters us all and provides us with amazing gifts, including the oxygen that we need to survive, but also with fruits, medicines and much else. This tree is sometimes also known as the Octopus tree because of the way its branches hang, although other trees are given this name as well. To us the Octopus reminds us that the trees are all connected to each other through their roots, the water in the ground and the fungi beneath the Earth. They communicate with each other. The forest is a living community.

These trees often serve as food for the larvae of certain butterflies and moths and are known to attract birds, thus to our minds they are clearly friends to the faerie folk as well as to human kind. These trees can be grown in pots indoors and thus, in that way, have adapted to modern life in the world. Someday we will have homes in space with trees and forests in them helping to provide us with oxygen and surely these trees will be among them.

What This Oracle Means:

Getting this Wizard Myne is a blessing. But its blessings come mainly from community, the community of elfae and otherkin and of the trees and forests, the community of Elfin, Faerie and of the Shining Ones. Seek your others, your kindred and know that in getting this Wizard Myne you are part of a much larger web of relationship and interconnected being. You may feel alone out in the world, as many elfae do, but your connections actually run deep, deeper than the roots of the trees and farther, reaching out across the Earth and out into the Stars. You are part of this world but also of other dimensions, the realms of spirit and the supernatural.

You are sheltered in the magic of Elfin and connected to Faerie magic, which is not only of this world but beyond it. This is a three-dimensional world but you are a part of a fourth dimensional reality and there will always be a part of you that normal folk will never be able to perceive until they awaken to their own true natures and their individual part in this greater reality.

At the same time, remember to nurture and protect your own kindred as best you may. Be an umbrella to others, sheltering them from the storms of the world. Stay in touch and help others get together. There is great magic in doing so. And know that when you are in need, as you may be now, your elfin kin are sending you magic and blessings to help you.

Enchantment Spell:

Sheltered now by Elfin great
Blessings come my needs to sate

This Spell in Arvyndase:
Parcanïn mat la Êldat ralt
Elsordasli koso el'na goltli va barnsh

Pronunciation:
Pair - con - in mate lah L - date rail-t
Eel - soar - dace - lie eel'nah goal-t - lie vah bare-n-sh

Chapter 12:

Alder

KEYWORD: **RANGER**

TREE NAME IN ARVYNDASE: **OLÊTRE** (PRONOUNCED: OLE - L - TREE

ARVYNDASE NAME OF THE WIZARD MYNE: **THADLORI** (PRONOUNCED: THAY-D - LORE - RYE)

THIS TREE AND ITS MAGIC:

The Alder is part of the Birch family of trees. It is related to the third Ogham Fearn and to the month of January. We Silver Elves associated it with the Wizard Myne, Thadlori, which comes from the word Thadlor, which means Ranger in Arvyndase. Interestingly, the name for the Alder in Spanish is Alamo, which is also the name of a Mission in Texas (previously Mexico) where a group of about 250+

expatriate Americans and independent Mexicans rebelled against what they thought of as an oppressive government and made their last stand against an army of about 1,500 soldiers in a siege that lasted 13 days.

The name Alder is related to the root word El, which means red or brown and is clearly related to the words for Elves, Elf, Ælf, and Alb, although Graves (see *The White Goddess*) traces Alb back to the Greek word for white. The Alder is sometimes related to oracular ability, perhaps the Ranger ability to scout and follow tracks and also connected to protective and defensive capabilities. The Alder is a water loving tree for the most part, yet its wood is oily and both fire and water resistant, even their foliage and leaf litter tends to resist fire, and it is said that the original foundations for the houses in Venice where made of Alder.

The largest of its species are the red alder, but there is also black alder and green, although this last one seldom grows above 15 feet tall. There is also a white Alder that can be found in warm, dry climates. Like Rangers, these trees venture nearly everywhere. And like Rangers, the Alder is a pioneer species. In a symbiotic relationship with a certain bacterium, Alders are able to fix nitrogen into the soil and enrich it so that other species of trees can follow after them successfully.

The catkins, which is to say the slim cylindrical flowers of the Alder, are thought to be rich in protein, however, they are noted for having a bitter and unpleasant taste, and thus they are utilized more for survival purposes. Once again, giving us a ranger association. Some First Nations peoples of the Americas put Alder catkins in their smoking mixtures. Did Aragorn smoke Alder catkins?

WHAT THIS ORACLE MEANS:

This is an oracle of exploration and daring, but also of protection and security. It indicates that you may be at a point where you wish to expand or explore into the new and the unknown or perhaps even into slightly risky territory, but that you should do this from a place of stability and security that you can retreat to in times of danger. And use your oracles. You may not know exactly what is ahead of you but you can get a sense of it. You are venturing into uncharted territory, so engage your oracular and divinatory tools to inspire your intuition and catch a glimpse or at least few hints regarding what it is that you will be facing as you go forth. The only thing the map you have now says is: beyond this point, live dragons mostly likely, or something else equally dangerous.

So, go as prepared as you can. Be ready to adapt to changing circumstances, like the elfae you are. Our sisters Melryn and Adruil of the Elf Queen's Daughters used to say to us that one of the things that distinguished most elves from other folks was our great ability to adapt. This is certainly true of elven rangers. And while you may just be surviving and uncertain in this new and unfamiliar area for a while, and things may be a bit bitter; once you have established yours'elf and know your way around, circumstances will open up to you and greater success will come. So, endure, persevere and hang in there. And if things just don't work out at first and they become too hard to bear, retreat and try again later. Eventually, you'll achieve what you desire. And even in the exploration, you may gain knowledge that will be helpful for the future or for those who will come after you.

ENCHANTMENT SPELL:
Venturing forth into land unknown
In realms uncharted, I will roam

This Spell in Arvyndase:
Halfandas soch verva taru murkenan
Ver êldli murmavïn, El yon dune

Pronunciation:
Hale - fane - dace sore-ch veer - van tayr - rue muir - key - nane
Veer eld - lie muir - mave - in, Eel yone due - knee

Chapter 13:

Birch

KEYWORD: **GNOME**

TREE NAME IN ARVYNDASE: **PIHYR** (PRONOUNCED: PIE - HER)

ARVYNDASE NAME OF THE WIZARD MYNE: **NOMAN** (PRONOUNCED: NO - MAIN)

THIS TREE AND ITS MAGIC:

The Birch trees, like the Alder, are a pioneer species that tend to make the way and prepare the soil for other species to grow. Often, they renew a forest that has been razed by fire and bring it quickly back to life again. In a way, they may be compared to the survivors of a holocaust or apocalypse who endure and go on, in the course of time, to establish a new world. Usually, the image of individuals recreating the world in zombie movies, particularly when they are spreading knowledge of how to survive, is of Birch people.

The Birch is associated with the Ogham Beith (pronounced: bay) and with the first Celtic month of November (right after Halloween) and is also linked with the Proto-Germanic rune berkanan that is related to the Letter B, as is the case with the Ogham, as well.

We Silver Elves associate it with the Gnomish folk and the Wizard Myne Noman that comes from the Arvyndase word, Nomae (no - may), which means Gnome. This is not the Wizard Myne, however, that is related with the letter B. That connection belongs to another tree.

The name for its genus and that of the Alder is Betula, which is from Latin. However, that word is a diminutive that comes through the Romans from the Gaulish betua, the Old Irish bethe, and the Welsh bedw, thus from the Celtic tribes (who never actually called thems'elves Celts) nor actually thought of thems'elves as entirely related for the most part.

The Birch comes in various colors of gray, white, black, silver and yellow, although we elves call the silver and white Birches, the Shining Trees, and these are particularly beloved by we who are elfin folk. And traditionally, the Birches overall have been associated with the Faerie world. But then, many trees are.

The reason we associate it with gnomes principally comes from the fact that its bark is used for making paper, among other things. It is a symbol of communication and knowledge, as is the ancient idea of gnomes, before they became garden gnomes in much the same way the faerie folk were diminished into cute little flower fairies. Gnomes have long been a symbol of knowledge and wisdom, communication and the continuance of culture. Note that Birch bark was also used by some First Nations peoples for making their homes and for making waterproof canoes. So, it also bears the idea of preserving and protecting and of connecting through travel. Note, further, that birch is used for tone-wood in guitars, speaker cabinets and often drums, all of which reinforce the idea of communication and culture.

These elves once saw a television program about how one might survive after a worldwide near extinction event and the expert, giving tips about what to do in this circumstance, said one of the greatest resources a person had would be libraries with books on all sorts of ways to do things and thus could gain knowledge on how to continue on. This is the spirit of renewal that comes with this tree, the spirit of the gnomes who preserve culture through writing and pass it on through time aided by these shining trees of new beginnings and a new era of Elfin.

WHAT THIS ORACLE MEANS:

This oracle is about starting again. Not starting something totally new, but starting again from scratch after things didn't entirely work out or collapsed utterly. You may have failed previously, been here before and left. However, even though things didn't work out the first time, you now have experience and knowledge that will help you do better this time. Maybe you are thinking of getting married again, for the second or third time. Remember what went wrong previously and adapt and change so that this time you will do much better. And remember, you are also setting an example that others may follow in the future. So, follow the example of those who have come before you and succeeded. Gain what wisdom you can from others who have been through this previously.

You are a pioneer; not venturing into totally unexplored territory but into a world where nearly everything went wrong but now you know, or at least have some idea, of how to make things work out this time. How to improve what you're doing. And, if it doesn't pan out this time, perhaps it will the next. Don't give up, be a shining example of endurance and determination and give it another try. This time you just might succeed.

Enchantment Spell:
This time I will succeed
And draw to me all that I need

This Spell in Arvyndase:
Wyr mern El yon redae
Nar omhyr va el wyl dij El golt

Pronunciation:
Were mere-n Eel yone re - day
Nair om - her vah eel will dye-j Eel goal-t

Chapter 14:

Hornbeam

Keyword: Grimlin

Tree Name in Arvyndase: **Trodryn** (pronounced: trow - drinn)

Arvyndase Name of the Wizard Myne: **Grymlynca** (pronounced: grim - lin - cah)

This tree and its magic:

While related to the Birch and Alder, the Hornbeam is an extremely hard wood that is sometimes called ironwood or musclewood because of the muscular look of its trunk. It is related to the Wizard Myne Grymlynca, which comes from the Arvyndase word for Grimlin. Note that the Arvyndase word for paperwork is Grymlynka (grim - lin - kay). These grimlin folks are natural bank clerks and civil servants, for paperwork doesn't deter them. They love the sense of order it provides and they often like to keep lists. And you don't want to be on their list if you can possibly avoid it. At least, we elves surely don't. These grimlins want everything organized precisely and can be utterly unyielding as individuals, especially in positions of authority and they nearly always strive for being in such positions even if they are only minor post where they can be petty tyrants and martinets.

Grimlins are also often lean, mean fighting machines who are very rule oriented, frequently finding work as policeman or other enforcers of the law or the military and they make natural Hall Monitors (see our book *Elven Psychology* for more about Hall Monitors as a psychological tendency). They are often fanatics, especially about the doctrines, dogmas and cultural expectations of their chosen or more often inherited religion and society. In fact, it generally suits grimlins to live in theocratic societies where the principles and restrictions of their religion are also the laws and rules of their culture. They ever try to force everyone else to live the way that they believe to be the right and only way to live.

Hornbeams tend to be medium sized trees, as grimlins are also inclined to be medium but hard bodied and hard minded people. This tree is seldom used in general carpentry since its wood is so difficult to work. Thus, grimlins are usually in societies of their own, finding it hard to fit into general society whose people seem to be less serious about life and more into indulging themselves. Grimlins are often ascetics.

This tree is called hornbeam because its wood is seen as being similar to horn, as in the horn of a bull or goat, which is also reminiscent of the nature of grimlins who may not have horns that show on the surface but none-the-less are hard headed individuals ever willing to goad, butt or gore those they disapprove of.

WHAT THIS ORACLE MEANS:

If you get this as an oracle in response to a question then you will probably have to deal with red tape, forms to fill out or hardnosed by the book bureaucrats of some sort. Naturally, you want to avoid this if you can, but probably in this circumstance you won't be able to do so. And most likely, while you may wish to complain or rebel, that seldom turns out well. In fact, rebelling or protesting usually only plays into their hands, putting you even deeper into their power.

On the other hand, if you can bend the rules, find a loophole, it is possible that you may get away with doing that, but usually the easiest and most efficient thing to do is endure the situation, be hard within your own s'elf, and just go along with what you have to do and get to the other side and get it over with as soon as you can. Don't linger in this situation any longer than need requires.

Don't do anything that will prolong this experience for yours'elf or make it so you have to deal with these individuals or this situation any longer than you need to. Keep smiling, mainly to yours'elf, because they may take a happy, playful elfin smile as mocking them. Play along with their game, play by the rules, pretend you take them seriously, and get it over with and move on with your elfae life. Don't get entangled with them. They can be very hard to deal with and are very hardnosed people. Treat them with respect as they absolutely hunger to be respected, and then slip away as soon as you can.

ENCHANTMENT SPELL:
You will not bend and that's okay
I'll play your game and be on my way

This Spell in Arvyndase:
Le yon kon fynd nar dij'da dåda
El'yon jol le'na los nar te ton el'na yer

Pronunciation:
Lee yone cone fend nair dye-j'dah dah - dah
Eel'yone jole lee'nah lowce nair tea tone eel'nah year

Chapter 15:

Hazel

KEYWORD: **DIVINATION**

TREE NAME IN ARVYNDASE: **CORIL** (PRONOUNCED: CORE - RILE)

ARVYNDASE NAME OF THE WIZARD MYNE: **RAFEVAR** (PRONOUNCED: RAY - FEE - VAYR)

THIS TREE AND ITS MAGIC:

The Hazel tree is associated with the Ogham Coll and the powers of wisdom and prophecy. We Silver Elves relate it to the Wizard Myne Rafevar that comes from the Arvyndase word Rafeva (ray - fee - vah), which means Prophecy. The Hazel nearly always forms multiple trunks, which the elves take to mean that there are many possibilities flowing into the future and finding the way that is right and best for each individual is one of the great quests of life. One gains wisdom by being true to ones'elf and choosing the way best suited to one's own nature. If you are true to your own instincts and intuition, you cannot truly go wrong for among all other things that you will encounter in taking that course you are bound to eventually find and develop your true s'elf.

The fruit of the Hazel is the hazelnut, which gives it a nutritious and nurturing aspect. Its wood was used for making wattle, which is a composite material for making houses, also for withy fences (woven, almost basket-like, fences), and for frames for the circular or rounded coracle boats. Thus, there is an aspect of stability (the house), of delineation and discrimination (the fence) and of exploration (the boat), indicating that wisdom comes from having and leading a balanced life that is well nurtured (the nut).

Hazel trees are sometimes harvested or coppiced, which is to say cut down to their stump, and they will spring up new shoots in response. So, there is strong indication here of endurance beyond all challenges and hardship, even of beginning again if need be. Some of the cultivars of the common Hazel produce a gnarled walking stick or enchanter's cane, as we elves like to call it, associating the Hazel with enchanters and wizards. For wizards are noted for their powers of prophecy and wisdom and enchanters usually see far more than they ever let on and have such wisdom that few realize how wise they are.

There are certain fungi and mushrooms that need the Hazel to grow upon, and its nuts are beloved by the red deer, the dormouse and the red squirrel, in particular, although other animals love them as well. There are also species of lichen that depend upon the Hazel for their growth. Thus, there is an indication that wisdom provides not only for itself but for others as well. A house is only as stable as the land it is built upon.

WHAT THIS ORACLE MEANS:

If you draw this as your oracle, then the possibilities before you are many. You may have to discriminate between them. It is unlikely that you can do everything or accomplish all that you envision, at least not immediately, so pick the best and most feasible course and perhaps the one that by its nature will lead you to greater things yet. Take your next step with the far future and your personal vision in mind.

Interestingly, prophecy often comes from knowing the past. Like the saying 'those who ignore history are doomed to repeat it', those who know history can avoid some things and repeat others that have worked previously. Know your past. Know yours'elf. Don't repeat your mistakes, and yet stay true to your vision and focus upon what can realistically be achieved, what will bring you stability and provide you with the tools and circumstances that will enable you to venture even farther forward into the new.

And be as generous to others as you reasonably and practically can be. The more successful you become the more others will look to you for help, guidance and possibly support. Let your association be symbiotic as much as possible, but share your success and this will lead to increased possibilities and thus ever more success in the future. Use your power wisely and spread it about creating a wide base for yours'elf and your kindred. A wise leader delegates authority. There is much you can do, you best be about the business of doing it.

ENCHANTMENT SPELL:

I see the future bright and clear
All I wish for now draws near

This Spell in Arvyndase:

El ten tae lasel ilu nar vyrn
Wyl El felj fro mat omhyrlu kol

Pronunciation:

Eel teen tay lay - seal eye - lou nair vern
Will Eel feel-j fro mate om - her - lou coal

Chapter 16:

Tabebuia

KEYWORD: **SELKIE**

TREE NAME IN ARVYNDASE: **ELDAEROMPET** (PRONOUNCED: EEL - DAY - ROAM - PEET)

ARVYNDASE NAME OF THE WIZARD MYNE: **FOCIDAN** (PRONOUNCED: FOE - SID - DANE)

The Silver Elves.... 67

THIS TREE AND ITS MAGIC:

The Tabebuia is sometimes called the Trumpet Tree, although there are other trees and shrubs that bear that name as well. It is sometimes called Roble, but that is Spanish for Oak and thus is a bit of a misnomer. Most are used as flowering trees for their beauty, but some are used for timber. It is subtropical for the most part, mostly found in the Caribbean and adventive by nature, which means it likes to spread to new regions and areas, this tendency aided by the fact that its seeds are windborne. It cannot be easily contained. The wood is medium weight and is noted for enduring salt water very well. Due to these facts, we Silver Elves relate this tree to the selkies, mer-folk and sirens of the seas.

The selkies are adventive in nature, going from the sea to land and back again. The siren's call is the trumpet of the seas, it calls people to the sea and Tolkien wrote that the Elves, once they had seen and heard the sea felt very drawn toward it. Sailors have long called this The Call of the Sea, a desire to sail and be upon the vast and open plains of water. That attraction of the sea is truly the siren's song. And the flowering and beauty of this tree reminds us of the mer-folk who even when they are shown as being fierce are still amazingly beautiful.

We associate this tree with the Wizard Myne Focidan, which comes from the Arvyndase word for Selkie, which is Focida (foe - sid - dah), which itself is related to the word for Seal (as in an animal), Focidae (foe - sid - day). It is the liminal creature of the land and the ocean, ever going between the two.

Interestingly, parts of some of this species of tree are sometimes added to the entheogen Ayahuasca, which has long been used by South American shamans to obtain visions. However, it is not psychoactive in itself and is probably added for flavor. So, the siren's song is really the call of the sea, and the mermaid's beauty simply an additive feature. Also, this tree is sometimes planted by beekeepers as it is used by bees for making honey, as well as being beloved by hummingbirds for its nectar. There is a sweetness here and a certain sort of magic that the sweet things in life tend to arouse.

WHAT THIS ORACLE MEANS:

If you receive this Wizard Myne as an oracle, then you are probably feeling the call to move, migrate or sensing the call of adventure. Possibility is summoning you with its siren song but remember reality can be very different than one's imagination. The sea can be dangerous as well as beautiful and going forth unprepared can lead one into great danger or the possibility of failure. Still, that doesn't mean you shouldn't take the chance; that you shouldn't move, or go on that trip, or go to that gathering or whatever it is that is luring you to it. However, you should go as prepared as you can be and be as adaptable and flexible as possible. And remember, while things may not turn out exactly as you desired or imagined, and they seldom do, that doesn't mean that something wondrous won't develop out of this adventure. The experience of the adventure itself often makes all its difficulties and challenges worthwhile.

There is another possibility as well. And this is that someone is attempting to enchant you into doing something that seems to hold great promise. And it may very well be so, but look at it closely. What are their true motivations? What do they expect to get out of it? And even though they say and act like they are your friends, even though they themselves may be very attractive on the surface, are you sure you can really trust them? Beauty is not a guarantee of reliability and trustworthiness. We're not saying not to do whatever it is that calls to you, but to do it wisely and know, in as much as possible, what you are doing and what the risks are. Remember, if things go very wrong, it is quite possible you will have no one to blame but yours'elf for being heedless; and the spirits, for their part, know that those who seek to lure you to your doom and their own advantage and profit, aren't going to take any responsibility for you or even for their own part in what you've done.

ENCHANTMENT SPELL:

You are attractive as can be
But beneath the surface of the sea
There's much that I can only see
By gazing to the depths of me

This Spell in Arvyndase:

Le da chanako tat vek te

Kana usco tae shurfa u tae oto

Norn'da lent dij El vek norae ten

La olsdas va tae dorwynli u el

Pronunciation:

Lee dah chay - nay - co tate veek tea

Kay - nah yousce - co tay sure - fah you tay oh - toe

Norn'dah lean-t dye-j Eel veek nor - ray teen

Lah ole-s - dace vah tay door - win - lie you eel

Chapter 17:

Saguaro

KEYWORD: **THE NUMBER 1**

TREE GROUP NAME IN ARVYNDASE: **NEDALPA** (PRONOUNCED: KNEE - DALE - PAH)

ARVYNDASE NAME OF THE WIZARD MYNE: **LEFÅLYN** (PRONOUNCED: LEE - FAH - LYNN)

---

70 .... The Elfin Book of Trees for the Elven Druid

THIS TREE AND ITS MAGIC:

The Saguaro cactus, which is often seen as an icon of the American West, is a tree-like cactus that can grow up to forty feet tall. It is native to the Sonoran Desert of Arizona and Mexico and can also be found in parts of California. Note that the sorcery of Don Juan Matus of Carlos Castaneda's books often takes place in the Sonoran Desert. So, there is an aspect of elven sorcery here.

These trees can live to one hundred and fifty years old. While they often have branches or arms that grow out, some are a simple trunk without arms and this armless tree is called a spear. Thus, we Silver Elves relate this Wizard Myne to the Number 1, that looks like a spear, and to the elf spear and also to the desert elves. Its Myne name, Lefålyn, comes from the Arvyndase word Lefål (lee - fahl) that means spear.

The Saguaro is able to store up large amounts of water, which helps it subsist during the long periods of desert drought. It has numerous spines that are also, in their way, spear-like or dagger-like. And it produces white waxy flowers from the months of April to June that create a nectar that is beloved to honey bees, long nosed bats, particularly, as well as, white-winged doves. But, it also attracts woodpeckers, hummingbirds, orioles, the gilded flicker, a type of tit, and also the house finch, all of which contribute to its pollination.

It produces a ruby red edible fruit that can contain up to 2,000 seeds. Some birds, such as the Gila woodpeckers, purple martins, house finches, and gilded flickers create nests inside the Saguaro, but abandon these nests each season to create new ones. This leaves the old nests available for flycatchers, wrens and elf owls, although non-native and more aggressive birds have been invading their territory thus making it hard for the elf owl to find shelter. Where have we heard that story before?

WHAT THIS ORACLE MEANS:

In receiving this Wizard Myne, one is advised to prepare for possible difficult or lean times ahead. One might be wise to save, rather than spend, at this point, to be strong and stand up for ones'elf without being aggressive, speak your truth without demeaning others, even if they are rude to you, and give as generously as you can when you can do so. For in this way, you will gain support when the time comes that you really need it. Be a shelter for others and help them endure the hard times as well and, in doing so, you will increase your spiritual and magical clan and find a niche in an otherwise hostile territory. The key here is in making alliances.

It is possible that you are in an area where there is not much in the way of elven culture, or elfae friends or kindred and while migrating elsewhere may be a solution, it also may be the case that you simply cannot do so at this time because your job or support system is tried up with the particular area or situation you are currently in.

It is difficult being an elfae in the modern world and often finding those we can relate to as kindred elfin in our vicinity is hard as well, and this requires incredible resolve and perseverance and quite often we must compromise and hang out with those who are most elfin-like while they may not actually be elfae or, at least, know and identify as such. We might call this Hanging with the Unawakened. You are a 'Stranger in a Strange Land' (as the Wilhelm/Baynes translation I Ching says), or really, a Stranger in Your Own Land and only the most resilient of elves can stay true to their path under these circumstances. Most folks cannot bear the loneliness and thus fade back into the world but even if you do so, it is quite possible that Elfin, in the form of other elves, will come along in time to find you and you will be stirred from your nap and refreshed and can start once again, renewed and more experienced. The Elven Way is always there and available, even when we are not treading it.

ENCHANTMENT SPELL:

I shall endure and will succeed
Though times be hard all that I need
Will come to me by kin most true
Together we'll the future brew

This Spell in Arvyndase:

El van jalat nar yon redae

Nåt mernli te zos wyl dij El golt

Yon koso va el la eldi erst lod

Eldan eli'yon tae lasel adur

Pronunciation:

Eel vane jay - late nair yone re - day

Not mere-n - lie tea zoe-ss will dye-j Eel goal-t

Yone co - so vah eel lah eel - dye ear-st load

Eel - dane e - lie'yone tay lay - seal a - dure [as in endure]

Chapter 18:

Hackberry

KEYWORD: **ELFAE**

TREE NAME IN ARVYNDASE: **POLINPYNA** (PRONOUNCED: POE - LINE - PIN - NAH)

ARVYNDASE NAME OF THE WIZARD MYNE: **ÊLFAR** (PRONOUNCED: L - FAIR)

THIS TREE AND ITS MAGIC:

Among the experts, there are different systems of classification and sometimes disagreements about which trees belong to which family. The Hackberry tree is sometimes placed with the elm family, although it seems immune to Dutch Elm Disease, but the APG

III system puts it in the hemp or cannabis family, which appeals to these elves greatly and feels quite right to us. We associate it with the Elfae, the mixed and combined elven, elfin, elvish and faerie and fae folk and with the Wizard Myne Êlfar, that comes from the word Êlfae.

This is a truly ancient tree that goes back at least to the Miocene period of Europe, from about 23 to 5 million years ago, and Paleocene of North America and Eastern Asia, approximately 66 to 56 million years ago. The Roman author Pliny the Elder called its family the Celtis, which reminds us of the Celts whose variety of tribes, to our elven minds, were essentially elfae. It is more commonly called the Hackberry or Nettle tree.

This tree does flower, although the male flowers tend to be longer and fuzzier than the rounder and usually greener female flowers. And it produces a small pea sized fruit or drupe that is edible in many species, and has been described as having a dry but sweet flavor that some people feel is similar to the date.

Some of these trees are grown as ornamental trees, and one species works well as bonsai trees. They tend to be drought resistant. Honeybees love them for the sweet berries and certain caterpillars depend upon them as well. And its wood is used to make cabinets, while a tea can be made from the berries. Overall, this tree reminds us of the diversity of the Elfae, their endurance through the ages and even through periods of cultural drought for the elfin, and our determination, none-the-less, to bring something sweet and wonderful into the world, filling it with beauty, while softly and quietly protecting ours'elves.

WHAT THIS ORACLE MEANS:

In getting this Wizard Myne as an oracle, it is an indication that this is a very uncertain situation. There are certainly opportunities available to you, but the question is at what point do you make your entry in order to make the most of them. You are on the outside looking in. Finding the right connection is vital and approaching at the right time crucial. Where, oh, where do you fit into the prolificacy of Elfae being? If you find the right people, the right place, the right connections and introduce yours'elf at the right time, this may turn out to be very sweet for you.

But although we share a common culture, we elfae, like the Celts, are not one tribe but many tribes. And the tendency for people to misunderstand us, categorize us incorrectly and hold to their own opinions about us despite what we say and believe of ours'elves is so common we've simply come to expect it from them.

So, this is all about finding the right moment of approach and biding your time until you see a real opening for you. Don't get impatient. Watch carefully. The way will present itself to you. If you endeavor to force your way in prematurely, you may fail, or more than likely simply waste a lot of time with those who are not quite right for you in the first place. Feel strong in yours'elf and be true to your own nature and your kindred will come. Endure; you have the strength to do so. This may seem like it will take forever, or that the right one(s) may never come, but that is not the case. Elfin is watching out for you and when you realize that reality, you will understand that the moment awaits you just as much as you await the moment and your kindred seek you as you endeavor to find them.

ENCHANTMENT SPELL:
Swift the river as it flows
I'll enter in where wisdom shows

This Spell in Arvyndase:
Vys tae lowa tat ter shurlu
El'yon contyn ver ern zardpos tekelu

Pronunciation:
Viss tay low - wah tate tier sure - lou
Eel'yone con - tin veer ear-n zair-d - poe-ss tea - key - lou

Chapter 19:

Dogwood family

Keyword: **The Letter: Z**

Tree Group Name in Arvyndase: **Konuelpa** (pronounced: co - new - eel - pah)

Arvyndase Name of the Wizard Myne: **Zåndu** (pronounced: zahn - due)

This Tree and its Magic:

The Dogwood species can be found throughout much of temperate and boreal, sub-arctic Eurasia and also in North America. There are also species in China and Japan and they are especially abundant in southeastern United States. In the past, it was called the Dogtree and the Hound's tree and its fruits are sometimes called dogberries or houndberries. However, dogwood seems to originally come from the term dagwood, due to the fact that its slender stems of very hard wood were used in the past for making 'dags' or daggers, skewers, and arrows. Thus, we elves relate it to the letter Z and the Wizard Myne Zåndu, which stems from the Arvyndase word Zån that means 'bolt,' as in an arrow or dart. For we relate this tree to the elf arrow or elf bolt that tradition says was ensorcelled with magic, shot from hiding, and made ill those whose skin it pricked, since it was toxic (a poisoned dart).

However, before it was named dogwood it was referred to as a Whippletree. The whipple is part of a horse-drawn cart. It connects the draw-pole of the cart to the harnesses of the horses in a line. The name stems from the fact that the Whipple tree was carved and used to create this part of the cart.

Most of these species create small berries that are usually edible, although some can be mildly toxic to humans (especially when they are ensorcelled) but the birds love them. They are said to be high in vitamin C and thus utilized to combat colds.

The Dogwood is also used for making walking canes (what we elves call enchanter's canes) and for arrow making, as mentioned previously, but also for the construction of mountain dulcimers (an elven instrument) and for creating fine inlays. It has also been used for the making of golf club heads or 'woods' and it was further used, in strips, for the earliest laminated tennis rackets. Pioneers in the Americas fashioned the twigs to brush their teeth by peeling off the bark, biting the twig and then scrubbing their teeth with it.

WHAT THIS ORACLE MEANS:

In getting this Wizard Myne as an oracle, it is likely that you are in a situation where someone is doing something a bit wicked, pursuing self-interest at the expense of others, and you feel compelled to do something about it but have neither the power nor the authority to do so directly. Thus, you must be subtle, perhaps even sneaky and underhanded, in dealing with this issue. You must act from the shadows. You are called to block their wicked activities, but do so in secret for to confront them openly is to suffer unnecessarily yours'elf and the point is to make them regret what they are doing and make it so that pursuing their evil course costs them more than they will profit by doing so. They may not be developed enough to understand morality, but they will understand cause and effect when their acts are costly, especially when the effect results in their own suffering and loss.

While obstructing them and hindering their efforts to do ill, try to make it a bit of a game (like golf or tennis) for yours'elf, make obstructing them fun. Get into the joy of hidden opposition. Yet, at the same time, remember this is not really about punishment, nor is it about revenge, this is about getting them to understand that it is easier in the long run and much more to their advantage to play nice, get in harness with everyone else, which is to say cooperate with those who are pulling in the right direction, so they find that doing the right thing for everyone is also best for their own selves.

It could be possible that all you are able to do is shoot hidden bolts of magic at these miscreants from your secret sanctuary. And while these elves, for the most part, don't use dark magic, or tread the left-hand path, there are times when those who pursue the dark ways must experience a bit of their own toxic medicine if they are to be saved from their own ignorance. The point, however, is to incline them toward the light and that is best done when they don't know who is opposing them and when it seems as though Nature and the Universe are actually the true source of their obstruction. For in the long run, that is exactly what is happening. Act on the behalf of the Universe and the Elfae folk overall.

ENCHANTMENT SPELL:
You are wicked but you'll see
The Shadow you arouse is me

This Spell in Arvyndase:
Le da konaf kana le'yon ten
Tae Dasår le alesi da el

Pronunciation:
Lee dah co - nafe lee'yone teen
Tay Day - sahr lee a - lee - sigh dah eel

Chapter 20:

Dipterocarpaceae Family

KEYWORD: **THE NUMBER 2**

TREE GROUP NAME IN ARVYNDASE: **FROFABORELPA** (FROE - FAH - BORE - EEL - PAH)

ARVYNDASE NAME OF THE WIZARD MYNE: **FROFLYN** (PRONOUNCED FROE-F - LYNN)

THIS TREE AND ITS MAGIC:

The Dipterocarpaceae family of trees and shrubs contain about 16 genera and approximately 695 species that are for the most part tropical lowland rainforest trees. The family name comes from the Greek words di, meaning two; pteron, which means wing; and karpos, which is the word for fruit, all this because of the two-winged fruit that these tree produce. Therefore, we Silver Elves associate these trees with the Wizard Myne Froflyn, which comes from the Arvynadse word frof, or wing. This myne is used to symbolize the Number Two, and is further associated with Faerie Wings and by extension Elf Ears, which are the symbolic representations of the faerie and elven peoples.

Besides being harvested by Man for timber, these trees are valued by the elfae for balsam, for their aromatic essential oils and for other resins that they create. We elves love our aromatic essential oils and we expect that the faerie folk do as well. In fact, we put them on nearly every day.

These trees can rise to great heights, some reaching 260 feet tall, about 80 meters, and generally grow above the rest of the trees in the forest reaching for the sky, as faerie wings allow the faeries to ascend to great heights. It is said that these trees have 'crown shyness', which is to say that when they become mature, they do not let their crowns touch each other, an indication to the minds of these elves of individual uniqueness and nobility. In fact, for the elven, uniqueness and eccentricity are signs of nobility.

In Borneo and other places where these trees grow in abundance, it is said that up to 90% of these trees in a particular section of the forest will all bear fruit at the same time. This is called 'mass fruiting' and its evolutionary purpose is to overwhelm potential predators with abundance, (a very elven way of going about things). The predators then eat their fruits and propagate them all over the forest as they migrate from place to place seeking another area where these trees are in the process of fruiting en masse.

One of the major contributors to this process is the bearded, wild boar that tirelessly forages the jungle, roots about in the earth and reshapes the soil surface and at the same time in doing so accelerates the decomposition of organic matter. Its browsing clears the undergrowth, which improves the access of tree roots to needed soil nutrients. Note that the blue boar was often used as a symbol of wild power and warrior spirit by the Celts. The native folk of Borneo see this bearded boar as an ambassador from the spirit world of the forest, the realm of the elves and faerie folk, and possibly the Celts saw them this way as well.

WHAT THIS ORACLE MEANS:

While modern faeries don't usually have physical wings, nor do most incarnate elves have pointed ears, the faeries do like to create and wear their wings from time to time and we elves don our elf ears to declare who we are spiritually in our hearts (feelings), minds and souls (our connection and link to others). Thus, if you get this Wizard Myne as an oracle, it is time to be daring enough to reveal who you truly are, at least to those you can trust, and let the Light of Elfin and Faerie shine anew through you and out into the world around you.

It is not that you can trust everyone. But we do have the great wise bearded spirit boar (possibly blue, which denotes the second ray of

Love-Wisdom, what the Elf Queen's Daughters used to refer to as our Shield of Love, see *The Elf Magic Mail: The Original Letters of the Elf Queen's Daughters with Commentary by The Silver Elves*, vols. 1 & 2) to protect us. And we have our own mature understanding that tells us it would be naive to think that everyone will accept us for who we really are, and those who take any sign of difference as permission to bully and persecute those unlike them do exist.

But they are not everywhere and they usually feel very uncomfortable venturing into Faerie or Elfin. Not everyone will accept you for who you truly are and know yours'elf to be, but surely there are those around you who, while they may not totally understand your elfae nature will be openminded enough to let you wear your wings of spirit or your noble elf ears without making fun of you or harassing you for doing so. They may even find it quite intriguing, while others of your kind may very well join you.

In other words, be yours'elf. Wear your elfae crown as the unique individual that you are and stand tall in the world, independently, and lead the way for others. Find those with whom you can trust to share this inner truth, and nurture and protect each other and let your faerie or elf or otherkin out for a run, or a soar.

Enchantment Spell:

(faerie)
I spread my wings and I fly
Up into the spirit sky

(elf)
My ears are pointed you can see
I am elf and I am free

This Spell in Arvyndase:
(faerie)
El wyd el'na frofli nar El fos
Rep verva tae tari faln

(elf)
El'na polli da lyntün le vek ten
El da êlda nar El da alo

Pronunciation:
(faerie)
Eel wid eel'nah fro-f - lie nair Eel foe-ss
Reap veer - vah tay tay - rye fail-n

(elf)
Eel'nah pole - lie dah lent - in lee veek teen
Eel dah l - dah nair Eel dah a - low

Chapter 21:

Persimmon family

Keyword: **Dark Elves**

Tree Name in Arvyndase: **Banfu** (pronounced: bane - few)

Arvyndase Name of the Wizard Myne: **Daslyn** (pronounced: dace - lynn)

---

82 .... The Elfin Book of Trees for the Elven Druid

THIS TREE AND ITS MAGIC:

The Persimmon family of trees bears the genus Diospyros that has over 700 species of deciduous (seasonally shedding leaves) and evergreen shrubs and trees. Most of these trees live in the tropics, while a few species may be found in more temperate regions. Some are noted for their hard, heavy, dark timber, and these are commonly referred to as ebony trees, while some of these trees are especially valued for their fruit and are noted as the persimmon side of the family. The persimmon in ancient Greece was seen as being the Fruit of the Gods, the Divine Nectar. These trees were said to be common in the lowland dry forests Maui Nui, which is what geologists call a prehistoric Hawaiian Island that was constructed from seven volcanoes, which later became smaller islands with the rising seas. According to esoteric scientists, Maui Nui was said to be part of the great ancient civilization and island continent of Mu.

We Silver Elves relate this Wizard Myne to the Dark Elves and the name for the Myne Daslyn comes from the Arvyndase word for Dark, which is Das. We do this because of the dark mahogany trees but also because of the Persimmon, the Fruit of the Gods, which if eaten before it is ripe will be hard, acrid and bitter. Therefore, this fruit symbolizes the fact that enlightenment doesn't usually come quickly but is a matter of time, effort and maturity. Mahogany on the other hand is a hard, dark wood, and symbolizes both strength and protection. We need to be strong to pursue enlightenment and we need to protect ours'elves as elfae as we tread the path of the Elven Way. Thus, these trees represent the passage from the dark (in this case symbolizing ignorance but also strength and primal power) toward the light through the ingestion of the fruit of enlightenment. It is a passage from pure force to the true power of enchantment, subtlety and indirect influence, the power of awakening, persuasion and illumination.

The Dark Elves are often mistaken by some folks with the Unseelie Elfae, and surely some of them can be Unseelie. The Unseelie are usually parasitic in expression and nearly always hostile toward Mankind, although they will sometimes form uneasy alliances with them, just as criminals form uncertain alliances with each other but are seldom sure whom they can really trust.

But the Dark Elves are not necessarily Unseelie, and all elves and others, all life and all being is destined to develop, evolve and reach enlightenment in time. Therefore, the dark elves, in a way, represent a transition from our more animal s'elves to our more illuminated beings. But there are aspects of the animal nature that we do not wish to lose, for this dislocation from our inner natures would be unfortunate. We are not becoming utterly different from animals nor divorcing ours'elves totally from Nature but rather we are developing our animal instincts and abilities to their highest and most powerful state. Not getting rid of our animal instincts and natures but refining them and in that way possibly making them even more powerful.

WHAT THIS ORACLE MEANS:

Power is one thing, wisdom is another. It is good to have power but if used unwisely will bring great misfortune upon you. Be wise. Use your power wisely.

If you receive this Wizard Myne in response to a question put to the oracle, then it is best that you gain some patience and wait. It is true that you may have the power to force your will upon the situation and make what you desire happen, but that is not really wise, and will turn out poorly in the long run, evoking unnecessary regrets, which can all be avoided with just a touch of s'elf mastery.

This situation needs time to ripen. Hold back, bide your time, let things develop on their own and at their own pace. Don't interfere. If you can restrain yours'elf, it is most likely that you will get what you desire with almost no effort required at all. It will come to you like a ripe persimmon falling from a tree. And if you give things time to mature, the result will be all that much sweeter for the waiting. Be strong within yours'elf and use the power you have to discipline yours'elf, your desires and your inclination to act before the time is ripe.

People are repelled by those who seem desperate and attracted to those who are calm and confident about thems'elves and their abilities. Don't be desperate. Be confident in yours'elf, be serene and let the Universe and the Magic serve you. If you do so, this will turn out to be a very tasty treat and well earned, with minimal investment of energy.

ENCHANTMENT SPELL:

Calmly, I do watch and wait
Time will bring me gifts most great

This Spell in Arvyndase:

Elwynla, El ba jort nar her
Mern yon cura el retonli erst ralt

Pronunciation:

Eel - win - lah, Eel bah jour-t nair here
Mere-n yone cur - rah eel ree - tone - lie ear-st rail-t

Chapter 22:

Heath family

KEYWORD: THE LETTER L

TREE GROUP NAME IN ARVYNDASE: ELODELPA (E - LOAD - EEL - PAH)

ARVYNDASE NAME OF THE WIZARD MYNE: LYNTOAR (PRONOUNCED: LYNN - TOE - AIR)

THIS TREE AND ITS MAGIC:

The Heath family of flowering plants, shrubs and trees, also known as the Heather family, are usually found living in acrid and otherwise infertile growing conditions. They are survivors. This family includes the cranberry, blueberry, huckleberry, and rhododendron, which includes azaleas, and numerous other heaths and heathers. Among this family is also the Arbutus, or Madrone species. Their flowers tend to be hermaphroditic as are many elfae and otherkin in disposition and sexual preference if not in actual form.

The Heather is linked to the Ogham Ur and is related to healing. In the ancient Druidic poem, The Battle of the Trees it says: "The heath gave consolation to the toil-spent folk..." (see *The White Goddess* by Robert Graves). We Silver Elves associate these trees with the Wizard Myne Lyntoar that is derived from the Arvyndase word Lynto, which means deliver, as in 'set free,' such as in the Christian prayer, '... deliver us from evil...'. The Arvyndase word Lyntoara (lynn - toe - air - rah) means deliverance.

The madrone tree is seen as balancing the light and the dark (the tree of the knowledge of good and evil?). The First Nations people of Northwestern U.S.A. have a tale of how the Madrone was used by its people to survive the Great Flood by tying their canoes to it on top of a mountain, thus bringing deliverance. Therefore, we elves connect this tree family to the World Tree, called the Yggdrasil by the Norse, and seen as an Ash tree by some folks, Oak by others, and other trees depending upon the prominent tree of their region. In the bible, the world tree becomes the two trees of Paradise, which Tolkien followed when writing of the two trees of Valinor.

To we Silver Elves, this is one tree family, that represents the center of Elfin as well as the magnetic center running through the Earth, with a positive, Madrone, and negative, Heath/Heather, pole. Also, we relate it to the Yin and Yang energies whose intertwining is part of the Tao, two seemingly opposite forces that are really part of the same power or state of being. Not separate but two sides of the same coin. Note that the Madrone is red, the color of leadership, initiation and activity, and of the first ray; and heather often has purple flowers, the color we Silver Elves associate with the seventh ray of ritual and ceremonial magic that involves the invocation and evocation of elementals and devas, which is to say the powers of Nature, the Universe and of the Elfae folk and the Shining Ones.

What This Oracle Means:

In deriving this Wizard Myne in response to a question put to the oracle, then it is advised that you hold firmly to your principles, don't waver, don't give up the path, cling to your elfae or otherkin nature, know who you are and don't let others' doubts or disapproval dissuade or infect you. You may feel exhausted by the world and struggling hard to keep afloat within it; you may feel that you are the only elf, faerie, or other in the world or, at least, anywhere in your vicinity; but don't yield to the world. Don't let it wash you away in its current of popular fads and consumption and basic wrongheadedness about nearly everything. Hold on to what you believe and inwardly know to be true.

At the center of Elfin is the World Tree, be it Oak, Ash, Thorn, Madrone or whatever. Embrace the wisdom you have gained from your association with that realm. Don't second guess your inner feelings about who you truly are. Stand tall and stand out, like the Madrone and be a leader among your people, and at the same time, be not so far above them as to be removed from them. Be healing unto your people, like the Heath, for they have labored, too, and they also need succor.

Be the tree at the center of your own eald, your demesne, your realm that others can depend upon and encourage them to be their own central tree as well, until we have a forest of elfae being growing upon the Earth once again and the world that was thought by so many as only a dream becomes a reality born of our being.

Enchantment Spell:

I stand firm amid the storm
And to me all my kindred swarm

This Spell in Arvyndase:

El lotz byrn onid tae zalvor

Nar va el wyl el'na eldivu yom

Pronunciation:
Eel low-tz burn oh - nide - tay zale - vour
Nair vah eel will eel'nah eel - dye - view yom

Chapter 23:

Eucommia family

KEYWORD: **UNICORN**

TREE GROUP NAME IN ARVYNDASE: **UKURNELPA** (PRONOUNCED: YOU - CURE-N - EEL - PAH)

ARVYNDASE NAME OF THE WIZARD MYNE: **USELDI** (PRONOUNCED: YOU - SEAL - DYE)

THIS TREE AND ITS MAGIC:

Eucommia trees live primarily in China but, according to the fossil record, they had wider distribution in the past. It has only one living species, Eucommia ulmoides, which is near to extinction in the wild. However, because it is highly valued as a healing herb in traditional Chinese medicine and its bark is often sought after, the Chinese cultivate this tree for its healing properties. Eucommia is thought to be a power herb, which is conceived to be second only to

Ginseng in its value and potency. The bark of the eucommia tree is considered one of the elite herbs for maintaining the integrity and function of the musculoskeletal system. It is also an herb that is utilized for balancing the endocrine system and it is seen to support normal, healthy sexual functioning. In Chinese natural medicine, Eucommia is the primary herb utilized for creating a healthy, flexible and strong skeletal structure. It has great value in the development and maintenance of muscles, ligaments, bones and tendons and is used for helping repair these areas if injured.

We Silver Elves connect it to the Unicorn but also to the Pegasus, the winged horse of Greek Mythology, because this tree produces a winged samara, that looks rather like the 'helicopter' winged seed of the elm tree, only this tree produces a samara with two wings and one seed between them, thus reminiscent to us of the Pegasus, the flying horse.

This tree is sometimes referred to as the China Rubber tree because of the fact that a torn leaf will ooze latex that will hold the leaf together. It is also called the Hard Rubber tree; however, it is of a different family than the rubber trees of Southeast Asia or the ones of South America. Because of its rubbery nature, we are reminded of the child's saying 'I am rubber, you are glue, your words bounce off me and stick to you,' that is used when one is subjected to name calling insults. This brings to our minds the Unicorn in its purity and its ability to be above the normal fray of the world.

We associate this tree with the Wizard Myne Useldi that comes from the Arvyndase word Usel, which means 'above' and indicates operating from a higher level of intelligence, being and understanding.

WHAT THIS ORACLE MEANS:

If you draw this Wizard Myne as an oracle, it means that you need to rise above the situation. No matter what others say about you, don't get dragged down to their level. They are not worth it and being principally ignorant, their opinions aren't really worth your interest or concern. The fact that they criticize you in this instance, and seek to tear you down, by itself, indicates their lack of understanding and the inferiority of their position. Be like rubber. And if you feel a bit hurt, you need not; but still, even so, if you do feel insulted, know you are stronger than they and hold yours'elf together and endure.

More than likely these people are just trying to rattle you because of their own hidden feelings of emptiness and their lack of inner confidence in anything but the enculturated opinions they've been raised with and have come to cling to out of a fear of venturing beyond the norm. They are not strong enough, as yet, to be the unique individuals they are destined to be and so they seek to tear down those who are and whom they secretly envy.

You are above all that. Be a Pegasus Unicorn in this situation and simply fly away from it all. Look at things from a higher perspective, from the point of view of your more advanced and evolved s'elf, and don't worry about what these others say or think. This situation requires a new approach, an unusual solution. It won't be fixed by doing the same old thing. It is only by seeing the wider perspective of the situation, as though you were observing it from the sky, that you can come to understand the entirety of what is needed in order to go forward. This is a situation that requires greater intelligence, not greater force. Step back, look from on high, and you will see the path that is obscured to those who are way too close to the situation and way too emotionally involved to look beyond themselves and their knee-jerk reactions and opinions. And it just may well be that you simply need to move on and leave them stuck in their limited worlds and world views.

ENCHANTMENT SPELL:

From above I see it all
And take no part with tooth or claw
I am not touched nor disturbed so slight
But embrace the path I know is right

This Spell in Arvyndase:

An usel El ten ter wyl
Nar rud kon sun ena can sa tarqa
El da kon fostïn konsa bothïn re nofa

Kana byrha tae tål El ken da mard

Pronunciation:
Aine you - seal Eel teen tier will
Nair rude cone soon e - nah can sah tair - qwah
Eel dah cone foe-st - in cone - sah both - in ree no - fah
Kay - nah ber - hah tay tahl Eel keen dah mare-d

Chapter 24:

Acacia

KEYWORD: **FAERIE**

TREE NAME IN ARVYNDASE: **WYKORLI** (PRONOUNCED: WICK - CORE - LIE)

ARVYNDASE NAME OF THE WIZARD MYNE: **FARRIFAR** (PRONOUNCED: FAIR - RYE - FAIR)

THIS TREE AND ITS MAGIC:

Acacia trees and shrubs are commonly called wattles and are part of the pea family. Wattle is thought to be from an Old Teutonic word referring to 'weaving' for in Old English they used the word watul in reference to the interwoven branches and sticks that were used to form fences, walls and roofs, etc. Thus, there is some link surely to witchcraft, magic, the wicca and weaving as a magical art in general, which elfin spells are often used for charging in the course of their making. Whispering spells as one weaves, weaving spells into rugs, clothes and other woven items.

We Silver Elves relate this to the Wizard Myne Farrifar, which comes from the Arvyndase words, Farri (faerie) and Far (dance), therefore it means faerie dance and represents Faerie as a place, realm and a state of being rather than as individual faeries or fairies. Faeries Collective, we might say or the realm of Collective Faerie Being.

These trees and shrubs are found in all regions of the Earth, which includes alpine environments, woodlands, rainforests, grasslands, and even coastal dunes and deserts. Like Faerie, these trees are found nearly everywhere. People often think of Faerie and faeries as being strictly of Western European origin but fairy tales are really a worldwide phenomenon, as Evans-Wentz mentions in *Fairy-Faith in the Celtic Countries*. Also see *American Elves* by John E. Roth about the faerie folk of the Americas and further note the various tales from cultures around the world of devas, dragons and all sorts of faerie, elfae folk and otherkin.

Some of the species of acacia are found to contain psychoactive alkaloids, while others possess potassium fluoroacetate, which can be used as a rodent poison. Like Faerie, itself, these plants are wondrous to some and deadly to others. Be not a rat in Faerie unless you be an intelligent, magical Faerie Rat.

Some of the Australian species of these trees are fire resistant. Faerie and faeries have taken the heat through the centuries and have endured. Also, the seeds of some of these species can have as much as 25% more protein than is to be found in most grains or cereals. Plus, they store well for extended periods of time because of the hard covering of their seeds.

This tree and related shrubs have also been utilized to make various implements, including weapons. It is also used for fuel and in the making of musical instruments. Faerie, as a place, is psychically nutritious and provides one with more energy than living in the world of the Normals does, which for its part can be quite draining.

WHAT THIS ORACLE MEANS:

In connecting to this Wizard Myne and getting it as a sign, it is time to look to Faerie as a source of spiritual nutrition and strength. It may seem like you are all alone in the world without any faerie kin around you, struck in a place that has little to do with Elfin and Faerie, but Faerie can grow nearly anywhere. Look about you and you may very well see bits of Faerie in some of those around you who don't even know of or recognize their elfae being. It is just a matter of the right approach, using the charms of enchantment and your personality that will awaken that seed of Faerie within them and get them to come out and play, at least for a little while.

And if there is truly nothing of Faerie that you can find in your environment, be the seed that sprouts into Faerie life. Be the elf, fae, faerie, or other that you truly are, even if you are doing so in a sort of camouflaged way, and sprinkle faery dust or pixie powder about you and see who is attracted to the sparkle. Some people hide in the dark and fear the light of Faerie, but others will be intrigued and it is these that need but a gentle nudge to awaken something deeper within them. Something that speaks to their soul in ways that the normal world can never do.

If you weave your charms carefully, and with a bit of delight, you may find that your unassuming magics find response in others and they, in turn, may lead you to opportunities and connections you otherwise would not have or encounter. You may take a little heat from the ignorant but you can endure it and as long as you don't try to force anything upon them, keeping it all very light and playful, and don't attempt to push it in their faces, everything should turn out well. They, after all, are good at ignoring things they don't want to see or believe in.

ENCHANTMENT SPELL:

Faerie, Faerie everywhere, enduring, rising strong
And every seed a part of it bringing all for which we long

This Spell in Arvyndase:
Farri, Farri lotymern, talosdas, luftdas mylth

Nar lotym dern na sun u ter curådas wyl fro tild eli awath

Pronunciation:
Fair - rye, Fair - rye low - tim - ear-n, tay - lowce - dace, loof-t - dace mill-th

Nair low - tim deer-n nah soon you tier cur - rah - dace will fro tiled e - lie a - wayth

Chapter 25:

Orchid tree

●

KEYWORD: **THE NUMBER 0**

TREE NAME IN ARVYNDASE: **CHIDALDA** (PRONOUNCED: CHI - DALE - DAH)

ARVYNDASE NAME OF THE WIZARD MYNE: **FLUERI** (PRONOUNCED: FLEW - EAR - RYE)

THIS TREE AND ITS MAGIC:

The Orchid tree, which is also a member of the Pea family, is principally an ornamental tree grown for its beautiful orchid-like flowers. It is found across the tropics. They are frequently cultivated in Southeastern China, India, Sri Lanka, and Vietnam but can also be found in Hawaii and other warm coastal areas of the United States. They can grow up to nearly forty feet tall or from six to twelve meters high. Their blossoms can be found in various shades of red, pink, purple, orange, or yellow, and are frequently aromatic. They can be propagated by seed or cuttings, and while they do well in alkaline soils, they do not thrive in salty conditions.

We Silver Elves associate this Wizard Myne to the Number Zero, and also to the Flower Fairies, those beautiful beings that are a diminution of the legendary Fair Folk who could be both beautiful and dangerous. We love the Flower Fairies, surely, but they can seem quite frivolous as beings, the faerie version of the "dumb blond" stereotype, beautiful but whimsical and empty headed. The name of the Myne is Flueri, which stems from the Arvyndase word Fluer, which means flower.

This is not to say that beauty and gentleness are not great powers in themselves. They are filled with charm and enchantment and should not be underestimated. In fact, one of the chief powers of the flower faeries is the ability to get one to take them for granted and not even look to see the magic they are weaving even as they do so right before one's very eyes.

WHAT THIS ORACLE MEANS:

If you receive this Wizard Myne as an oracle, it indicates that there is little you can do at present, other than make things as beautiful as you can, as pleasing as possible and therefore you can take action only upon the surface of things. This Myne is connected to the I Ching hexagram # 22, sometimes called Grace but we Silver Elves refer to it as Beauty (see *The Elven Book of Changes*).

Some people look down upon those folks who just dress up as elves or faeries and have a good time at Faery Gatherings but don't seem to take our culture more seriously. They see these folks as posers and frown upon their seemingly frivolous natures and deride them for what they see as their lack of commitment. However, remember that those who look down upon those elfae who are just putting their toes in the waters, so to speak, are usually uncertain about their own elfae nature but cannot admit their uncertainty to thems'elves as yet. Embrace your others, however frivolous they may seem, they are children in a sense, needing encouragement and nurturing.

Embrace the flower fairies, they are more than they seem usually, and even when they are not, they make nice camouflage for us in a world that can, at times, be hostile to elfae folk. We can always use them as a disguise if necessary and pretend we are just as frivolous as they if we need to do so to pass through that world.

And, after all, they are just playing and we elfin folk love to play. Besides, at this point in the game, there really isn't much that you can do of significance, anyway. So, bide your time and be content with waiting until the cycles change and more serious magics can be enacted.

Enchantment Spell:

I pause and smell the flowers
Their beauty to enjoy
And when the time doth come around
Great magics I'll employ

This Spell in Arvyndase:

El bers nar sum tae fluerli
Tam'na eloa va taelsa
Nar nas tae mern båver koso anabo
Ralt êldonli El'yon melus

Pronunciation:

Eel beers nair sue-m tay flew - ear - lie
Tame'nah e - low - ah vah tay - eel - sah
Nair nace tay mere-n bah - veer co - so a - nay - bo
Rail-t l - doan - lie Eel'yone me - loose

Chapter 26:

Brazilwood

KEYWORD: **ENCHANTMENT**

TREE NAME IN ARVYNDASE: **SARAKACALDA** (SARA - CAKE - ALE - DAH)

ARVYNDASE NAME OF THE WIZARD MYNE: **SOFAN** (PRONOUNCED: SO - FANE)

THIS TREE AND ITS MAGIC:

This flowering tree, which is another member of the pea or legume family, has an orange-red heartwood. It is generally found in Brazil, thus its name. This wood creates a red dye that was valued in the past, particularly for dyeing velvet. We elves love velvet, lace and silk, and silk velvet is our favorite (silk is a material, velvet is a weave, as is lace, although we might call lace a stitch or a knit, and silk lace is also beloved by us but cotton lace is nice as well). This tree has an Asian relative called Sappanwood that also produces a red dye.

However, this tree is best noted for its use in making bows. Not the bow of bows and arrows, but the bow that is used for playing stringed instruments. We elves, as a people, are fabled archers, but we are also legendary musicians. This tree speaks to that aspect of our being and culture.

We relate this Wizard Myne to the power of Enchantment and the name of the Myne is Sofan, which comes from the Arvyndase word Sofa that means Velvet. Music is certainly something that holds the power of enchantment, that can reach to the depth of one's soul and encourage one's imagination to soar to the heights of possibility. Elven magic, for the most part, is enchantment. A magic that is based upon beauty and, in its way, sensuality (rather like velvet) and on the stirring of the heart strings of the individual.

At the same time, while this tree produces beautiful and fragrant yellow flowers, whose petals have a blood red spot upon them, the branches, leaves and fruit all bear small thorns. Our enchantments while beautiful are not naive. We are innocent in the world but not innocents. We elven will not allow ours'elves to be easily taken advantage of.

WHAT THIS ORACLE MEANS:

You may wish to use your elven bow and shoot an arrow or two at someone, but if you receive this Wizard Myne in response to a question put to the oracle, then it is better that you use the musician's bow rather than that of the archer. We understand the impulse to strike back, we really do, and in some cases that is appropriate, but this is not the case here. And it can be hard not to strike back at those assholes, but resist the temptation, for you will only get entangled deeper into their folly when it is best if you can depart from them altogether. This is a situation that calls for elven enchantment rather than elven martial arts. Beauty, intelligence and grace, not muscle, are the solution here.

Even if they have been rude or insulting to you or yours, smile, treat them with kindness, and watch as they become confused, frustrated and even a bit insane (more than they already are), as they try to process why you aren't responding in the knee-jerk fashion they have come to expect. In fact, it is quite possible that no matter what you say or do they will be so anticipating you to react in a certain way that they will think you have done so, whether you have or not. But don't be put off. Smile, keep your enchantments flowing, point out the truth clearly, serenely and without malice, and at first opportunity leave them behind.

It doesn't really matter what they think. After all, their thoughts are merely rote responses that they've learned and have never changed, being, as they are, reinforced by their own isolated society. The fact that you have done something unexpected will puzzle them. It will set their minds to spinning, for a brief period, and cause most such individuals to avoid you in the future for they do not like having their stereotypes color out of the lines. It makes them think and question and, really, they don't like thinking very much.

ENCHANTMENT SPELL:

I'll hum a tune and give a smile
And you'll not notice all the while

This Spell in Arvyndase:

El'yon zerm na nis luth na fiso
Nar le'yon kon dothar wyl tae jern

Pronunciation:

Eel'yone zeer-m nah nice lou-th nah fie - so
Nair lee'yone cone doe - thayr will tay jeer-n

Chapter 27:

Honey locust

KEYWORD: **NIXIE**

TREE NAME IN ARVYNDASE: **OSTÅFETRYN** (PRONOUNCED: OH - STAH - FEE - TRINN)

Arvyndase Name of the Wizard Myne: **Wåkser**
(Pronounced: Wahk - seer)

This Tree and its Magic:

Honey Locust trees are also called the Thorny Locust due to their thorns that can grow from an inch to eight inches in length. This is another member of the pea or legume family of trees and is usually found in the moist soil of river valleys. However, it is highly adaptable as a species and is generally seen as being both invasive and aggressive. In fact, this tree can endure urban conditions, such as compacted soil, alkaline soil, road salt, and both heat and drought. It's a survivor.

On the other hand, these trees often grow up fast and they do tend to have a relatively short life as trees go, of only about one hundred and twenty years or so. They produce very fragrant cream-colored flowers that appear in clusters. They are beautiful in their own way, but can be dangerous.

We Silver Elves connect this tree to the Nixies, those water sprites that are noted by legend for being aggressive and hostile to Mankind, beautiful and we might say fragrant, but with sharp teeth and claws, luring Men to their deaths or, at least, to be used and preyed upon. The natural habitats of the nixies are springs, ponds, rivers and their surrounding areas, but they have expanded in modern times and are frequently found in and around modern 'watering holes,' such as bars, strip joints, night clubs and other places where they can use their beauty to draw the unwary into their clutches. However, like the honey locust tree these creatures often have shorter lives than most fae, being prone to drug addiction and alcoholism. Being a bit of a parasite can take its toll on a person.

This Wizard Myne is named Wåkser after the Arvyndase word Wåkse, which is our word for Nixie. While these beings are often female, there is also a male variety that are called Nixes, or Nix singular.

What This Oracle Means:

If you receive this Wizard Myne as an oracle, then you need to be really careful. Quite possibly, there is someone you are encountering in your environment or in these current circumstances, who may be a danger to you. This person may seem friendly, may even be beautiful and alluring, but don't be tempted, they are most likely out to use you for all they can get out of you and will give you nothing substantial in return, except perhaps the clap or herpes or large credit card debt. They may, quite possibly, be out of your league as far as beauty goes, and that, in itself, should serve as a warning. Does it seem too good to be true? Tread carefully if you don't wish to be used and thrown away later after they have gotten all that they wish from you. They are out for themselves and you are just seen as their prey. They are masters of glamor and while they may be quite lovely in appearance, look beneath the surface into their souls and you will discover that, indeed, in this case their beauty really is only skin deep.

On the other hand, nixies sometimes don't bother with the elven. We have little of material value that interests them really and sometimes, just in recognition of our rather spiritual nature, they wish nothing to do with us. Our presence can make them feel uncomfortable and a bit guilty about their Unseelie proclivities. So, if this person rejects you, appreciate the fact that you have been blest and accept the rejection for the kindness it really is. You got lucky this time. Move on to where your spirit will be appreciated and reciprocated. And if you insist on going forward, and involving yours'elf with them, at least wear protection.

Enchantment Spell:

Beneath the surface I do see
Beyond the face you show to me
And seeing true I'm free to leave
Cutting through the web you weave

This Spell in Arvyndase:
Usco tae shurfa El ba ten

Hyrlon tae fyli le teke va el
Nar tendas lod El'da alo va dorpa
Vakdas joul tae sent le tols

Pronunciation:
You-ss - co tay sure - fah Eel bah teen
Her - lone tay fill - lie lee tea - key vah eel
Nair teen - dace load Eel'dah a - low vah door - pah
Vake - das joe - yule tay seen-t lee tolls

Chapter 28:

Laburnum

KEYWORD: **GOBLIN**

TREE NAME IN ARVYNDASE: **KIFLYN** (PRONOUNCED: KI [RHYMES WITH HIGH] - FLYNN)

ARVYNDASE NAME OF THE WIZARD MYNE: **GOBLYNA** (PRONOUNCED: GOB - LIN - NAH)

THIS TREE AND ITS MAGIC:

Laburnum tree is commonly called the Golden Chain or Golden Rain tree. It is another tree in the pea or legume family and its natural setting is in the mountains of Southern Europe extending from France to the Balkans. Indian laburnum, which is generally referred to as the Golden Shower tree, is a distant relative this tree.

The Laburnum tree leaves are trifoliate and thus appear similar to clover in appearance. They produce yellow pea-flowers that come out in long leafless chains, leading to the name Golden Chain. However, the fruit of this tree and all its parts are poisonous, although usually not fatally so.

Due to all this, we elves associate this tree with the Goblins, and the Wyzard Myne Goblyna, based on the word Goblyn, which is the word for Goblin in Arvyndase. However, this tree is also used for cabinetmaking and inlays. It is utilized for making various musical instruments, including wind instruments, such as recorders and flutes, and it was once a very popular wood for the creation of Great Highland Bagpipes. Some people would argue that Bagpipes are a form of torture, although we Silver Elves love Bagpipe music.

Grimlins and some others may wish to enslave you and make sure you know you are a slave, but Goblins can be very clever, so they let you think you are free even while you are enslaved. They will tell you your chains are made of gold and that they will make the world rain gold upon you if you just do what they tell you. They are full of unfilled promises luring you to spend more and more. They will raise prices enormously and then lower them a little and tell you how much you can save by buying things you don't really need or actually want. But, unfortunately, beneath all that there is often a poisonous greed that taints nearly everything they touch.

WHAT THIS ORACLE MEANS:

In getting this Wizard Myne, it is likely that someone is making promises that they will be unable and unlikely to keep. They may wish to you to buy something, or invest your time and money into this or that, and paint glorious stories of the great benefits and rewards you will eventually reap, but the hype is much greater than the actual possibility and while you may get something out of this relationship or situation, it won't be anywhere near as much as you were originally promised.

This is not to say that Goblins never do anything of worth. As we say, you might get some reward from this, but forget all the wonderful projections about the "big score," or the glorious future. That just isn't going to happen. They may promise you that a golden rain will shower upon you from a magic rainbow but they are really just taking a piss and you will be a sucker if you fall for it. Don't get taken.

So, go into this situation with your eyes open. Look at it from all the angles, and be realistic and practical about it. This is really a lot like gambling. If you can't afford to lose your investment, totally, then don't invest. The chances are good that you will lose out in this situation. If you can afford the risk, okay, but if not, don't take the chance. It is really not worth it.

ENCHANTMENT SPELL:

I am not fooled by flowery word
And see the truth of what I've heard

This Spell in Arvyndase:

El da kon gibïn la fluerath mol
Nar ten tae lodver u wu El'tir lysïn

Pronunciation:

Eel dah cone guy-b - in lah flew - ear - aye-th mole
Nair teen tay load - veer u woo Eel'tire liss - in

Chapter 29:

Black Locust

KEYWORD: **UNSEELIE**

TREE NAME IN ARVYNDASE: **NORSFETRYN** (PRONOUNCED: NORSE - FEE - TRINN)

ARVYNDASE NAME OF THE WIZARD MYNE: **ÛNSELE** (PRONOUNCED: UN - SEE - LEE)

THIS TREE AND ITS MAGIC:

The Black Locust tree, another of the pea or legume family, is sometimes called the 'false acacia' tree. Acacia, if you will look at chapter 24, is related to Faerie as it exists as a place, realm or demesne of Faerie being, thus we associate the Black Locust tree with the Unseelie Fae, those beings who in reaction to the persecution from Mankind and others have responded in kind, which is to say, in unkind ways, seeking vengeance and revenge for the wrongs that have been done to them and to the persecution of faerie kind overall, thus they often view Mankind, or Man-unkind, as we sometimes call them, and the normal mundane folk, as their natural prey.

The Black Locust tree has incredibly hard wood, one of the hardest woods of all, so these are a tough people. It is a hardy tree; however, it is also prone to heart rot. Hatred, even when it is justified, as it often is for these folks, still harms the heart. On the other hand, unlike most tales of the Unseelie, these trees do not tolerate shade well, but prefer sunny climes. But, we might say that the Unseelie are rather angry about being cast into the shade by Mankind, and feel that they are superior as a species in every way, and long for the spotlight that they feel that they rightly deserve that has been unfairly taken from them. They resent having to hide their light under a basket so to speak, take second place or be considered second class citizens when they are so much better and more knowledgeable than those who arbitrarily place themselves above them and who often undeservedly steal the credit for themselves when it is the Unseelie who actually did most of the work.

These trees are sometimes noted for being an invasive species, taking over from other species of trees and dominating their region, just as the Unseelie have taken on the habits of domination, thus seeking to beat Man at their own game. But they are also a pioneer species, who thrive and bring back trees after fire or some other destruction that has caused a region to be barren. They bring back Faerie in their own invasive fashion seeking to push out Man and replace them with our kind.

Note that these trees are also subject to a virus that causes what are called witch's broom growths. Thus, they promote, even at their own expense, the possibility of the influx of witches into an area. They make an area responsive to magic, especially the magic of using will power and force to achieve what one's desires, rather than that of using enchantment.

WHAT THIS ORACLE MEANS:

If you receive this Wizard Myne in response to a question put to the oracle, then it is likely that you are called upon to set things straight, clear the air, and perhaps even put someone in their place who has gotten a bit out of line and perhaps a mite above thems'elves, assuming authority that they don't actually deserve or naturally possess. However, it is important to realize that this individual may have valid reasons for their irritation and agitation and for their complaints, and these should not be ignored for that will only lead to more problems later. Give their protests a true and honest hearing.

It is possible that there is nothing you can really do to help this person. Their hate against society may be justified but, alas, in this case, it is not helping to make things better and while you wish you could ease their hearts and help them, you have little in the way of power to do that and it is quite possible they have no interest in listening to you anyway.

It may also be that they are arbitrary throwing you in with those they hate merely because you don't immediately agree with them or because, on the surface, you seem to be part of this or that group by whom they feel oppressed. They are simply stereotyping you based on race, gender, spiritual belief or some other factor in the same way they have been stereotyped, pigeonholed and persecuted.

You may be in a situation where you are called to reprimand this individual, but do this with as much sensitivity as you can even though they, thems'elves, haven't demonstrated much in the way of sensitivity to others. Do not react with vengeance in mind, as they are inclined to do. Set an example of courtesy and understanding and superior intelligence, without acting superior, as best you are able to do so.

And remember, guard dogs can be useful. However, you don't want them running off the leash, wreaking havoc everywhere, and they may need some discipline and training, but if you befriend them, they will die to protect you. Still, you don't want them accidentally or mistakenly biting your friends. Or even biting those who are hostile toward you but not acting upon it unless the time comes when defense is truly necessary.

Enchantment Spell:

You have suffered it is true
And there is little I can do
But the harm they did was not my act
So now your claws you'd best retract

This Spell in Arvyndase:

Le tir igurïn ter da lod
Nar norn da zil El vek ba
Kana tae gras tam baïn daïn kon el'na din
Re mat le'na tarqali le'tirïn rildor dafa

Pronunciation:

Lee tire eye - goo-r - in tier dah load

Nair nor-n dah zile Eel veek bah

Kay - nah tae grace tame bah - in dah - in eel'nah dine

Re mate lee'nah tayr - qwah - lie lee'tire - in rile - door day - fah

Chapter 30:

Chestnut

KEYWORD: **THE NUMBER 6**

TREE NAME IN ARVYNDASE: **CASTAN** (PRONOUNCED: CASS - TANE)

ARVYNDASE NAME OF THE WIZARD MYNE: **ANSTA** (PRONOUNCED: AINE-S - TAH)

THIS TREE AND ITS MAGIC:

Before the onset of agriculture and the planting of the potato, the chestnut was the main staple food for the woodland folk, thus we associate this tree with the wood elves, as well as the number six, and the name of this Wizard Myne is Ansta, which is based upon the Arvyndase word Anst (aine-st), which is our elven word for Lore and thus we further associate this Myne and this tree with elven and faerie lore.

Unlike most nuts, chestnuts are primarily composed of carbohydrates, which is to say they provide energy for the body but if overdone it can lead to fat. Balance is always an important part of elven society and we wish neither to do too much or too little. Creative activity is balanced with recreation and seriousness with humor.

There is the old expression of "that old chestnut" referring to a story, joke, adage or other tale that has been told so many times it has become redundant and tedious. Thus, our association with this tree to elven lore, which while it can be valuable and interesting, should be taken with a grain of salt. Some folks accept the lore without question, but we elves question nearly everything, particularly things about us and our kindred, and while we find the lore interesting we are constantly looking at in a new light, the light of change, reality, our personal observations of our people and our own understanding of ours'elves and of our people, our culture and our history.

Alas, these trees, much like we elfae ours'elves, are subject to many pests, and to potential diseases, although the diseases we elves are prone toward tend to be less of the physical nature and more of psychological (and occasionally psychical) assaults from the dominant culture around us ever seeking to get us to conform, to give in to their way of thinking, dress as they believe we should and otherwise imitate them in all the ways they hold to be socially approved and accepted. While we, most often, find these arbitrary social rules to be ludicrous, meaningless, and senseless.

What This Oracle Means:

When getting this Wizard Myne as an oracle, one is called to examine ones'elf, one's life, what one feeds ones'elf mentally, psychologically, spiritually and physically and be sure one has a nutritious diet that fulfills one's needs on all planes of being without indulging in excess except upon a rare occasion.

One may also wish to consider the ancient tales and lore concerning our people and try to decipher how much of it is really valid and how much is the nonsense made up by others about our people, and how much of it, while it may have been true at one time, no longer holds validity for us in the present.

Try not to be redundant. Don't rest strictly upon the authority of the past and instead look at what is going on with fresh eyes and a practical understanding of what life is like for we elfae in the modern world. Nurture yours'elf on ancient values but don't let them overly restrict you. Bring the light of your own elven experience and understanding to bear on this situation.

Honor the ancestors, but realize they were, like us, spirits striving to better thems'elves and while they were surely not perfect, they did the best they could for the times they lived in. Treat them with respect but don't necessarily follow their example except for their example of aspiring toward becoming better elfae, each of them in their own way, and each of us in ours.

ENCHANTMENT SPELL:

I do what's best for me and mine
Now, the future, and throughout time

This Spell in Arvyndase:
El ba wu'da rildor fro el nar el'na
Mat, tae lasel, nar joulzes mern

Pronunciation:
Eel bah woo'dah rile - dorr fro eel nair eel'nah
Mate, tay lay - seal, nair joe - yule - zees mere-n

Chapter 31:

Beech

KEYWORD: **THE NUMBER 4**

TREE NAME IN ARVYNDASE: **NERON** (PRONOUNCED: KNEE - RONE)

ARVYNDASE NAME OF THE WIZARD MYNE: **MESEL** (PRONOUNCED: ME - SEAL)

THIS TREE AND ITS MAGIC:

The Beech tree is part of the Celtic tree alphabet and is linked to the Druid Few Phagos. Current classifications recognize ten to thirteen species of this tree in two distinct subgenera, Fagus and the Engleriana. The first is clearly the tree the Celts and their Druids were familiar with, while the second, the Engleriana, is natively be to found exclusively in East Asia and are low-branching trees, often composed of several major trunks that have a yellowish bark.

This tree is associated with ancient knowledge and old writings in Celtic lore, since this tree doesn't heal over things that are carved into it, such as Legolas loves Tauriel or whatever and such signs remain for the life of the tree. However, since the Druids and Celtic were an oral tradition and didn't usually write things down, we elves link this tree to the Number 4, a number symbolizing permanence, and to the Wizard Myne Mesel, which comes from the Arvyndase word Mes (pronounced: miece and rhymes with niece) and is our elven word for Sign, such as an

Elf Sign. Note the Arvyndase word Mese (me - see) is the word for Sibyl, the prophetess and seer of the ancient world.

This tree for us is not about books and lengthy writing, even though the name Beech is linked to the word for book in Old English bōc and Old Norse bók, and in words in German, in modern Dutch, in Swedish, and in Russian. This tree, to we Silver Elves, is rather about writing in terms of Signposts carved into these trees in the forest to give short messages and directions. Go this way to Eldåfaryn (Elfhaven), or Danger Ahead, Trolls! or whatever. These are short messages of significant content helping kindred to find their way to Elfin and hopefully to avoid potential dangers upon the way.

What This Oracle Means:

If one draws this Wizard Myne as an oracle, one is called to look for a sign. If you are confused and need direction, especially concerning the Elven Way and the direction of the path of your spirit, then an elf sign will surely come to you shortly. Be alert, but not too hasty. Make sure it is an actual sign not simply a response to wishful thinking. Being magic wielders by nature we tend to draw what we wish to us, but if we are not careful we can fool ours'elves. Remember true signs are often repeated and reinforced by other signs so wait for confirmation before making any significant moves.

Also, in dealing with others, look to the signs that they make. Listen to what they say, but pay closer attention to the way they say it. Heed well their tone of voice, observe their body language and facial expressions and, of course, pay even closer attention to what they do. Talk is one thing, action is another. As the saying goes: Actions speak louder than words. Look for the truth in their behavior.

And, leave your own signs for those who will follow after you. Share what you have learned on the path so that others may profit from your experience. Show others the ways that worked for you.

Enchantment Spell:

Grant me sign the path to know

The way to Elfin do now show

This Spell in Arvyndase:
Kiv el mes tae tål va ken
Tae yer va Êldat ba mat teke

Pronunciation:
Kive [rhymes with dive] eel miece tahl vah keen
Tay year vah L - date bah mate tea - key

Chapter 32:

Tanoak

KEYWORD: **WIZARD**

TREE NAME IN ARVYNDASE: **RUCYDAECH** (PRONOUNCED: RUE - CID - DAH - EACH)

ARVYNDASE NAME OF THE WIZARD MYNE: **ZÅRDOAR** (PRONOUNCED: CZAR - DOE - AIR)

THIS TREE AND ITS MAGIC:

The oak tree is associated with an Ogham few, but that is the next tree, not this one. This tree also bears an acorn but one that is harder, and has a woody nut shell similar in that way to the Hazel tree. Many ancient aboriginal peoples preferred this acorn to the other oak acorn, due to its higher tannin content that makes it easier to preserve and store. Roasted, these seeds can be used as a coffee substitute, but if it tasted better than coffee it would surely be used that way more often. During the American Civil War, Confederate soldiers, who had no coffee due to the Union naval blockade around their borders, roasted acorns and used them in just this way, although we suspect they would have much preferred real coffee. In fact, they would often trade tobacco, which they had, with Union soldiers who had coffee.

The tannin from its acorns has also been used for tanning leather and a mulch made of its leaves will discourage grubs and slugs from feasting in one's garden. Thus, there is an aging and transformative quality to this tree, as well as a protective aspect to it.

We Silver Elves relate this tree to Wizards and the Wizard Myne Zårdoar, which comes from the Arvyndase word Zårdoa, which means wizard. Elven Wizards are similar to druids, although having perhaps a bit harder shell. They protect us from the grubs and slugs of the world so our Garden of Elfin can grow, bloom, flourish and prosper.

WHAT THIS ORACLE MEANS:

In getting this Wizard Myne as an oracle, there is a natural blessing that comes with it. A bit of luck will come your way, even if you are in difficult circumstances. Things might not be ideal but there is a way forward if you are resilient and adaptable.

In fact, in receiving this oracle there is a good possibility that you may not have everything that you need to achieve your designs, and while you are called on to transform this situation, you need to do so by making the most of what is already available to you, while being sure that you bring no harm to others by your actions.

Also, the situation you are facing may take a little time to develop. Don't be hasty. Be a wizard and let most of what happens develop on its own without interference. It may be that if you don't get entangled in this situation and don't insist on forcing your will upon it and trying to make things occur in a particular way that it will resolve itself on its own or, at the very least, require very little from you but patience. In the meantime, do what you can to hold your own, protect yours'elf and your kin, without being aggressive outwardly. Use protective and defensive measures exclusively.

ENCHANTMENT SPELL:
I may not have the best of tools
But what I have will do
I'll make a magic fine and strong
Enchantments great and true

This Spell in Arvyndase:
El me kon tir tae rildor u hansli
Kana wu El tir yon ba
El'yon kord na êldon sisan nar mylth
Syrandirli ralt nar lod

Pronunciation:
Eel me cone tire tay rile - door you hanes - lie
Kay - nah woo Eel tire yone bah
Eel'yone cord nah l - doan sigh - sane nair mill-th
Sir - rain - dire - lie rail-t nair load

Chapter 33:

Oak

KEYWORD: **DRUID**

TREE NAME IN ARVYNDASE: **ECH** (PRONOUNCED: EACH)

ARVYNDASE NAME OF THE WIZARD MYNE: **CELFROD** (PRONOUNCED: SELL - FRODE)

THIS TREE AND ITS MAGIC:

The Oak has traditionally been associated with Druids and we elves see it linked to our elven druids as well. In the traditional Ogham, it is connected to Duir and related to protection, strength and a doorway to the mysteries. We see it as joined to the Wizard Myne Celfrod, that comes from the Arvyndase word Celfro (sell - fro), which is our word for Druid. We should note that this tree, the Quercus or Oak tree, is part of the Beech family, as is the Beech itself, of course, the Tanoak and the Chestnut tree.

This tree produces both male flowers, which come out as catkins, a spike-like flowering found on trees such as Willow and Hazel, (catkins are usually downy, pendulous and pollinated by the wind) and smaller female flowers, indicative that the Druids, and surely the Elven Druids, had and have members of both genders. Magic, knowledge, wisdom and understanding don't belong to any one gender.

The wood of the Oak is dense and hard, thus the association with strength and protection. And its wood was used in the construction of ships, thus we would add the notion of exploration, perhaps into the mysterious unknown, to this tree's qualities and magical powers. But it is also used in the making of barrels for the aging of various spirits, such as wine, sherry, brandy, and whiskey. Another link to the world of spirits, we might say.

Alcohol was one of the first hallucinogens used in civilizations for getting out of this world and connecting with the parallel dimensions. It is an inferior technology, being potentially addictive and destructive to the body, but its use in this way by some of the ancients cannot be denied, such as the ancient Greek cult of Dionysus with its connection to satyrs, centaurs, and sileni (who were satyrs with horse legs and therefore a sort of centaur/satyr mix).

We might point out again that Oak was used to age the spirits, which is to say, to smooth and mellow them out and give them flavor through maturity, and we might extend this idea to the notion that wisdom comes in time with age and experience and the effort to study and grow wiser. It is not merely a matter of aging itself but of aging in the Oak, which is to say, aging while following the Path of Druids or of the Elven Way.

What This Oracle Means:

In getting this oracle, one is called to develop ones'elf and one's spirit in whatever field or fields one has chosen to pursue. Study, write, create, paint or whatever it is you do and do it as best you can and ever seek to do it better. Rid yours'elf of bias, especially gender bias, but do your best to eliminate all prejudice and preconceptions from your outlook and thinking. Study Nature, the Universe and the world as it is, without a priori assumptions, and see what your observations and experience tell you about it.

Also, look to the future and your increasing development as a spiritual and spirited entity. Don't assume you have already achieved what you perceive in your visions, but assume quite rightly that you are capable of achieving all that you will. If you need training, get it. Find those who already are successful at what you desire to do and learn from their example.

At the same time, it may be that you will encounter those who already present themselves as being wise, when they are actually far from it; who think they have all the answers when they haven't even asked the questions; and who make claim to experience that only exists in their imaginations. Be kind to these. Let them go on their way undisturbed. You don't need to point out their folly. Nature and reality will surely do that soon enough.

ENCHANTMENT SPELL:
Better and better at what I do
Mastering all that I pursue

This Spell in Arvyndase:
Rilfa nar rilfa zan wu El ba
Antrodas wyl dij El taor

Pronunciation:
Rile - fah nair rile - fah zane woo Eel bah
Ane - trow - dace will dye-j Eel tay - or

Chapter 34:

Boojum family

KEYWORD: **AIR**

TREE GROUP NAME IN ARVYNDASE: **SERIALDA** (PRONOUNCED: SEE - RYE - ALE - DAH)

ARVYNDASE NAME OF THE WIZARD MYNE: **SARTHA** (PRONOUNCED: SAIR - THAH)

THIS TREE AND ITS MAGIC:

This tree is a desert cactus that is found mostly in Baja, California, a peninsula in Mexico extending down from California, although this tree can also be found on the mainland of Mexico, however it is less populous there. These trees can reach heights of about seventy feet. The indigenous Seri people believe that if one touches this tree/plant, it will cause strong winds to start blowing, thus we Silver Elves associate this tree with the wind elementals and the sylphs who are the air spirits. We link it to the Wizard Myne Sartha that is derived from the Arvyndase word Sarth, which means Sylph.

Air is a symbol of the mind, of communication, or thought, ideas and imagination. It is a powerful energy that sustains our lives, for without air we would die in minutes, while we might survive a lack of water for a day or two, we cannot live long without air. Thus, the magic of air and the ability to arouse the winds is a great power and indicates the ability to communicate effectively, to set the world in motion through ideas and to sustain one's life and spirit through thoughtforms and their ability to manifest our wishes, and through the energy that air brings, carrying vital oxygen into our beings.

The power of air also gives us the idea of the atmosphere, of the sky and of connecting to the heavens, which is to say, connecting with the Shining Ones, those advanced beings who have previously mastered what we are encountering now, and seek to help and guide us toward the inner realms and dimensions of Elfin where our magic is ever more powerful and we can be all that we wish to be.

WHAT THIS ORACLE MEANS:

In getting this oracle, you are called to pay close attention to what you say, the atmosphere you create through your words and communications and to observe others and the moods they create around them with their words. Words have power to heal or harm, very real power, magical power. Ideas have changed and affected the world, sometimes for the better, sometimes for the worse, sometimes better for some people but not for others. Elfin has enlightened our lives but others seem unmoved by it. Others find power or solace in various religious beliefs that do not even stir us in the slightest fashion, not even arousing a breeze within us.

Elfin is an idea that can bring magic into the lives of others, stir their hearts and imaginations, and can make life better when one strives to realize its power and vision into one's life. Be like Elfin. Make the world a better place with the words that you say. Use your spells and enchantments, casting them upon the winds, blowing them into the air. Instill your magical tools and spells with your breath. And especially, here in the place of the sylphs and air elementals, say your spells out loud so that the air will vibrate with their energy and they will expand outwardly into the world around you. Here you have the power of the air, use it.

Mastery of the air, of ideas and speech are great powers. You may consider taking a course in public speaking. Increase your ability to communicate and make sure that what you do communicate is rooted in the true, the real and the possible. In that way, you give substance to your words so that they have genuine power. And, use this power wisely. The world you will be changing is your own.

Also, this oracle gives a blessing for travel, especially air travel, but sail boats or other modes of transportation that use the air would be included here, such as hang-gliding, parachuting, etc.

Enchantment Spell:

I cast this spell into the air
And find my will established there

This Spell in Arvyndase:

El jaka wyr moja verva tae eron
Nar låc el'na yon norsetyrïn norn

Pronunciation:

Eel jay - kay were moe - jah veer - vah tay e - rone
Nair lock eel'nah yone nor - see - ter - in norn

Chapter 35:

Persian Ironwood

KEYWORD: **WITCH**

TREE NAME IN ARVYNDASE: **PYRSEÄN FERIALDA** (PER - SEE - ANN FEE - RYE - ALE - DAH)

ARVYNDASE NAME OF THE WIZARD MYNE: **ZIDORYN** (PRONOUNCED: ZIE - DOOR - REN)

THIS TREE AND ITS MAGIC:

This tree is part of the Witch-Hazel family and thus we link it to witches, wicca, witchcraft and to the Wizard Myne Zidoryn that comes from the Arvyndase word Zidor, which means witch. Alas, this tree is greatly endangered as a species, as were witches who were and are persecuted, tortured and killed for their magical practices even in modern times in places such as Africa and India and the Middle East.

The Persian Ironwood tree is drought tolerant and, like witches, it has endured harsh conditions and still survived. It is found mostly in Northern Iran but a related species can be found in China. The bark of this tree has a smooth, pinkish-brown coloration; however, it flakes away to reveal green, pink, brownish red, and pale-yellow patches. Beneath the outer exterior of what the world sees, there are depths and variations to witches that are only revealed by their magic. These are ancient trees and could be 23 million years old or older as a species. Witchcraft is an ancient practice extending to prehistory and passed on through the ages mostly by direct contact and oral tradition. Witches teach each other.

Witches initiation each other. The same is true of elves and elfae folk in general.

There are many elven witches, for we elves are usually magic wielders who pursue, study, practice and perform numerous styles and technologies of magic. Our sisters of the ancient Elf Queen's Daughters were most certainly practicing witches, although like most elfin, enchantment was their chief style of magic. And among those who are not necessarily elven or faerie folk, we are probably closest to the witches, for they have been good to the elves and we, for our part, have done our best to reciprocate their kindness with our own.

What This Oracle Means:

In drawing this Wizard Myne, you are called to do your magic, but carefully, perhaps secretly, revealing yours'elf only to those who you are certain you can trust. There are people in the world who would not only despise your witchcraft, your magic, ridicule it and criticize it, but there are those who fear your magic and would and will do all that they can to harm you and prevent you from your work. Be not afraid, but be wise in this case. We have endured for ages, we will continue to do so. And remember, magic that is done in secret is harder to counter and interfere with.

So, proceed in this situation subtly and with caution. See what strings you can pull but do so quietly and unobtrusively. This isn't about standing out, but continuing on and, in this instance, success depends upon discretion.

Also, find those you can trust and make alliances. Even if they are not exactly of your kind, not elves or faeries or other; still if you can trust them, then they be elf friends true and that is all that you really need in this situation.

Enchantment Spell:

Stealthily, with barely a sound
My whispered spells touch all around

This Spell in Arvyndase:

Tårtvarathla, ena elfåla na deth

El'na sushoïn mojali fost wyl anabo

Pronunciation:

Tart - vayr - ayeth - lah, e - nah eel - fah - lah nah deeth

Eel'nah sue - show - in moe - jah - lie foe-st will a - nay - bo

Chapter 36:

Hickory

KEYWORD: **THE LETTER O**

TREE NAME IN ARVYNDASE: **VAFORM** (PRONOUNCED: VAY - FORM)

ARVYNDASE NAME OF THE WIZARD MYNE: **OGÅRI** (PRONOUNCED: OH - GAR - RYE)

THIS TREE AND ITS MAGIC:

The Hickory tree belongs to the Walnut family of trees. It is an ancient tree going back about 34 million years, although the shell of its nut has become harder through time in response, mostly likely, to rodents and other predators. Its wood is hard, dense, unyielding and shock resistant. There are other woods that are stronger, and others that are harder, but no others that demonstrate its combination of strength, toughness, hardness, and stiffness.

We relate this tree to the Letter O and to the Arvyndase word Ogåri, which comes from our elven word for Ogre. Among the many uses of the wood and nuts of this tree, it has been utilized for making canes that were used for 'caning' or beating people, especially young boys by their teachers and head masters. We elves have experienced a caning or two from ogres ours'elves. Although, there are also many other and more positive uses for this wood, so we should remember that while such Ogres can be cruel, hard, stiff, tough and very strong, there are also things one can learn from them. They are petty tyrants, but even petty tyrants have their uses if you know how to handle them appropriately.

And it should be remembered that part of their hardness, certainly the hardness that surrounds their nut, comes about because of what they have endured in time. They have learned to protect themselves through hard experience. They are the way they are because of what they have suffered, and it is good to keep that in mind when dealing with unyielding individuals such as these.

Also, Hickory is susceptible to the absorption of moisture, much more than many other species of wood, and because of this it is inclined to shrinkage, warping or swelling as the humidity changes and is therefore also subject to wood rot and corruption. By extension, these individuals, while hard, can also be moody, arbitrary and at times, rotting from within and open to bribes and other influences of various forms.

WHAT THIS ORACLE MEANS:

In getting this Wizard Myne, you are most likely dealing with some very hard and unyielding individuals who are difficult to deal with, obstinate and while they appear stiff and unchanging are sometimes rotten to their core and slowly decaying from within. Kindness is unlikely to influence them, and reason certainly holds little value in their world, although they are fond of using rationalizations themselves; but gifts and things that appeal to their self-interest and to their prejudices sometimes may affect them. They are products of cruel behavioral conditioning and seek to treat others in the harsh ways with which they were programmed.

Be cautious in proceeding. It may be that you will wind up taking a lump or two in the process, but be careful as well of becoming like they are. This is most important. Don't let their hatred and cruelty infect you.

Become hardened, it you need to be, but not stiff and unyielding. Be strong and tough but don't let this rot your heart and destroy your essential goodness nor let this harsh treatment pervert your understanding that all spirits were innocent at one time and inwardly yearn to return to that state of being no matter what they may say or do. Be fair, be an example to others, and be compassionate as much as you can be, even when they have shown little compassion. Be better than they, but don't make this obvious to them for they will make you suffer even more for doing so.

ENCHANTMENT SPELL:

I shall endure and stronger rise
Be greater than you realize

This Spell in Arvyndase:

El van talos nar mythfa luft
Te raltfa rena le briobar

Pronunciation:

Eel vane tay - lowce nair mill-th - fah lou-ft
Tea rail-t - fah ree - nah lee bry - oh - bare

Chapter 37:

Walnut

✝

KEYWORD: **THE LETTER H**

TREE NAME IN ARVYNDASE: **JULAN** (PRONOUNCED: JEW - LANE)

ARVYNDASE NAME OF THE WIZARD MYNE: **HYRNFAR** (PRONOUNCED: HERNE - FAIR)

THIS TREE AND ITS MAGIC:

The walnut is actually a drupe, not a nut in the true sense. These drupes need to be stored in cool temperatures with low humidity otherwise fungal molds can develop and form dangerous aflatoxin. Walnuts are one of the thirty-eight substances that are utilized to prepare the Bach Flower Remedies, which can usually be found as herbal remedies in natural food stores. Therefore, we Silver Elves associate this tree with Elven and Faerie healers and herbalists. Healing magic is surely one of the greatest of magics. There are few powers as potent or unassuming it its way than healing magic and few as ancient as it and the alchemical magic of herbalism.

We link this tree to the Wizard Myne Hyrnfar, which comes from the Arvyndase word Hyrnfa that is our elven word for Healthier. It is a curiosity of Arvyndase that usually the suffix -fa at the end of a word represents -er in English. Thus, normally, Hyrnfa would mean Healer. However, the word for Healer in Arvyndase is Hyrnlor, for the suffix -lor is added when someone is particularly respected for what they do. Thus, Hyrnlor would literally be Heal-ian, rather like magician or pediatrician. Healthy, by the way, would be Hyrnath, which literally means heal-ly, and usually healthier would be formed as Hyrnathfa (literally heal-ier), but here we have an exception due to the high regard that elves afford to healing and healers. To be healthy and healthier is to be a healer in the elven way of thinking.

Walnut husks have been used in the past to create durable ink for writing and drawing and may have been used in this way by artists such as Leonardo da Vinci and Rembrandt. Its pigments have also served as a brown dye for fabric and for dyeing hair. Thus, the Walnut has a symbolic aspect to it of being transformative and enduring, as healing is meant to be.

WHAT THIS ORACLE MEANS:

In getting this Wizard Myne, there is a need for healing magic for yours'elf or for others in your environment. It may also be that the situation you are asking about requires some healing. But it also means that healing is possible, that this is not a hopeless situation but one that can be improved by healing magics on every dimension and plane.

Also, this is one case in particular where herbs can play an important part of your spells. We often see herbs used in stories about witches and magic, but most of us don't actually use various herbs in our spells, although incense, in that way, is an herb really and is often utilized in this fashion. And, in this instance, if you have or can obtain some walnuts and can enchant them with your spells, you can then put them about in places where you wish healing to occur or give them to people who may need a bit of healing.

Also, honor the healers. This is very important. Bless the healers with your magic and spread healing into the world. Further, herbal remedies, such as the Bach Flower Formulas, may be just the thing you happen to need in this case to get things moving in the right direction. And if you can't find certain herbs in your environment, use Bach Flower combinations to assist in your magic.

ENCHANTMENT SPELL:

Healing, healing all about
I disperse all illness with a shout ... Hey!

This Spell in Arvyndase:

Hyrndas, hyrndas wyl basar
El rytya wyl naltu ena na ontar ... Ae!

Pronunciation:

Herne - dace, herne - dace will bay - sair
Eel rit - yah will nail - two e - nah nah ohn - tair ... A!

Chapter 38:

Wingnut

KEYWORD: **THE NUMBER 17**

TREE NAME IN ARVYNDASE: **FROFHAR** (PRONOUNCED: FOE-F - HAIR)

ARVYNDASE NAME OF THE WIZARD MYNE: **JILOTAR**

THIS TREE AND ITS MAGIC:

The Wingnut tree is native to Asia and is related to the Walnut, although its wood is not quite as dense or strong as the Walnut's. It is so named because its nuts have wings on either side, although there is another related species, the Wheeled Wingnut that has one wing that wraps around the nut tenderly enclosing it.

We Silver Elves relate this tree to the Number 17, a very magical number for us, and to the Elven Visionaries and to the Wizard Myne Jilotar, which is derived from the Arvyndase word Jilotey (ji - low - tay) that means Visionary. Sometimes the word Wingnut is used to describe someone with extreme views that may not be entirely in touch with reality. However, we elves note that Peter Jackson's film company is named WingNut and he had the vision to create *The Lord of the Rings* movies that others thought to be un-filmable. He is a true visionary as well as a great artist.

Therefore, we need to remember that those whose views and ideas don't necessarily fit into the norm or what is generally thought of as being attuned to reality, sometimes see a greater reality that others are not as yet able to perceive. Some wingnuts are surely crazy, maybe most of them, just as most mutations in Nature fail. But sometimes, there is a great visionary that opens us to new worlds we weren't even sure actually existed or could exist. These are the elven visionaries who gift us with a glimpse of the possibilities of the future.

WHAT THIS ORACLE MEANS:

In getting this as an oracle, you are called to have faith in your own visions. However, it doesn't hurt to link these visions, as best you can, to reality. Many visions are vague sightings of Elfin seen through the mists and we must connect them to reality through our own lives and actions, letting our magic manifest into the material world what had only existed previously as potentiality. Just because others don't understand, doesn't mean that you are wrong. Be true to yours'elf.

At the same time, have some compassion for others who also have visions of the future. Do not condemn or dismiss them out of hand. Just because their views don't conform with the socially accepted opinions of the world or even with what science currently thinks, doesn't mean they are wrong. Science is ever questioning and reconsidering. You may not agree with them, or see what they see, but encourage them to keep looking and envisioning ever deeper. This may not be the vision for you, but it may be for them and others. As long as they don't attempt to force their views on you or others, they should be encouraged.

The question isn't, is the vision immediately practical, but will it, in fact, bring about a better world? Does it divide people unnecessarily? Discriminate and promote prejudice? Does it allow some to accept it, while others are free to go their own way? Everyone must be free to choose their own path. Does this vision promote that reality? Or is it a vision meant to enslave others to its exclusive way of looking at the world?

ENCHANTMENT SPELL:
I see a future bright and true
A better world for me and you

This Spell in Arvyndase:
El ten na lasel ilu nar lod
Na rilfa telth fro el nar le

Pronunciation:
Eel teen nah lay - seal eye - lou nair load
Nah rile - fah teal-th fro eel nair lee

Chapter 39:

Brazil Nut

KEYWORD: **LIGHT ELVES**

TREE GROUP NAME IN ARVYNDASE: **ÊLDATHARELPA** (PRONOUNCED: L - DATE - HAIR - EEL - LAH)

ARVYNDASE NAME OF THE WIZARD MYNE: **LUNAR** (PRONOUNCED: LOU - NAIR)

THIS TREE AND ITS MAGIC:

The Brazil Nut tree is a member of the Paradise Nut family. It is related to blueberries, cranberries, gutta-percha, sapote, persimmons and phlox. This tree is commonly found in South America. The Brazil Nut tree can grow to 160 feet tall, with a trunk from three to nearly seven feet in diameter. This makes it one of the largest of trees in the Amazon rainforests. It can live for 500 to 1,000 years. They usually only produce fruit in pristine forests, dependent for pollination upon a large bodied bee that isn't generally found in forests that have been disturbed. So, there is an aspect of purity here and of primal being.

In the past in North America, brazil nuts have been sometimes referred to as 'nigger toes,' as a racial slur and a joke by the ignorant. These nuts are often put in boxes of mixed nuts for sale; however, during transportation and the jiggling and vibrations that entails, the brazil nuts tend to rise to the top, this is called the 'brazil nut effect'.

All of this leads us Silver Elves to associate this tree with the Light Elves and the Wizard Myne Lunar, which comes from the Arvyndase word lun that is our elven word for light, as in sunlight or moonlight.

There are actually three words for light in Arvyndase. There is lun, but there is also fef (feef), which means light as in not heavy and there is rolyn (row - lynn), which specifically indicates a healing light. All of these are appropriate for describing the Light Elves who are advanced elven in the process of becoming Shining Ones, on their way to Elfin or Paradise, and will, as they ascend to the more expansive dimensions, surely live to 500 years or more in the same bodies.

And, they are certainly those who, when subjected to the shaking and jockeying for position of the world, tend to rise to the top, spiritually if not materially. Rising rather in the true world, the world of magic and energetic being. Also, these developing individuals of advanced spiritual character are sometimes subjected to ridicule and slurs, even when these slurs are just about them choosing to dress differently than others. But then, the ignorant will seize any excuse for exercising their prejudices.

WHAT THIS ORACLE MEANS:

Getting this Wizard Myne is surely a blessing for you. All you need to do to make the most of the blessing, this bit of magic coming your way, is to be true to your spiritual path, as purely as you can, trusting in the Shining Ones, those beneficent spiritual forces more advanced than us, to pollinate your being so you can prosper and grow. Delve into the pristine forests of elfin being. The inner world of magic and potentiality that exists alongside of but, most of the time apart from, the outer world where the ignorant struggle with each other instead of cooperating for mutual success.

The world and the circumstances you are currently facing may be difficult for you. You may be subjected to various slurs and ridicule from the envious, from those who seek to put you down in the mistaken notion that they will then rise up in your stead. But they are really burdening themselves with weights that will hold them down until they truly denounce and leave the dark and ultimately dead-end path they are on.

Be true to yours'elf, ignore the taunts and jibes of the ignorant, and continue on your way unaffected by their opinions. After all, their comments about you are really only a reflection of their own insecurities and have nothing to do with you at all. You will rise in the spiritual hierarchy of the world, although there may be nothing of an outer sort, except your increasingly powerful character and developing magical potency, to signify this fact. There is no sense in waving around titles, they are meaningless. It is the aura of your being, the enchantment of your personality, the strength of your soulful spirit that truly informs others of who you really are and the significance of your achievements. You need say nothing, your spiritual radiance speaks for itself.

ENCHANTMENT SPELL:
I clear the way as I clear my self
Rewarded by great spirit's wealth

This Spell in Arvyndase:
El vyrn tae yer tat El vyrn el'na eln
Bonoïn la ralt tari'na doljver

Pronunciation:
Eel vern tay year tate Eel vern eel'nah eel-n
Bo - no - in lah rail-t tay - rye'nah dole-j - veer

Chapter 40:

Crapemyrtle

KEYWORD: **THE LETTER M**

Tree Group Name in Arvyndase: **Ronsmyrtos** (pronounced row-ns - mer - toe-ss)

Arvyndase Name of the Wizard Myne: **Mone** (pronounced: moe - knee)

This tree and its magic:

The Crapemyrtle tree, also spelled Crepe Myrtle, although incorrectly, is a member of the Loosestrife family of trees, shrubs and plants that are native to the Indian subcontinent, Asia and Oceana, but can be found in warm environments around the world. They are mostly known for their colorful flowers and are used as ornamental trees.

We Silver Elves link this tree to Mankind, to the Letter M, and the Wizard Myne Mone that comes from the Arvyndase word Mon (Moan), which is our word for Man. Crapemyrtle is a beautiful tree but must be cut back each year to allow for new growth. However, if they are cut back too much, the tree will produce whip like shoots that issue forth from the unattractive stumps that are too weak to support flowers.

Mankind, to the elves, are a developing spiritual race, whom we often admire for their great beauty and courage but who need some cutting back or discipline in order to get them to flower. At the same time, too much discipline often ruins them. And they are frequently far too ready to apply too much discipline to their own kind and others, turning them into ugly whips that then seek to lash out at others.

Crapemyrtle is often and traditionally seen as a symbol of marriage and potential success in marriage and union. But, we must remember that this is the Loosestrife family, and many of the images we see in movies and television, and in reality, of the modern, normal marriage of Men and Women portray constant complaining, bickering and strife. We suppose this is meant to be drama, but really it is just sad. A good deal of this arguing needs to be cut back in order for the marriage to blossom. But, if no complaints are allowed, then the marriage will suffer as well. The key is in the proper balance.

What This Oracle Means:

Marriage can be beautiful but it can also be stressful and filled with strife as well. Seek the beautiful in the relationships you are in, seek what will endure (for Crapemyrtle flowers will bloom for a long time). Some discipline is needed, but mostly and principally it is a matter of s'elf discipline. Disciplining others, as in one's family, must always be done with a bit of restraint and caution, lest we destroy the good that we seek to foster. Don't let loose strife into your relationships. Life is stressful enough as it is, already.

But you should know that these days everyone, even women, are known as Mankind. In reality many, perhaps most, of those who are called Men, are really elves, faeries, pixies, grimlins, goblins, trolls, orcs, and various other kinds of being, all lumped together as if we were all the same. In actuality, the name Man is a tattered blanket that obscures a large variety of other spiritual races beneath it.

While we elves can physically intermarry and interbreed with Mankind, our marriages to them and some of the other spiritual races, don't often work out very well due to their lack of spiritual development. They are too inured to strife for the taste of most elfin. They may look beautiful, but be cautious whom you marry and whom you trust as a friend. Getting this Wyzard Myne is a warning about getting involved with the wrong people. Treat them with courtesy but don't become entangled in their lives or let them deeply into yours. If you do so you will surely regret it. Many of those folks are just not ready for the higher realms of elfin being as yet. Find those who are.

Enchantment Spell:

My very own will come to me
And from all strife we will be free

This Spell in Arvyndase:

El'na lefa os yon koso va el
Nar an wyl scurv eli yon te alo

Pronunciation:

Eel'nah lee - fah ohss yone co - so vah eel

Nair ane will scurv e - lie yone tea a - low

Chapter 41:

Mallow family

KEYWORD: **THE LETTER F**

TREE GROUP NAME IN ARVYNDASE: **VAMALELPA** (PRONOUNCED: VAY - MALE - EEL - PAH)

ARVYNDASE NAME OF THE WIZARD MYNE: **FELDARI** (PRONOUNCED: FEEL - DARE - RYE)

THIS TREE AND ITS MAGIC:

The Mallow tree family has the Baobab, the Bombax or Silk-cotton tree, the Bottletrees, the Kapok, the Durian, the Balsa, the Cacao and the Linden, which is also known as Basswood or Lime, although it is not, in fact, related to the tree that produces the lime as a fruit. The Baobab, on the other hand, has a fruit with a velvety shell (we elves love velvet in all its forms) that is approximately the size of a coconut, and is said to have a taste like citrus sorbet and is a good source of vitamin C, potassium, carbohydrates, and phosphorus.

The ovary of the Silk-cotton tree matures into a husk containing seeds covered by a fiber similar to cotton, although it has short fibers that cannot be spun and is thus unsuitable for making clothes. The Bottletree, sometimes called Kurrajong has had its bark used for making fishing line. The Durian produces a fruit that has an odor that some people abhor but others love this fruit. We Silver Elves have a friend from Thailand who adores it. It seems to be an acquired taste or perhaps an inherited one.

The Linden tree produces a fiber that was used by the Ainu people of Japan, who are reputed to be connected to the ancient elven and faerie tribes (see Nicholas De Vere *The Dragon Legacy*), for weaving their traditional clothing. And the Cacao tree, well, it produces chocolate, which is known, like the persimmon, as the food of the gods, and we elves certainly can't disagree with that.

Thus, we associate these trees with the Letter F, and the Wizard Myne Feldari, which comes from the Arvyndase word Feldar that means Divine. We also associate it with Elf food and Faerie food that legend warns people not to eat or drink because one will be compelled to stay in Faerie or Elfin. We elves, however, don't compel anyone and elfin food is not addictive in the sense indicated by lore, rather elf food is like chocolate. Having had it, one wants it again and again. Especially, dark chocolate. We love dark chocolate.

WHAT THIS ORACLE MEANS:

In receiving this Wizard Myne, whatever the question you asked of the oracle, the reply says look to what you love. Look to what turns you on, what makes your boat float, rocks your life in a good way and encourages you to be a better person, a better elfae, a better artist or whatever you are and to pursue it with all your heart.

Your magic, your art, the thing that rouses you, makes you feel like life is worth living, your passionate pursuit of what truly interests you and fills you with wonder, is the thing that connects you to the Divine. It is the fishing line of the spirit and it is helping you to find your way to Elfin and to a better world. It will clothe you in magic and touch your soulful spirit and help you realize your connection to the all of Life in the most harmonious and successful way. Do what you love. Pursuit your true interest and connect everything else to that. This is the path to success.

Having tasted of Elfin, having felt it deep within us, like having experienced love, we want that link to continue forever and it can and will. But the best way to strengthen this tie is to foster our own creative spirit and that of others. Don't waste time with those things that don't really stimulate you, unless true compassion compels you to do so. Follow your delight. This is the way.

ENCHANTMENT SPELL:
The Call is strong, I follow gladly
I am quite sane, but I pursue it madly

This Spell in Arvyndase:
Tae Koar da mylth, El loqi veltla
El da ven dan, kana El taor ter kokola

Pronunciation:
Tay co - air dah mill-th, Eel low - qwi veelt - lah
Eel dah veen dane, kay - nah Eel tay - or tier co - co - lah

Chapter 42:

Mahogany family

KEYWORD: **THE LETTER E**

TREE GROUP NAME IN ARVYNDASE: **SETENIAELPA**
(PRONOUNCED: SEE - TEEN - NIGH - AH - EEL - PAH)

ARVYNDASE NAME OF THE WIZARD MYNE: **ELPAD**
(PRONOUNCED: EEL - PAID)

THIS TREE AND ITS MAGIC:

The Mahogany family of trees and shrubs includes the Mahogany tree but also the Neem tree and the Bead tree. They are noted and used for the making of soaps, vegetable oil, insecticides, and, of course, Mahogany is highly valued for its wood. The Neem is most valued for it uses as medicine, while Mahogany is symbolic of strength and protection and is said to be able to resist lightning strikes.

Therefore, we elves associate this tree family with the Elven Family, the Letter E, with preventive medicine, and with the Wizard Myne Elpad, which comes from the Arvyndase word Elpa (pronounced: eel - pah) and means family and is related to the Arvyndase word elpadon (eel - pay - doan) and is our word for 'coat of arms' or 'family crest'.

The best way to deal with disease, and the easiest really, is to prevent it. The strongest individuals, those mostly able to endure crisis and the lightning strikes of life are those raised and nurtured in loving families. Others may be physically strong, or hardened and appear tough on the outside but usually true pressure unravels them. They often lack the psychological strength to persevere through extreme pressure. Our Elven family makes us strong. Strong as individuals and surely stronger together.

Also, these trees, while they appear bisexual, are said to be 'cryptically unisexual'. Most elves also tend toward what appears to be bisexuality but, really, we are unisexual or androgynous, we see no real or significant differences between the genders. Elves are elves whether we are male or female, and that is what truly matters to us. We are not a culture with strict divisions between the male and female, nor do we have different social codes and expectations for each gender. We don't have double standards.

What This Oracle Means:

Look to your family, particularly your elfin, elfae, faerie family for support and aid in this matter. If your family is strong, or you were raised in a loving and nurturing family, you will see to the heart of this issue and resolve it easily. If you were not raised in a strong and loving family, it is time to seek one or create one, as best you are able in the world. Especially, look for those who were raised in a loving and nurturing atmosphere. If you link yours'elf only with fractured souls, there will be no one to serve as an example of this lovingness. No one that really knows what is needed to heal you, or this situation, psychologically. Find those who are emotionally more together than you and learn from their example.

And realize that at the heart of the Elven Family is friendship. Friendship is at the root of all elven relationships. Find your true elfae friends, even if it is only one person, who share your love of Elfin and Faerie and whom you know you can trust, whether they be male or female, the same gender or different. We are not saying you should be bisexual, if you are not naturally so, or homosexual, but that you need to find your true friend or friends regardless of gender and from that build your elven family and out of that your eald, your elven demesne, will grow and prosper. Create an elven vortex (coven) and do your magic together. This is the answer to your question.

Enchantment Spell:

We stand together, united as one
Create our world by what we've done

This Spell in Arvyndase:
Eli lotz eldan, atåråïn tat ata
Talys eli'na telth la wu eli'tir baïn

Pronunciation:

E - lie low-tz eel - dane a - tah - rah - in tate a - tah

Tay - liss e - lie'nah teal-th lah woo e - lie'tire bah - in

Chapter 43:

Fig and Banyan

KEYWORD: **ELFIN**

TREE NAME IN ARVYNDASE: **GRUN** (GREW-N)

ARVYNDASE NAME OF THE WIZARD MYNE: **ÊLDATI** (PRONOUNCED: L - DAY - TIE)

THIS TREE AND ITS MAGIC:

The Fig trees also include the Banyan tree which is a favorite of the we Silver Elves. The Banyan is a tree that sends down shoots from its branches, in order to support their wide reach, but which also, in time, becomes a trunk for another tree that is the same tree. So, the banyan, if allowed to grow and has enough room, will become one tree that is also many trees. Because of this, we associate this tree with Elfin as a place and a space of mystical, magical elvish being. We link it to the Wizard Myne Êldati, which comes from the Arvyndase word for Elfin, which is Êldat (pronounced: L - date). It is similar to the motto of the United States, which is E pluribus unum that means one out of many or one from many, although here we have one creating and supporting many or many that are one. Thus, it is a symbol of elven spiritual community.

Fig trees are pollinated by Fig wasps who spend their larval stage inside the figs. Most of these wasps are pollinators but others of them merely feed off the plant. This is rather like elves in the modern age. Most of us pass on our culture to others, but some merely absorb the magical energy of Elfin but do little to contribute to it at this stage. We tolerate them all. Some are not quite ready for the Great Work.

Fig trees are seen as a keystone species in many tropical forest ecosystems, which is to say they are vital to the life of the forest and have greater power and influence than their numbers would suggest. They provide for many species.

Interestingly, fig wood was used for making mummy caskets in Ancient Egypt. This gives us a connection to the legendary longevity and the link to the life eternal of the Elves when we are in Elfin.

Of course, figs are probably most noted for their fruits, for the food they provide humanity but also for many of the other creatures and residents of the forest. Elfin is not for elves alone, but open to all sincere magical folk. We elves nurture everyone, as best we may, each toward the fulfillment of their own true nature.

WHAT THIS ORACLE MEANS:

In getting this Wizard Myne, you are called to look to your spiritual roots and connections to Elfin. Most elves and elfae in the modern world feel alienated, alone, see thems'elves as loners surrounded by individuals and cultures that they can't really relate to. We are few and far between and it is hard to find other elfin, especially those who are developed enough as spirits to work with us toward the common goal of creating Elfin upon the Earth.

This makes it difficult for us, but it also serves to either move us to turn inwardly and strengthen our connection to Elfin as it exists within us or, for those who are not quite strong enough to bear the loneliness of our path, to fall back into the world conforming with the status quo in order to find companionship.

And yet, there is a third choice, as there nearly always is with elves. One can retain one's elven being, while associating with like-minded people who, while they may not be elves exactly, are elfin enough to accept one for who one truly is and in doing so make them elf-friends. Thus, one continues in the world while keeping one's link to what is really important and vital in one's spiritual life. As the Stephen Stills song goes, "If you can't be with the one you love, then love the one you're with."

ENCHANTMENT SPELL:
Ever together in Elfin bright
Drawn to the world to share the elf light

This Spell in Arvyndase:
Vari eldan ver Êldat ilu
Omhyrïn va tae telth va mati tae êlda lun

Pronunciation:
Vair - rye eel - dane veer L - date eye - lou
Ohm - her - in vah tay teal-th vah may - tie tay l - dah loon

Chapter 44:

Mulberry

KEYWORD: **THE LETTER A**

Tree Name in Arvyndase: Morynda (pronounced: more - ren - dah)

Arvyndase Name of the Wizard Myne: Antrathyn (pronounced: ane - tray - thin)

This Tree and Its Magic:

The Mulberry tree is related to the Fig and thus Banyon tree, which are both members of the Mulberry family. Its fruits undergo significant changes as they develop. The immature fruits tend to be white, green, or pale yellow; however, in most species, as the fruit develops, it turns pink and then red as it ripens, after that it will turn dark purple or blackish. It has a sweet flavor when fully ripe.

The Mulberry is heavy with pollen, which is why it is banned from many cities, due to its effect upon those with allergies and asthma. However, it is only the male mulberry trees that produce pollen. On the other hand, female mulberry trees create all-female flowers that attract pollen and dust from the air, purifying it. Interestingly, a male mulberry tree can be cut back and female scions can be grafted to it, creating a female tree and thus eliminating the irritating pollen problem.

We Silver Elves link this Wizard Myne to the Letter A and to the Myne Antrathyn, which comes from the Arvyndase word Antrath (ane - tray-th), which is our elven word for Mastery. Elven mastery is s'elf mastery and this leads to mastery in the world. But, the goal here is not outer mastery but inner mastery and thus development and evolution as an elf and an elfin spirit. This tree symbolizes our refinement and development as individuals (as we become in a certain sense more feminine as males and more masculine as females, balancing our beings) and as we ascend the planes and dimensions of magical being toward becoming ever more elfin as individuals and ever more like the Shining Ones who have passed this way before us.

What This Oracle Means:

In drawing this Wizard Myne, one is called to master this situation by mastering one's own s'elf. In whatever way you are dealing with things, if they are giving you a problem, there is probably a way that you can deal with them better. How do you improve your ability to function in the world? How do you step up your game? Improve your technique? How can becoming more elfin make you more successful in dealing with the world? These are the questions to ask yours'elf.

At the same time, getting this Wizard Myne can be a sign of spiritual development and progress. The Path is never-ending and while you have clearly advanced on the spiritual planes, don't let your success tempt you into assuming you have achieved all that you need to achieve. There is always more to do. Always more to be and become, ever greater and ever higher. Keep transforming and the magic will reward you with increasing power and adeptship. Devoted practice, with an effort to ever improve, leads to perfection, so do your magic and always strive to do it better.

This mastery will give you greater power in the world, certainly it will grant you increased facility in dealing with others. But, don't be fooled into thinking that success in this world represents spiritual success, or that failure in the material world is due to a lack of spirit. That can be the case, but it isn't necessarily so. And remember the same holds true for others as well. Don't judge people based merely on their success or failure in the world. These are transitory things. Look to what is true, real and eternal.

Enchantment Spell:

Ever greater I become
Step by step the way is won

This Spell in Arvyndase:

Vari raltfa El casae
Cid la cid tae yer da bemïn

Pronunciation:

Vair - rye rail-t - fah Eel cah - say

Sid lah sid tay year dah beam - in

Chapter 45:

Eucalyptus

Keyword: **Fire**

Tree Name in Arvyndase: **Driflawela** (pronounced: dry - flay - wee - lah)

Arvyndase Name of the Wizard Myne: **Furni** (pronounced: few-r - nigh)

This tree and its magic:

We Silver Elves relate these trees to the elemental of fire, whose spirit is traditionally said to be a salamander, but we associate it with the Phoenix that burns up and then rises again from their own ashes. These trees are some of the tallest trees in the world. They rise high like fire and are not very tolerant of frost or extreme cold. Due to the fact that Eucalyptus oil is extremely flammable; these trees, once they have caught fire, may very well explode. And bushfires spread with ease along the oil saturated atmosphere of their tree crowns. However, like the Phoenix, the Eucalypts have developed long-term fire survivability because of their ability to regenerate after they have burnt.

Therefore, we link these trees to the Wizard Myne of Furni that comes from the Arvyndase words Fur (few-r), which is our elven word for fire, and Furn, which is our elven word for blaze. For they do make a great blaze when alight.

These are ancient trees, shown by the fossil record to have existed 35 and 50 million years ago, arising just after Australia and New Guinea separated from Gondwana, which is the name of a supercontinent that was in existence from the Neoproterozoic until the Jurassic and that was composed of territories that included South America, Africa, Antarctica, Australia, the Indian Subcontinent and what was to become the Arabian Peninsula. While these trees mostly exist in Australian in present times, they were, according to the fossil record, originally found in South America. Like fire, they moved.

Among the many uses of these trees, including their astringent oil that, like fire, is noted for purifying things; its wood is often used in the creation of didgeridoos, that magical and mystical instrument of the Australian Aboriginal peoples. Once, years ago, these elves where at an elf gathering where one evening a musician played didgeridoo music through an amplifier in the dark of a night illuminated only by campfires and starlight and it was hauntingly and beautifully magical.

WHAT THIS ORACLE MEANS:

Fire represents energy, and in getting this oracle, you are being told to pour energy into the issue at hand. Go for it, deal with it directly, pour yours'elf into this relationship, situation or circumstance and if everything should go wrong, if everything crashes and burns, and this is surely possible, then know that you will rise again from the ashes. Ask, and if you are rejected, don't worry about it. Don't take rejection to heart. It was the asking that was important in this case, not the answer whatever it might be.

Of course, it might be better if you could use a little bit of caution, just a bit, and avoid the more combustible aspects of this situation so you don't have to start all over again from the beginning. However, in this instance, action is to be preferred to caution, and doing is the theme of the day. Success will prove you right, while others may have doubted you. And failure is just a temporary setback. You will do better next time.

Overenergetic behavior is not advised in most cases, but here we have the exception to the rule, and again, as we say, if it turns out to be a mistake, don't give up, renew yours'elf, start from the inner seeds of your being and build yours'elf up again. This may be a manic phase, to be followed by a depressed phase, but the energy will come once more and you will rise renew and filled with enthusiasm.

ENCHANTMENT SPELL:
Direct I go right to the core
Get all I wish and even more

This Spell in Arvyndase:
Stran El tas mard va tae dor
Pål wyl El felj nar jåja gilf

Pronunciation:
Starin Eel tace mare-d vah tay door
Pahl will Eel feel-j nair jah - jah gile-f

Chapter 46:

Myrtle

KEYWORD: **THE NUMBER 1,000**

Tree Name in Arvyndase: **Torpmyrtos** (pronounced: torp - mer - toe-ss)

Arvyndase Name of the Wizard Myne: **Murvasår** (pronounced: muir - vay - sar)

This tree and its magic:

The Myrtle trees and shrubs contain high levels of salicylic acid, which is related to aspirin. These trees have been seen as sacred by many cultures and are valued for their fragrant essential oil, their beauty, and their medicinal properties. However, while their berries are edible they taste rather like pepper.

The myrtle is one of the four sacred plants of Jewish tradition and is used to represent one of the different types of personality that make up a community. The myrtle is said to indicate those who have performed good deeds but have no knowledge of or development with the Torah and are thus thought of as being good folk without true spiritual knowledge.

We Silver Elves relate this tree to the Wizard Myne Murvasår, that comes from the Arvyndase word Murvasa (muir - vay - sah), or Unawake. It is also related to the number 1,000, for there are thousands of these beings, who are truly good, loving, healing, magical elf folk, but who are unaware of and unawakened to their elven natures and often have not, as yet, fully developed their spiritual understanding in any direction, nor have they developed the power of elven courtesy, in many cases, and may seem a bit peppery to other folks.

There are multitudes of unawakened elfae folk. In fact, they may never awaken in this lifetime, for not all elfin folk are as obsessed with Elfin and Faerie culture as we are. They are often too busy trying to save the world, save the creatures of the world and right the wrongs and injustices of the societies they live within. They have relinquished their elven identities for a higher purpose. Yet, to our minds, they are still elfin and we embrace them as elf friends and nurture their being as best we are able.

What This Oracle Means:

You may know of folks who are beautiful, wonderful, that seem very elven or elfae or faerie-like to you, but who do not associate with those concepts and whose attention is tied up into the world as it is promoted and accepted to be by the majority of folk, yet seeking, with all their hearts, to transform it and make it better. Although, sometimes, they are just caught up the in world as it is and pursuing their personal interests within it. They see the world as the path to success for them and never consider any alternative. And yet, still they are elfin beings and you cannot help, being the advanced elfin you are, recognizing this aspect of their character. Our Elf Sight allows us to see into the hearts of people and to perceive the body of light that surrounds their material body.

However, if you approach these individuals as elves, they may very well scoff at you, or being possibly more advanced as spirits, merely smile but show no real interest in our ancient culture. Accepting, but not really interested except in the most casual of ways. We can't persuade people to be elves. We don't convert people. We don't proselytize. We accept each one for who they present thems'elves to be at the moment and further and foster them as much as we can, based upon whatever level they are currently functioning upon.

And honestly, some of these folks may have no interest in our ancient culture and its modern manifestation, but still be more advanced elves than we very simple, humble wee Silver Elven folk. People are not awakened by force, but by charm and enchantment. Develop yours'elf and your personality and those who are aroused, attracted, intrigued and perhaps mystified will open their hearts and minds to you.

Enchantment Spell:

I see you and I see your soul
I honor you and bid you whole

This Spell in Arvyndase:

El ten le nar El ten le'na der
El entra le nar tak le loj

Pronunciation:

Eel teen lee nair Eel teen lee'nah dear

Eel een - trah lee nair take lee lowj

Chapter 47:

Guava

KEYWORD: **THE NUMBER 10**

TREE NAME IN ARVYNDASE: **TRORUS** (PRONOUNCED: TROW - RUSE)

ARVYNDASE NAME OF THE WIZARD MYNE: **ZIFTAN** (PRONOUNCED: ZIE-F - TANE)

THIS TREE AND ITS MAGIC:

The Guava tree is another member of the Myrtle family of trees. It is most noted for its fruit that has high pectin content and thus is excellent for making preserves, jellies, jams, and marmalades. Pectin is what makes jellies jell. One of our fathers, by the way, loved Guava jelly so we would always send him some from Hawaii, where we currently abide. Also, we much prefer guava jelly, when we occasionally have breakfast out, to the strawberry jelly that they usually try to pawn off on us. However, you have to be sure to ask for it.

Therefore, we Silver Elves associate the Guava tree with the number Ten, a number that represents both stability and change, as well as an advancement to a higher level of development. We further link it to the idea of Quickening, of advancing on the path and having things jell or come together for you on a higher level. This often happens a year or more after one's awakening when the original enchantment begins to wear off and one is faced with persevering (or giving up the path) and decides to commit ones'elf to the Elven Way or not. Therefore, we associate this tree to the Wizard Myne Ziftan, which comes from the Arvyndase word Zifta (zie-f - tah), which means Quicken.

Guava seed oil is especially rich in linoleic acid. Linoleic acid is one of two essential fatty acids for humans. It must be obtained through the diet. It is mostly colorless but sometimes appears as a white oil and is nearly insoluble in water. This is symbolic of the fact that there is something essential about the quickening to the elven soul. It is the sign we get that we are on the right path and although we are going somewhat against the flow of most of the rest of humanity and cannot mix well with it, it is the right and true direction for us. We are not only swimming against the current, we are swimming up a divergent tributary that flows from the rivers of Elfin.

WHAT THIS ORACLE MEANS:

You may have come to a place in your path where you are uncertain whether you should continue on or give in to peer pressure to conform to normal society and gain whatever acceptance, however provisional, such acquiescence offers. If you receive this Wizard Myne then you have most likely arrived at a turning point, a crossroads, and must choose your path from here. Choose carefully, for your entire future will depend, in many ways, upon the choice that you make.

However, if you are in doubt about your spiritual path, about pursuing or continuing on the Elven Way then ask the Spirits for a sign, speak to Nature and await the rely. A sign will come to you. Or if it doesn't, then surely that is a sign as well.

But remember, if you have come this far then there will be benefits to continuing on. We are not saying that the path will get easier, although once you put aside doubt and uncertainty that will inevitably make things easier. However, if you commit yours'elf to the Path, then your magical potency and powers will surely increase. And certainly, a bit of elven luck will come your way and the Shining Ones will take heed of you and send you energy to aid you as you progress further toward and into Elfin. But that is up to you.

ENCHANTMENT SPELL:
Here I am, the choice is mine
Continue on? Send me a sign.

This Spell in Arvyndase:
Jän El da, tae efor da el'na
Lortyn ton? Tek el na mes.

Pronunciation:
Jan Eel dah, tay e - for dah eel'nah
Lore - tin tone? Teek eel nah meese.

Chapter 48:

Southern Beech family

KEYWORD: **SHAPESHIFTERS**

TREE GROUP NAME IN ARVYNDASE: **SARNERONELPA** (SAYR - KNEE - RONE - EEL - PAH)

Arvyndase Name of the Wizard Myne: **Fodata** (pronounced: foe - day - tah)

This Tree and its Magic:

Southern Beech trees are part of the Nothofagaceae tree family. You can almost hear their slow southern drawl as the breeze stirs their leaves and branches. Nothofagaceae literally means false beeches or bastard beeches, thus we Silver Elves associate this tree family to the Shapeshifters, Werewolves and Pwcca/Pookhas and other form changers or skin walkers of the Faerie world (see C. J. Cherryh's novel *Faery in Shadow*). These are not the beeches related by the Celts and Druids to the Ogham Phagos. However, one might make such a connection by extension if they so desired. Sort of a cousin by marriage or something.

These trees bear a fruit that is a small, flattened or triangular nut, borne in cupules containing one to seven nuts. Every four to six years or so, these trees create an unusual abundance of seeds. This is known as the beech mast. We Silver Elves, however, associate this event with the Faerie Feast. The Faerie Feast is the largesse of Faerie cast upon the world sending blessings to all who encounter it, the sharing and spreading of abundance, the Noblesse Oblige of the Elfin. Therefore, these trees are linked to the Wizard Myne Fodata that comes from the Arvyndase word Fodat (foe - date), which is our elven word for Feast.

What This Oracle Means:

In this situation, adapt. Present yours'elf in whatever way you need to in order to succeed and continue on. Appear as one of them, whomever they are, or as near to them or related as you can manage. They don't necessarily need to know that you are an elf or fae or other. It may be better if they don't see the real you. Rather, be one of the gang. Pass through their world seen but unseen. Dress as they do. Talk as they do, or do whatever is necessary to get through their domain, get what you need from it, so you can continue on the path to Elfin unscathed. Shapeshift and become one of them, at least temporarily.

And, bring an offering. Bring a gift, a bottle of wine, a box of donuts, whatever it is that will make their day and make them feel glad that you came, thankful for your presence (presents). Be as generous as you can be. Befriend them. Not so much that they can truly see you. But enough so that they feel comfortable being around you and accept you as one of them, more or less. Smile, and then shine grandma on, or whatever. Let them think what they will. And if they make some friendly but mistaken assumptions, go with it. You are not here to shake their world, challenge their opinions or prejudices, or rock their boat, you are just getting what you need and then traveling onward to places they will never be able to go, at least in this lifetime.

ENCHANTMENT SPELL:

Through the world I pass unseen
While all I need from it, I glean

This Spell in Arvyndase:

Joul tae telth El gol murtenïn
Jern wyl El golt fro ter, El lumat

Pronunciation:

Joe - yule tay teal-th Eel goal muir - teen - in
Jeer-n will Eel goal-t fro tier, Eel lou - mate

Chapter 49:

Tupelo family

KEYWORD: **NAIAD**

TREE GROUP NAME IN ARVYNDASE: **ITOPYLWÅELPA** (PRONOUNCED: EYE - TOE - PILL - WAH - EEL - PAH)

ARVYNDASE NAME OF THE WIZARD MYNE: **TARSPRIT** (PRONOUNCED: TAYRS - SPRITE)

THIS TREE AND ITS MAGIC:

Nyssaceae or Tupelo family of trees are flowering trees that are sometimes included in the dogwood family. There are known to be thirty-seven species that fall into the following genera: there are the Camptotheca, which are called the Happy trees. There are the Davidia, commonly known as the Dove tree, the Handkerchief tree, the Pocket Handkerchief tree and also the Ghost tree. There is the Diplopanax (diplomatic?). There are the Mastixia (mass - trickies-a?). And there are the Nyssa or Tupelos. Most of these trees are found in China, Vietnam or Southeast Asia. The majority of Nyssa trees are highly tolerant of wet soils and flooding, and some of them need such conditions to thrive.

We Silver Elves link these trees to the Naiads, those somewhat ghostly water nymphs of Greek mythology and to the Wizard Myne Tarsprit that comes from the Arvyndase word for naiad, which is Tarspri (tayrs - spry). These are enchanting, haunting beings, rather like sirens, only more likely to be in fresh water ponds, streams, and lakes. They are the Ladies of the Lake of ancient legend. They are the spirits of water that often appear ephemeral and ghostly, like mist rising from a sacred spring. They will touch your heart, dab away your tears (like a pocket handkerchief) and soothe your soul and your longings. They are usually beautiful and alluring. Some care is called for however. One can be drawn into their world of feeling and emotion and have a hard time finding one's way out again, sink into depression and become ghostly to the world that no longer holds any interest to one. One's passions can be so consuming that one loses touch with the world and becomes totally absorbed in one's imaginings.

WHAT THIS ORACLE MEANS:

If you receive this Wizard Myne, then be mysterious in this situation or relationship. Don't chase after things or people. Hang back, take your time and lure people to you. Use your enchantments. Be diplomatic. Offer a kindly handkerchief if needed, but don't get involved unless asked to do so. Hold your advice to yours'elf. Don't offer it and if it is asked for be reserved in giving it because they will most likely ignore it anyway. But don't let that bother you. They are just using you as a sounding board to bounce their own thoughts off of. They don't really want your opinion except as a way to formulate their own thoughts. They will only take your advice if you happen to agree with their own thoughts.

On the other hand, let your feelings show. Don't hide them. But don't broadcast them either. Simply feel truly and genuinely, be sincere, not disingenuous, and let your feelings express themselves through your demeanor but not so much through your words or some emotional outpouring.

At the same time, don't get drawn into other people's trauma dramas. Let them express their emotions but don't get caught up in them. Be sympathetic but a bit elusive. Be hesitant with others in all your interactions. Only when they show that they really value you and your input should you feel free to offer your own insights concerning their situation. You are the Mist itself. You are the manifestation of the Mystery in the world. Your part at this time isn't to clear things up for them but to remind them, through your being, of the possibilities for happiness that come to those who seek the higher path. Be confident in yours'elf and let them make of you what they will. You are only a mirror for their own inner being.

ENCHANTMENT SPELL:

From afar I see you there
Come closer now for I do care

This Spell in Arvyndase:

An narlo El ten le norn
Koso veskfa mat fro El ba synth

Pronunciation:

Ane nair - low Eel teen lee norn
Co - so veesk - fah mate fro Eel bah synth

Chapter 50:

Ash

KEYWORD: **OTHERKIN**

TREE NAME IN ARVYNDASE: **IRANALI** (PRONOUNCED: EYE - RAIN - NAIL - LIE)

Arvyndase Name of the Wizard Myne: **Saoni** (pronounced: say - ohn - nigh)

This Tree and Its Magic:

The Ash tree is related to the Ogham Nuin and is also one of those trees known as a world tree, the Yggdrasil tree, that links the worlds together and thus symbolizes the Universe. The English name ash can be traced to the Old English æsc and from that to the Proto-Indo-European word for tree. On the other hand, the generic name Fraxinus comes through Latin from a Proto-Indo-European word for birch. Both words, however, were also utilized as a word for spear since the wood of this tree was used for ages to make excellent spear shafts.

We Silver Elves connect this tree with the word Otherkin, which is a generic word that represents all elves, elfae, fae, faeric and otherkind of all manner and sorts. Like the Ash tree or world tree it links all the worlds and faerie peoples together. We further associate it with the Wizard Myne Saoni, which is derived from the Arvyndase word Saon (say - ohn) that means Other. We are the Others, the otherworldly, the eternal aliens to the world of the normal folk from whom everything different is strange and not-normal.

And let us not forget that the shaft that is used to make the spear is really the wizard's staff with a sharp pointed end attached to it. Therefore, this is a tree of great magic, magic that can touch all the worlds, link them together and has consequently a very far reach. Therefore, the magic of this tree is not really about using force (the spear), unless absolutely necessary, but about using wisdom (the wizard's staff) and making connections between things. This is not a Myne of brute strength but of leverage and the wise and efficient use of power.

What This Oracle Means:

In getting this Wizard Myne, one is called to consider what connects one to others and what are the connections you can use to deal with and solve this situation. How can you bring the proper pressure to bear in the right place, at the right time, with the least amount of effort necessary to obtain what you desire? This is not a matter of power, or strength or force but of an understanding of how things work and how you can work them. Technique, not muscle, is the key to dealing with this issue.

You may feel very apart from the world and from those that are around you. You may think that you are a loner and feel alienated from the world. And surely, you are a unique being, since all elfae folk are truly unique and often eccentric. But here you are asked to consider how you are the same as others, what links you to them. What relationships can you call upon, what commonality exists that will aid you in connecting with others, possibly enlisting their aid, and through that achieving what you desire. High or low, roots or branches, trunk or top, it is all one tree.

ENCHANTMENT SPELL:

There is a thread of light I see
Runs through the world betwixt you and me

This Spell in Arvyndase:

Norn da na nes u lun El ten
Kellu joul tae telth cata le nar el

Pronunciation:

Norn dah nah niece u loon Eel teen
Keel - lou joe - yule tay teal-th cah - tah lee nair eel

Chapter 51:

Olive

Keyword: **The Letter U**

Tree Name in Arvyndase: **Olea** (pronounced: oh - lee - ah)

Arvyndase Name of the Wizard Myne: **Urmi** (pronounced: your - my)

This Tree and Its Magic:

The oldest known mention of the Olive tree goes back to Mycenaean Greek in the Linear B syllabic script from around 1,450 B.C.E. According to the fossil evidence the Olive tree goes back to at least 20–40 million years ago in the Oligocene period. Humans have been using and cultivating the edible fruit of the Olive tree for at least 5,000 to 6,000 years, and certainly since the early Bronze Age at about 3150 to 1200 B.C.E. Some of its wood fragments have been found in ancient tombs, suggesting a magical and spiritual significance to these trees and the idea that olives, olive oil or the olive branch has some currency in the Other World of the Afterlife. Olives are known to have been grown and traded commercially in ancient Crete back as far as 3000 BC and the Minoan civilization.

The oil from the olive has also been considered to be sacred. And the branch of the olive has been seen to be symbolic of abundance, glory, and peace. The branches were offered in ancient times to various deities to represent devotion and purification. They were placed on the heads of the victors of competitive games and conquerors of wars to crown their achievements. The oil was, and is still utilized, in current times in many religious rituals and was an oil of anointing. The term, extending an olive branch, which means offering peace, a truce, or a peaceful solution to a problem or conflict is still used today. And the Olive trees are some of the oldest living trees, their lives potentially extending to 2,000 years.

We Silver Elves relate this tree to the Letter U and the Wizard Myne Urmi that comes from the Arvyndase word Urm (your-m), which means Gold. Therefore, we related this tree, the olive branch, the olive and olive oil to Faerie Gold. Not the false faerie gold that is a rock or leaf glamoured by magic to appear to be gold for a short time, but true faerie gold, the gold of peace, abundance and prosperity.

WHAT THIS ORACLE MEANS:

In getting this Wizard Myne, it may be best if you extend the olive branch, seek a truce or compromise in the situation and put all your effort into working things out. If the others involved won't accept your offer then that is their own fault and they will eventually suffer due to their intransigence. At least, you will have done your best both magically and karmically to resolve things. You will be in the right place morally and strategically and can be justified in proceeding as necessary in keeping with the circumstances that thereafter arise.

Also, look to how you can profit from this situation, not at the expense of others but in a mutual exchange that is beneficial to all parties concerned. Commerce, trade, barter and thus prosperity and abundance are keys to peace and surely, in the long run at least, peace is vital to commerce. Which is not to say that there are not those who make profit off war and conflict, but that is ever a situation limited by the nature of war, which consumes but seldom creates or builds anything lasting. Nearly everything is wasted away in war. Here, we are looking for long term solutions to the problems you are encountering and mutual and shared success is the key to establishing the conditions for continued prosperity.

The true Faerie Gold arises not from conning others, tricking others, or being a parasite, but by creating bridges between individuals or groups for regular connection and profitable exchange. Poverty is often the cause of violence, crime and war. On the other hand, abundance and success, without greed, lead to the possibility of enduring success. Make nice and this will surely profit you in the long run.

ENCHANTMENT SPELL:

Let's make a deal so you will see
What profits me will profit thee

This Spell in Arvyndase:

Lao'eli kord na pado re le yon ten
Wu mormolu el yon mormo vele

Pronunciation:

Lay - oh'e - lie cord nah pay - doe ree lee yone teen
Woo more - moe - lou eel yone more - moe vee - lee

Chapter 52:

Foxglove

KEYWORD: **THE NUMBER 5**

TREE NAME IN ARVYNDASE: **GILEF** (PRONOUNCED: GUY - LEAF)

Arvyndase Name of the Wizard Myne: **Lorfaor** (pronounced: lore - fae - or)

This tree and its magic:

These trees most easily develop in sterile soils, after wildfires have raged through because otherwise, their seeds are prey to fungi in the soil. The fires purify the soil and thus make it suitable for the inception of these trees. Because of this, they are sometimes called Phoenix trees. But they are also called Princess trees and we Silver Elves associate these trees with the Number 5 and the Wizard Myne Lorfaor, which comes from the Arvyndase word Lorfao (lore - fae - oh) that is our elven word for Princess. Therefore, these trees are, to us, the Faerie Princess trees.

We should also remember that these are the Foxglove trees. There is an expression of treating someone with 'kid gloves', which means to be very careful and delicate with them. But what would treating someone with foxgloves mean? It indicates being clever but modest about the fact. Rather like the idea we encounter in stories about grifters, where the best con is the one where the individual never realizes they've been conned. So, this energy is about using power, but using it in such a way that it is mostly unseen.

Such is the way of princesses, and women in general, in male dominated traditional societies, where the women must use their intelligence and their feminine wiles to influence things without the men even realizing that they are being manipulated. These are trees of unseen magic. Secret magic, done in the dark, in the shadows, hidden from view and yet all the more potent because of this.

What This Oracle Means:

In receiving this Wizard Myne, one is called to influence a situation without anyone even realizing that one is doing so. At the same time, look behind the situation and see who is also moving things from the shadows. You may not be the only one putting magic into this situation, although women and elfae folk are more likely to use this power than men who have been led to believe force and power are the most important factors in any situation and pay little attention to suggestion and leverage.

You may offer certain ideas as advice. They will probably be rejected. But if you are subtle about it and give the individuals time to consider things on their own, and present the ideas without any attachment to their acceptance, you may find that in due time, your ideas will be taken up by these others. However, it is most likely that they will forget you ever even mentioned them in the first place and will present these ideas as though they were their very own thoughts, giving you no credit or thanks whatsoever.

This may seem to be a bit ungrateful of them. And surely it is, yet, at the same time, this is actually a good thing. If they present the ideas as their own they will fully support and endorse them. You don't need credit. You just need them to do what you suggested. So, praise them for their great and brilliant idea and put your support fully behind them. You are not seeking fame, you seek to transform the world.

And as to these others acting from the shadows, as long as their ideas are good, support them as well. But if they are not, your counter spells, your counter suggestions, will help reduce their influence. Really, the question isn't about getting your way no matter what, just for the sake of manipulating, but finding the best idea, the best solution and supporting it. This will make things better for everyone and that is always our ultimate goal as elves.

ENCHANTMENT SPELL:
Whispers from the shadows sound
To better ways, we are now bound

This Spell in Arvyndase:
Susholi an tae dasårli deth
Va rilfa yerli, eli da mat med

Pronunciation:

Sue - show - lie ane tay day - sar - lie deeth

Vah rile - fah year - lie, e - lie dah mate mead

Chapter 53:

Plane

KEYWORD: **THE LETTER C**

TREE NAME IN ARVYNDASE: **SHRONA** (PRONOUNCED: SHROW - NAH)

ARVYNDASE NAME OF THE WIZARD MYNE: **CHIOFKOR** (PRONOUNED: CHI - OAF - CORE)

THIS TREE AND ITS MAGIC:

Plane trees tend to be very tall trees, reaching from 100 to 160+ feet. They like to live near water, close to or alongside of rivers or in wetlands, but some cultivated versions have become drought resistant. It is possible that these were the trees Marco Polo noted as Dry Trees that battle any other trees that comes near them, although it doesn't exactly seem like a dry tree. It is known for certain that these trees provided the German camouflage pattern 'Platanenmuster' providing the first dotted camouflage pattern. Also, after pollination, the female flowers develop into achenes that form an aggregate ball that looks a bit like a caltrop (antipersonnel and anti-tire weapon composed

166 . . . . The Elfin Book of Trees for the Elven Druid

of three or more sharp nails or spikes arranged so that at least one of spikes always points upward from a stable base) that pierces feet or tires. These achenes are composed of multiple seeds around a ball whose attached bristles assist in the dispersion of the seed by the wind, much in the manner of a dandelion flower as it seeds and blows away in the wind or upon our wish enchanted breath. Only here, the wishes you may set forth probably have to do with being safe from your enemies.

Therefore, we Silver Elves associate this Plane/plain tree, with Elven Camouflage. We often say that besides Nature and the creatures within it, we were the first peoples to use camouflage for blending into the forest. We also associate it with the Letter C and the Wizard Myne Chiofkor that is derived from the Arvyndase word Chiofko (chi - oaf - co), which is our elven word for camouflage. This is the tree of the elven rangers who roam and explore the world unseen, merging in wherever they go and becoming one with their environment.

What This Oracle Means:

You may need to camouflage yours'elf. It is best if you can avoid conflict, but if conflict is necessary, never let them see you coming. Help your others to protect thems'elves as well. Show your kindred how to merge in the world. How to pass through it unseen. Be the elf you are, or faerie, or whatever, but don't let potentially hostile individuals even get a glimpse of your true s'elf. Pass for normal (or whatever they may be) in this situation, be as plain as possible, and yet inwardly remain true to your own unique s'elf.

Don't engage in conflict unless you have no choice but to do so. It is better to disappear in this case, to fade away, than to stand and fight, unless your kin are endangered and you have no other alternative. In that case, stand your ground if you must and drive off the enemy. But they will likely return again, even stronger, so mostly it is best to retreat from them. Decamp without them even realizing you have done so until after you are long gone and leave them to sink into the swamp they have created for thems'elves. If you do that, they will surely find someone else to argue and fight with in due time. This is basic Behaviorism. Give them no energy. Do not engage. Really, you want no part of them.

On the other hand, if they are just being a bit paranoid and afraid but are not necessarily hostile, soothe their fears. They have nothing to fear from you or our kind. Let them feel that you are really one of them, just like them, on their side, they have nothing to worry about. Everything is okay. Everything is going to be okay. They just need to chill a little. It is their paranoia that is the problem, although it is best if you don't mention that to them.

But best of all, simply go about your life and your magic unseen. Be the plane tree, Hiding in Plain Sight. Be there among them, reaching for the heavens and yet, unnoticed.

ENCHANTMENT SPELL:
You see me but you notice not
That I don't fit into your slot

This Spell in Arvyndase:
Le ten el kana le dothar kon
Dij El ba'kon rylth verva le'na checa

Pronunciation:
Lee teen eel kay - nah lee doe - thayr cone
Dye-j Eel bah'cone rill-th veer - vah lee'nah chee - cah

Chapter 54:

Mangrove family

KEYWORD: **THE WATER ELEMENTAL**

TREE GROUP NAME IN ARVYNDASE: **ORFORELPA** (PRONOUNCED: OR - FOR - EEL - PAH)

ARVYNDASE NAME OF THE WIZARD MYNE: **QUANTI** (PRONOUNCED: Q - ANE - TIE)

THIS TREE AND ITS MAGIC:

The Mangrove family of trees are water loving trees. Some of them produce wood that is especially useful for creating piling and for constructions that will endure underwater. They also produce tannins used in leather making. The most famous of these trees is the Red Mangrove that usually can be found in intertidal zones that are inundated by the ocean or sea on a daily basis. Most of the Mangrove trees are hermaphrodites blending both genders in their beings.

Therefore, we Silver Elves associate these trees with the elemental of water and the power of water magic and thus also with pure sensory feeling, our instincts and the unconscious aspects of our beings. Jung said that each of us has an inner being in our unconscious that is the opposite gender to our physical bodily manifestation. This idea links the unconscious to the hermaphroditic nature of these trees. We are both genders. One manifesting within, the other outwardly. We also relate these trees to the Wizard Myne Quanti that comes from the Arvyndase word Quant (q - ain't), which is our elven word for water.

Part of the roots of these trees will be found above water, and it is through these parts that they respire oxygen even though the bottoms of their roots are submerged, somewhat like a swimmer who turns their face above the water to breathe. They also have the ability to remove excess salts from their bodies that accumulate due to their salt water environments. In this way, they are able to live in communion with the sea, just as our individual unconscious and our feelings are connected to the greater, Collective Unconscious, and we can, in that way, find a means, as psychic beings, to filter out what would otherwise be an overwhelming influx of sensory, feeling, and psychic data.

WHAT THIS ORACLE MEANS:

It is hard not to be affected by this world and all the crazy stuff that is going on in the realms of Mankind and the normal folk. It is not simply the news and its tremendous input of information about tragedies that occur on a near daily basis, but there is the huge outpouring of paranoia, trauma drama, and often depression and despair that all the news provokes in the people who listen to it. And remember, a good deal of it is fake news, mostly propagated by those who are ever railing against fake news.

You may turn it all off, or tune it out, but if you wish to use the power of the water elementals on a broad basis, you will need to take it in without it overly affecting you. You don't wish to let the lunacy of the world drive you crazy. Don't let its madness make you depressed. It may feel like everything is rushing downhill toward an inevitable doom, but you need to rise above that. Don't get swept away by the tide of emotional outpouring, on a large scale or even on an immediate scale, due to the personal trauma dramas around you. Stay calm. Let your serenity soothe others. Take their depression and subtly lift it up. Let your more potent and peaceful feelings ripple out and affect the world for the better. Whisper your spells over a bowl of water, or to a rushing stream or into a quiet lake or pond. This is water magic. Remember, 40 to 60% of the human body is water. Water magic has great potential power.

If you are unclear about what is going on, then a dream will probably come to you to guide you on the path. The unconscious, while hidden, does leave signs. It is like an invisible being leaving footprints in the sand of your mind. Creating synchronicities to catch your attention. If you understand these signs and intimations correctly, they will lead you to Elfin for that is our ultimate destiny and destination.

ENCHANTMENT SPELL:

Stir the waters, gentle, calm
My whispered spells a soothing balm

This Spell in Arvyndase:

Rus tae quantli, elaf, elwyn

El'na sushoïn mojali na tolthdas sorsae

Pronunciation:

Roos tay q - ain't - lie, e - layf, eel - win

Eel'nah sue - show - in moe - jah - lie nah tole-th - dace soar - say

Chapter 55:

Hawthorn

KEYWORD: **FAERIES**

TREE NAME IN ARVYNDASE: **ACANTHA** (PRONOUNCED: A - CAN - THAH)

ARVYNDASE NAME OF THE WIZARD MYNE: **FARRIL** (PRONOUNCED: FAIR - RILE)

THIS TREE AND ITS MAGIC:

Celtic tribes of the Druids associated the Hawthorn tree with the Ogham Huathe. It is said to represent purity and purification and thus protection that is afforded to the innocent. We Silver Elves link it to the Wizard Myne Farril, which is derived from the Arvyndase word Farri (fair - rye) that is our elven word for faerie. Not Faerie as in the place or realm of Faerie, but faerie as an individual being in those and other realms and dimensions.

The Hawthorn is part of the Rose family of trees and shrubs, and it is also known as the Quickthorn, the Thornapple, the May tree, the Whitethorn, and the Hawberry. The Haw is the fruit produced by this tree that is said to taste like an overripe apple. These trees, like roses, have sharp thorns. Thus, it reminds us that Faerie as a place, and faeries as individuals, while they can be wondrous and beauteous, can also be prickly and dangerous at times to those who don't approach them with sincerity and courtesy. You must be pure to enter Faerie, you must be pure in your heart to follow the Elven Way.

This tree is also sometimes called the May tree and is associated with the May pole, and thus with marriage and romance. No marriage or real romance can survive without sincerity. Be true to yours'elf but also be true to your others and if you do that you will avoid nearly all the dangers that can abide in Faerie and in the world.

The generic name for this tree is Crataegus, which comes from a Greek word meaning strength, due to the strength of the wood, and from another Greek word meaning sharp, that refers to the thorns of some its species. The name 'haw's stems from the Anglo-Saxon word haguthorn, which indicates a fence with thorns, although it is also used to indicate the fruit of these trees. Faeries can be wonderful beings, but they have their personal boundaries and to attempt to go beyond them before one is invited is to provoke their pinches and pricks, not to mention their sharp and clever tongues. Be polite to the faerie folk; they do not abide discourtesy kindly.

Hawthorn is also said, in faerie lore, to mark the entrance to the otherworld, the world of Faerie. The password into Faerie is sincerity and courtesy. Whatever you say, say it nicely. And a bit of elegance would not go amiss either.

WHAT THIS ORACLE MEANS:

Sincerity is the key to all true relationships and friendships. It is our protection in the world. It gains us entry into Faerie. None who approach with hidden motives can pass the threshold into Faerie or, if they do, they will not much like what they find. For in many ways Faerie reflects us; it is a mirror of our own being. We get back exactly what we put into it only magnified and amplified by magic and enchantment.

So, it is that in this situation, you are dealing with faerie folk of various kinds. Be true to yours'elf but also be true in your intentions. That is one thing that nearly all faerie kind, no matter they be faerie or goblin, hold in general, a respect for those who are genuine. No tricks, no cunning, you may be clever but be clever courteously. Make no snide remarks. Make no thoughtless jokes, not even about yours'elf. Deride no one. Present your truth clearly, purely and without too much ornament. A bit flowery is okay, but don't overdo it. Make it simple and mostly unadorned, at least for now. Don't oversell it.

And if they turn out to be a bit thorny, or prickly, do your best to ignore it and continue quietly on. Be strong. Don't react in kind. Stand your ground, if need be, and wait. They are just testing you. If they can see that you are genuine and, if you don't try to force things, they may come around in time. Be strong and patient. This is a game about reality. So be real.

ENCHANTMENT SPELL:
Though you are prickly as can be
Ever true I'll be to me

This Spell in Arvyndase:
Nåt le da vikla tat vek te
Vari lod El'yon te va el

Pronunciation:
Not lee dah vike - lah tate veek tea
Vay - rye load Eel'yone tea vah eel

Some Photos of The Silver Elves with Our Favorite Tree and Plant Cousins

Heliconia mariae in Caines Botanical Gardens; Caines, Australia.

Metrosideros excelsa in Davenport, New Zealand, a coastal everygreen tree in the myrtle family.

Both the Metrosideros Excelsa and the Heliconia Mariae (pictured on the previous page) were identified by our elven brother, Jeffrey Anthony Fuentes, who is an anthropological scholar.

*Banyan Tree (just one tree),
related to the Ficus benghalensis.*

This beautiful majestic giant is home of many birds, in Queen Kapiʻolani Park in Honolulu, Hawaii.

Waimea Botanical Gardens on the North Shore, Oahu, Hawaii.

We elves love the huge shady trees in these gardens that are surrounded by plants in the araceae family.

Zardoa attuning to the energy of the forest at 9 Oaks Farm, Monroe, Georgia.

At 9 Oaks Farm, Silver Flame finds a special magical oak friend!

Chapter 56:

Apple

KEYWORD: **THE NUMBER 19**

TREE NAME IN ARVYNDASE: **JUFI** (PRONOUNCED: JEW - FIE)

ARVYNDASE NAME OF THE WIZARD MYNE: **LORFAER** (PRONOUNCED: LORE - FAE - EAR)

THIS TREE AND ITS MAGIC:

In the Celtic Ogham, this tree is associated with Quert and is linked to the idea of youth and beauty. Liz and Colin Murray in their book *The Celtic Tree Oracle*, express the opinion that this is the cultivated apple tree, but here we are dealing with both cultivated and wild apples. If you cut an apple in half you will see that it forms a pentagram, often seen as a symbol of witchcraft and magic. It is said that Merlin had an apple orchard that mystical and magically followed him everywhere he moved. We are of the opinion, however, that Merlin, like Johnny Appleseed, went about planting Apple trees wherever he roamed. The same orchard didn't follow him exactly, but its seeds went with him everywhere being spread far and wide. He was creating abundance for everyone.

We Silver Elves link this tree to the Number 19, and to the Wizard Myne Lorfaer, which is derived from the Arvyndase word Lorfae (lore - fay), which is our elven word for Prince. Therefore, this is the tree of the Elven Prince, who is usually a cultivated individual but, much like Legolas, Tolkien's Prince of the Mirkwood Elves, also inclined toward being a bit wild and adventurous as well. We elves are refined beings but also primal beings in touch with our feelings and our instincts.

We Silver Elves used to live on a plot of land that had once been an apple orchard and still had some apple trees growing in a row on the acre behind us. One of the things we noticed about these trees is that mistletoe, known to be sacred to the Druids, grew abundantly upon them. We'd get a good-sized sprig to put above our doorway each Yule and gave some to our neighbors as well. In this way, we were helping the trees by removing a parasite, while enticing kisses for our own s'elves.

WHAT THIS ORACLE MEANS:

In this situation, give generously, but not necessarily directly, but rather invest in the present in such in way that the seeds you plant today will bear fruit and create abundance in the future. Do this in any way that you can, with money, or magic or just plain help and energy. Do things now that will help Elfin bloom in the course of time. Don't look for or expect immediate results. This is unlikely to happen. Here you need to look to your Vision, look to the future and what you wish your world to be and become.

Also, you may be a very refined, cultured and educated person. You may have wealth or other privileges. You may be wise and an expert in exoteric or esoteric lore or both. But don't let this show directly any more than a seed tends to show its roots as it begins to take root. Let your refinement manifest as a reflection of your being, not an elaborate or extravagant main stage show you put on. Like makeup, less is better. Subtlety speaks louder than theatricality. Let people sense your education and cultured nature. You don't have to prove that you're intelligent and it is unwise to make people feel that they are less wise or knowledgeable than you. Nurture everyone and these will be the seeds that will create an orchard of abundance for you and them in times to come. Like Merlin, do this wherever you go.

And be a bit wild as well, if that is your nature. Not ostentatiously so. Again, this is not about making yours'elf the center of attention but letting your personality, whether refined, or wild and primitive, be a natural expression of your being.

ENCHANTMENT SPELL:

Everywhere I go I seed
The magic that we all do need

This Spell in Arvyndase:

Lotymern El tas El dern
Tae êldon dij eli wyl ba golt

Pronunciation:

Low - tim - ear-n Eel tace Eel dear-n
Tay l - doan dye-j e - lie will bah goal-t

Chapter 57:

Prunus: Almond, Peach, Apricot, Plums, Cherries

KEYWORD: **THE NUMBER 1,000,000**

TREE GROUP NAME IN ARVYNDASE: **KOLNABOR** (PRONOUNCED: COAL-N - A - BOAR)

ARVYNDASE NAME OF THE WIZARD MYNE: **ELDÂELAR** (PRONOUNCED: EEL - DAH - E - LAIR)

THIS TREE AND ITS MAGIC:

Prunus trees include the Almond, the Peach, the Apricot, the Nectarine, the Plum and the Cherry. Their fruits are mostly drupes which is to say a fleshy covering for an inner pit or seed. These, like the Apple, are part of the Rose family of trees. However, unlike the Ogham that associated the Apple directly with youth and beauty, we Silver Elves link these trees with Elven Longevity and thus in that way to beauty and youthfulness. The beauty and youthfulness of age, so to speak.

In fact, the name of this Wizard Myne, Eldåelar, comes from our Arvyndase word Eldåela (eel - dah - e - lah), which literally means Elf Life and is our word for longevity. We elves are rumored in lore to be blessed with long lives, but also to be beautiful and youthful long into our lives. Thus, potentially we could live for a 1,000,000 years and still look like we are in our twenties or thirties. What good does it if we live to a thousand years if we are no longer youthful as individuals? Thus, these trees represent one of the primary trees of elven culture, the Tree of Life Eternal and Youth Never-Ending.

In many Asian mythologies, the Peach tree and sometimes the Cherry tree are said to grow in the gardens of the gods and to bear a fruit that grants immortality to whomever should eat it. Thus, we have the Chinese stories of Monkey, the King of the Monkeys, who tricked his way into heaven and stole the fruit of the Gods. The Cherry tree, especially the cherry blossom varieties, are also noted for their great beauty. These are the trees of beauty ever renewed.

The Almond, while it is used to symbolize charm, sweetness, and a delicate nature, also represents fortitude in the face of sorrow, wisdom gained through experience and vigilance and watchfulness. While we may grow old and yet still seem young, part of our beauty comes from the sorrows we have borne and overcome. We may appear youthful and be youthful in spirit and body, but we have learned the lessons of living in the world and are neither naive nor heedless in doing so.

What This Oracle Means:

Keep a youthful attitude no matter how old you may be. If you are aged, then have some sympathy for the young. Don't fall into the trap set by the normal culture that ever seeks to divide us, one race from another, one religion from another, young from old, male from female. There are differences due to upbringing and generational experiences, but these are small compared to the things we truly share with each other. Don't presume that your music was better just because it happened to be what you liked when you were young, or that the youth today are all lazy or s'elf indulgent or ignorant or whatever. That is all propaganda. Youths throughout time have been s'elf indulgent. It's what they do. It's part of the process. The old have been complaining about the young as far back as the Ancient Greeks and probably before that. We can hear echoes of cave men complaining about 'the youth day'.

And if you are young, don't presume that the older and elderly are all ignorant and out of it. It is true that there are things they haven't experienced that you have, but the same is true of them. See the beauty and the essential spirit, which is to say the potential immortality of all beings, all souls. You may be young now, but when the elderly are reborn again, they will be younger than you. And it just goes on and on, round and round in a never-ending spiral of becoming. It is true that many of the old have given up and have just gone along with the flow of things to get along and survive, but then there are others, still living free according to their own intuitions, inclinations and the dictates of their eccentric personalities (these are usually elfae folk). And people, whomever they may be, will often surprise us. Don't expect the unexpected; don't expect anything at all. See what actually manifests. Be a scientist and observe.

And ever keep in mind that our true bodies are our energetic bodies, our bodies of light, and these are truly immortal. In that way, we are all equal.

Enchantment Spell:

However, I may appear to be
Within I'm young and ever free

This Spell in Arvyndase:
Poso, El me forno va te
Enaver El'da tylf nar vari alo

Pronunciation:
Poe - so, Eel me for - no vah tea
E - nah - veer Eel'dah tile-f nair vair - rye a - low

Chapter 58:

Pear

KEYWORD: **VAMPIRE**

TREE NAME IN ARVYNDASE: **IRUM** (PRONOUNCED: EYE - ROOM)

ARVYNDASE NAME OF THE WIZARD MYNE: **VÅNSHEL** (PRONOUNCED: VON - SHE-L)

THIS TREE AND ITS MAGIC:

The Pear tree is another of the Rose family of trees. They are mostly noted for their fruit, although they also produce lovely flowers. We Silver Elves relate this tree to the Wizard Myne Vånshel that comes from the Arvyndase word Vånshe (von - she), which is our elven word for Vampire. From our point of view, vampires are primarily otherworldly beings, who are often, but not always, dark elves or dark fae and who are, alas, frequently Unseelie Fae, which is to say they tend to prey upon Mankind and are parasitic in nature, at the same time being beautiful and nearly immortal. Of course, whether they are Unseelie or not has to do with whether they are parasitic in their blood taking or symbiotic in doing so. Do they kill to live, like much of Mankind, or do they take a little and promote the wellbeing of their donor in exchange for their blood?

We make this connection because the fruit of the pear tree is another fruit that is often deemed as the giver of immortality and is, like the cherry, apple, and peach, seen as also being symbolic of youth and beauty. Immortal beauty that the vampires possess according to legend and lore.

There is also the expression, things have turned 'pear shaped,' which is used to mean things have gone terribly wrong. There is a potential darkness here that must be taken into consideration.

What This Oracle Means:

If you receive this Wizard Myne then, while this situation or relationship seems to have great potential, it is also quite possible things will go pear-shaped. Whether this occurs or not depends greatly upon the people involved, their motivations, intentions and actions. Is there someone in this circumstance who is merely into things for their own gain and will suck you or the situation dry if they can? Someone who is just feeding off the situation and the people involved? Examine the situation carefully and the people in it. If you find a vampire involved you may wish to withdraw from it entirely, although that can be hard if you have already invested a lot of time, money and/or energy into it. Still, it is better to lose some than lose it all. You may wish to cut your losses while you can.

Most important is to make sure that you are not the one draining the situation. If that were the case, while you might gain in the short term, the long-term effects of karma would be harsh. Do what you can to assist all those innocents involved and proceed, if you do continue on, with care. Protect yours'elf.

There is also a question here concerning vegetarianism. This is one of the most disputed questions in the elfae community. Those who eat meat love to taunt those who don't and talk about Nature being red in tooth and claw most often unknowingly quoting Alfred Lord Tennyson's *In Memoriam A. H. H.* Some vegetarians, on the other hand, can be utterly fanatical at times, even to the point of violence. We Silver Elves simply accept that some elfae are advanced to the point where they strive not to kill to live, while others have not as yet understood the significance of this devotion to non-violence except in s'elf defense. The choice is yours, but if we, as individual spirits and as an elfae people, are truly to become immortal in physical bodies, we must stop preying on others to do so.

ENCHANTMENT SPELL:
I give care in all I take
Ever seek to reciprocate

This Spell in Arvyndase:
El luth synth ver wyl El rud
Vari hed va aserorey

Pronunciation:
Eel lou-th synth veer will Eel rude
Vair - rye heed vah a - sear - row - ray

Chapter 59:

Sorbus: Rowans, Whitebeams

Keyword: **Protection**

Tree Group Name in Arvyndase: **Quantwytre** (pronounced: Q - ain't - wit - tree)

Arvyndase Name of the Wizard Myne: **Kafad** (pronouncd: kay - fahd)

This tree and its magic:

Sorbus is another group of trees and shrubs of approximately 100 to 200 species in the rose family, or Rosaceae. These trees are known as the Whitebeam, the Rowan, the Service tree, and the Mountain-ash, although this last is not related to the true Ash tree. The Rowan is linked to the Druid's Ogham of Ruis, which gives one protection from enchantments and dark magics and enables one to see through glamors and glamouré, the magic of casting illusions. Using this magic, you will be able to see who people really are behind their charms, enchantments and personas.

We Silver Elves also relate these trees to the power of protection from dark magics; and to be surrounded by these trees is to establish an aura of protection for ones'elf, one's loved ones, and one's home. Therefore, we link these trees to the Wizard Myne Kafad, which comes from the Arvyndase word Kafa (kay - fah) that is our elven word for protect, and to the word Kafådur that means protection.

In many ways, the greatest protection we have is not static isolation but the whitebeam of light that we project, the starlight of our being, that surrounds our aura. This protection builds up as we perform service or wild service, which is to say unexpected acts of kindness, creativity and magic spreading blessings to all around us.

What This Oracle Means:

Things may not be entirely what they seem in this situation. Someone may be interfering and attempting to manipulate things from hiding and in secret, however, the magic of this Wizard Myne enables you to see through their pretense and look to the very heart of things. With this Myne, you cannot be fooled or deceived, although you may not wish to let them know this or have them aware that you see them for who they truly are. Don't confront them, work around them with your own unseen counter magics.

This aura of protection is especially strong if you have regularly built up your aura and surrounded it with an orb of protective white light. Do this now; do this regularly. Also, there is a blessing that comes to those who have been kindly and friendly with no expectation of reward. Creative kindness for the pure joy of it.

So, you need not worry overmuch. They may cast spells from the shadows. They can stick their voodoo dolls with as many pins as they wish. They cannot penetrate the magic that shields you and all their darkness will merely bounce back upon them. Try to bless them, none-the-less, and trust that their self-inflicted suffering will help wise them up. Continue to set an example of wondrous elfin being in the world and in the various dimensions and planes of manifestation and trust that you are headed exactly in the direction you are meant to, which is the realization of your own true s'elf and nothing and no one can prevent that in the long run, except you. You alone in the course of your incarnations decide your destiny.

ENCHANTMENT SPELL:
No matter how great may be the disguise
The truth is still clear to my elfin eyes

This Spell in Arvyndase:
Kon trolar po ralt me te tae tasem
Tae lodver da vila vyrn va el'na êldat arli

Pronunciation:
Cone trow - lair poe rail-t tea tay tay - seem
Tae load - veer dah vie - lah vern vah eel'nah l - date air - lie

Chapter 60:

Bedstraw family or Coffea

KEYWORD: **BROWNIES**

TREE GROUP NAME IN ARVYNDASE: **MYRTEELPA** (PRONOUNCED: MER - TEA - EEL - PAH)

ARVYNDASE NAME OF THE WIZARD MYNE: **URNAVIN** (PRONOUNCED: YOUR - NAY - VINE)

THIS TREE AND ITS MAGIC:

The Bedstraw or Madder family is the family of trees and shrubs of the Coffea or Coffee trees. We Silver Elves associate these trees with Brownies who, according to legend and lore, often take care of people's homes for them and are thus noted for being homebodies, rather in the manner of Tolkien's Hobbits who are, in our opinion, a type of brownie or perhaps gnome. The brownies like things comfortable and cozy, with the smell of coffee brewing in the air, making one feel that indeed life is worth living and there is something to look forward to, even if it is only a fresh cup or two of coffee or tea. We further link these trees to the Wizard Myne Urnavin that comes from the Arvyndase word Urnavi (your - nay - vie), which is our elven word for Brownie (as in the people, not the dessert, although we expect that Brownies love brownies and may have invented them. That makes perfect sense.)

We find it interesting that it is sometimes called the Bedstraw family. Did ancient peoples use its dried leaves to make bedstraw? Which is to say, was this tree used to make sleeping more comfortable and cozy? That would surely fit with the brownies, as well.

From the Madder comes red and sometimes yellow dye, and if you mix them you get the color orange, a color that brownies love almost as much as the color brown especially when it is muted or soft orange. It is said that if you don't treat brownies well, they will get mad and take revenge against you. They like their comfort and are not happy to have it disturbed and they appreciate thanks (contrary to some tales that say otherwise). If you don't want them dyeing their caps red and acting like vicious unseelie red caps, you'd better show some appreciation for all that they do for you. However, they expect more than mere words. Perhaps that is what the tales are about, Brownies upset and departing because people offered them only empty words of thanks in recompense for their efforts.

What This Oracle Means:

There are people who are seeking to help you, to serve you, to make your life more comfortable, to ease your way and all of this because they love you or wish to be friends with you, and seek to be a part of your life. Thank them for whatever service they perform. It is possible that you don't feel comfortable with some of them coming too close or being too intimate with you, but you can put them off with courtesy and kindness. Don't hurt their feelings even while you keep them at a distance. Show some compassion and reward them for what they have done and are doing for you. A kind word, a simple gift or two, a genuine and heartfelt thanks will not go amiss.

And show gratitude for the blessings of your life. There are forces unseen (as brownies are often said to be) who look after you and make your life better. Bless them as well and be thankful for the gifts from the Divine Magic that you receive. Your life may not be perfect, it may not be everything you wish and desire it to be, but still there are surely things to be grateful for and in showing your gratitude you attract more of these blessings.

And relax a bit. Take a bit of time for yours'elf and rest in the comfort of your, hopefully, cozy elfin home. Creativity and invention arise not just from an unrelenting pursuit of your art or your ideas, but from resting for a bit and letting your unconscious work and play as you sit back in your plush chair or lay on your soft couch or sofa and take in the aroma of fresh brewed coffee. All things in life work in cycles, tides and movements back and forth, to and fro, round and round again. That is the Tao.

ENCHANTMENT SPELL:
I thank you for all the things you do
You make life better, this is true

This Spell in Arvyndase:
El sond le fro wyl tae vessåli le ba
Le kord ela rilfa, wyr da lod

Pronunciation:
Eel sewn-d lee fro will tay vees - sah - lie lee bah
Lee cord e - lah rile - fah, were dah load

Chapter 61:

Rue family

KEYWORD: PIXIES

Tree Group Name in Arvyndase: **Jordelpa** (pronounced: jourd - eel - pah)

Arvyndase Name of the Wizard Myne: **Pykser** (pronounced: pick - seer)

This tree and its magic:

The Rue family of trees and shrubs consist of the Rue and the Citrus trees, which include the Orange trees, the Lemon trees, the Grapefruit trees, the Kumquats and the Lime trees. Non-citrus members of this family are the White Sapote, found in Mexico, and the Bael, also known as Bengal quince, Golden apple, Japanese bitter orange, Stone apple or Wood apple, and can be found on Indian subcontinent and Southeast Asia.

We Silver Elves link these trees with the Pixie folk, who are bright, even flowery at times, but can also be tart, like a lemon, lime or grapefruit, if provoked into being so. We associate it with the Wizard Myne Pykser that is derived from our Arvyndase word Pykse, pronounced: Pixie, and that's what it stands for.

By the way, the Grapefruit is apparently so called because they grow on the trees in bunches, resembling grapes in their growth. So, it is that Pixies often hang together in their close-knit groups. If you mess with one of them, you're messing with them all. So, too, if one of them likes you, the others are inclined to do so as well. You just need one to vouch for you. However, if you cross these folks, you will come to rue the day you did so.

And there is often something a bit wild and sometimes tricksy, according to lore, about these people. They are inclined toward pranks, just for the fun of it. It can be a bit of an initiation process with them, but mostly they pull their tricks on those who have sought to harm them or have taken advantage of them.

WHAT THIS ORACLE MEANS:

This is a tricky situation. There are people involved who are being a bit sneaky or cunning about things, manipulating the situation, but only because they feel they have been slighted in some way and do not wish to confront anyone directly. A certain caution is advised here because they may be right. Try to make friends with them. Endeavor to discover what is really going on and what their actual motivations may be and why, and do what you can to work things out so everyone gets their fair share of credit or money or whatever this discontent may concern.

If you approach this situation, and these people, in the right way, things will turn out for the best for everyone and certainly they will start looking out for your benefit as well as their own. They are not unreasonable folk, just a bit upset at the moment, or a bit paranoid. Soothe them and everything will begin running smoothly.

If you have unknowingly (or knowingly) offended them, then apologize and this will go a long way in making things right. If they have unknowingly or intentionally insulted you, forgive them. Rise above the situation and look toward the end result that you envision and do all that you can, in a direct and clear way without being tricky, to move things toward the realization of your vision.

ENCHANTMENT SPELL:

Tell me the truth so I can see
What's going on between you and me

This Spell in Arvyndase:
Fram el tae lodver re El vek ten
Wu'da tasdas ton vyrlan le nar el

Pronunciation:
Frame eel tay load - veer re Eel veek teen
Woo'dah tace - dace tone ver - lane lee nair eel

Chapter 62:

Willow family

KEYWORD: **BANSHEE**

TREE GROUP NAME IN ARVYNDASE: **SALIELPA** (PRONOUNCED: SAY - LIE - EEL - PAH)

ARVYNDASE NAME OF THE WIZARD MYNE: **BÅNSHEN** (PRONOUNCED: BON - SHEEN)

THIS TREE AND ITS MAGIC:

The Willow family of trees include the Willow tree, the Poplars and the Aspens, although Poplar and Aspen are really different names for the same trees. The Willow tree is often said to Weep, while the Aspen is said to Quake or Tremble in the wind. We Silver Elves associate these trees with the Banshee or Bean Sidhe, which means Woman of the Fairy Folk, who is said to weep or cry or wail (the wind) when someone related to the Faeries is about to die. Quaking and trembling, of course, are often associated with the idea of fear of what may come. Therefore, these trees are linked to the Wizard Myne Bånshen that comes from the Arvyndase word Bånshe (bon - she), which is our word for Banshee and denotes an individual with psychic foresight who can see impending difficulties or troubles before they arrive. We sometimes call these beings the Doom-Seers.

While the Willow might weep over misfortune and death, and the Aspen quake in anticipation of this doom foretold, in its manifestation as the Poplar it is said to symbolize victory. There is always a chance of avoiding the doom if we can heed the warning signs in time and take proper preventive measures. Most willows can root very easily from cuttings or even from broken branches that lie upon the earth, thus the Willow tells us we can always start over again, even after we have been broken. Also, the willow bark produces the main ingredient for aspirin, so we can, at the very least, soothe the pain.

What This Oracle Means:

There is clearly a potential problem looming. You can quake with fear, or weep or get depressed about things, and we wouldn't blame you if you did. But also consider what action you may take, if any, to prevent, avoid, or lessen (aspirin) and make less painful the difficulty that is coming.

And remember, even if you can't avoid it entirely, or even partially, you can always begin again in this lifetime or another to come. That part is what is truly inevitable, starting over. Death often seems unavoidable but it is Life that continues on and on and we shall be born again and again on this plane of being until we learn to live upon higher, more expansive and more subtle dimensions. So, fear not. This is just a hiccup. Just another burp in the Universe. Just another fart. A bit of Cosmic indigestion in your life. If you can't avoid it, well, that's just the way it goes sometimes. But it will pass and you can carry on into the future knowing that we have all been through this in one way or another, most likely one way and another, lifetime after lifetime. Even the Shining Ones have passed this way. We wish we had better news for you but sometimes, that's just the way things are.

Enchantment Spell:

I see it coming and step aside
If I'm unable to go and hide

This Spell in Arvyndase:

El ten ter kosodas nar cid wylaten
Nef El'da murasha va tas nar rim

Pronunciation:

Eel teen tier co - so - dace nair sid will - lay - teen

Neef Eel'dah muir - a - shah vah tace nair rhyme

Chapter 63:

Maple

KEYWORD: **SPIRIT**

TREE NAME IN ARVYNDASE: **ASHAR** (PRONOUNCED: A - SHARE)

ARVYNDASE NAME OF THE WIZARD MYNE: **NESER** (PRONOUNCED: KNEE - SEAR)

THIS TREE AND ITS MAGIC:

The Maple tree is probably most noted for maple syrup and for its seeds that bear a single wing and spin as they fall to the ground or blow in the wind like a helicopter. However, its wood is also used for tone wood for musical instruments because it makes a nice sound and because of the strength and resilience of this wood it is also used in archery as the core material in the construction of the limbs of a recurve bow, another nice elven aspect to it.

All this has led us Silver Elves to connect these trees to the energy and magic of Spirit, of the Shining Ones, especially as one progresses toward and develops into a Shining One. We further relate it to the

Wizard Myne Neser, which comes from one of the two Arvyndase words for shine. There is glis, which means shine as in light, and in this instance Shining Ones would be translated as Glisdas Atali, and there is Nese (knee - see) that indicates shine as in to polish or make shiny, as in shine your shoes. The idea here is not that one has already achieved one's shine, glis, entirely, but that one is polishing, nesedas (literally: shining), up one's light, in the process of becoming a Shining One. It is the continual effort and perseverance that is important.

And with that effort to shine, comes blessings, like pure maple syrup. But too much sweetness can be detrimental; so, some caution and discipline are advised. Remember especially, you only have one wing at this point. You can spin and hover, but you can't really fly high. Keep up the good work but proceed with care and diligence.

WHAT THIS ORACLE MEANS:

If you get this Wizard Myne in response to a question, then it says to continue on with what you are doing, whatever it is. At the same time, this Myne is about working on the planes of spirit. This isn't simply about achieving something in the normal world, but about using this task or situation or aspiration as a means of developing yours'elf and your spirit. In this case, short-term success is likely. You may earn your maple syrup, but the long-term success, your progress as a spirit is what is most important here. At the same time, it is by doing our best in the immediate and applying ours'elves in each moment, doing the best we can at every task we undertake, that we ensure our success in the long run.

This Myne brings a small blessing with it. A little bit of luck that, if you use it well, can grow. You are not ready as yet for high flying, but you are progressing and getting stronger as a spirit and that is what is really important. You are like a baby bird just pushed out of the nest. You are unlikely to be a strong flyer, but you will get there. Keep exercising those wings.

And whatever magics you do, do them on the planes of spirit and from the point of view of the spirit world, which is to say the underlying world of energy that is within and beneath all things. This really isn't about success in the material world, or at least not directly so. This is about your success as a spirit being, as an elfae or other, and as a personality. It is about your increasing power and influence as an individual. It is about shining (nesedas) yours'elf up so you will increasingly manifest as a Shining (Glisdas) One (Ata). It is about brightening and strengthening your aura.

ENCHANTMENT SPELL:

I shine my spirit everyday
And thus, I find the Shining Way

This Spell in Arvyndase:

El nese el'na tari lotymlea
Nar hern, El låc tae Glisdas Yer

Pronunciation:

Eel knee - see eel'nah tay - rye low - tim - lee - ah
Nair hear-n, Eel lock tay Glice - dace Year

Chapter 64:

Aesculus: Buckeye, Horse-chestnut

KEYWORD: **TROLLS**

Tree Group Name in Arvyndase: **Oknaelpa** (pronounced oak - nah - eel - pah)

Arvyndase Name of the Wizard Myne: **Trolli** (pronounced: troll - lie)

This tree and its magic:

Aesculus family of trees has the Buckeye tree and the Horse-Chestnut in it, although the Horse-Chestnut is not directly related to the actual Chestnut tree, rather its closest relative, beside the Buckeye is the Maple. These are flowering plants and trees in the Soapberry and Lychee family. They may also be called White Chestnut or Red Chestnut and, in Great Britain, they are sometimes referred to as Conker trees due to their association with a game they call conkers, which is played with the Horse-Chestnut seeds. A string is put through a seed and players take turns hitting each other's seed until one of them breaks.

This is actually an old troll game that we Silver Elves have ever called Bonkers, both because it involves trolls standing and taking turns bonking each over the head with a club until one of them gets a concussion or is knocked unconscious (which is harder than you might think because trolls have very hard heads), and because it seems to us elves that this game is just plain Bonkers, or crazy.

In modern times, they have, for the most part, given up using clubs. Instead, they stand and take turns punching each other in the face until one of them is knocked down and stays down. We suppose that they regard this change as slightly more civilized. We elves are still of the opinion that it and they are bonkers.

This Wizard Myne and these trees are associated with Trolls, obviously, and the Arvyndase name for this Myne is Trolli, which is our elven word for trolls.

What This Oracle Means:

You may get your false ego aroused and be tempted into a 'pissing contest' with someone. True ego, or ego strength represents a strong sense of one's s'elfhood. It is a feeling of personal security and confidence in ones'elf. But false ego is aroused when one's insecurities are provoked and one feels one's persona is endangered. True Ego, or ego strength, does not feel assailed by the challenges that others present to one's persona.

So, as we say, don't get drawn into a 'pissing contest'. You will most likely only wind up with piss on yours'elf, yours or someone else's or both, and even if you seem to win the contest, you are really just pissing your time and energy away for no lasting purpose. Not to mention the fact that the person you have pissed on or outdone will merely come at you again, attempting to undermine you in secret or behind your back if they don't feel strong enough to confront you directly.

Consider whether this situation or relationship is really worth your time at all. You may wish to simply withdraw from the whole matter. However, if you do decide to stick it out, just proceed directly and clearly toward your goal and ignore the taunt and chides of others. More than likely they are just jealous because of their own insecurities and it has almost nothing to do with you really. This is all their stuff.

Enchantment Spell:

It doesn't matter what you say
That's not a game I wish to play

This Spell in Arvyndase:

Ter ba'kon trolar wu le des
Dij'da kon na los El felj va jol

Pronunciation:

Tier bah'cone trow - lair woo lee deece
Dye-j'dah cone nah lowce Eel feel-j vah jole

Chapter 65:

Golden rain tree

Keyword: **Leprechauns**

Tree Name in Arvyndase: **Sarpurte** (pronounced: sayr - pure - tea)

Arvyndase Name of the Wizard Myne: **Wynfola** (pronounced: win - foal - lah)

This tree and its magic:

Golden Rain trees are another in the Sapindaceae family of Soapberry and Lychee trees. We relate these trees to the Leprechauns because of the association of Leprechauns with rain, rainbows, and gold. These are beautiful flowering trees; however, they spread easily and are sometimes seen as an invasive species. This may be why leprechauns, for their own part, are often reluctant to identity thems'elves as such, plus the old rumor that if you catch one, which is to say, recognize one for whom they truly are, they will have to take you to their pot of gold. Leprechauns will seldom identify thems'elves as such; although, like the Golden Rain tree, they are easy to distinguish and hard to miss.

In our own experience, when we've seen leprechauns here and there, they always hedge about admitting who they are. However, they need not do so. We don't see them as invasive and we're not after their gold. They are safe with the elves, but they don't always realize this fact. Ages of prejudice have made them cautious.

In a certain way, leprechauns are related to goblins, especially in their love of gold, to dragons, in their hoarding of treasure, to brownies in their rather downhome-ness and sometimes to gnomes in their love of lore. To some leprechauns, the greatest treasure is knowledge, although, that still doesn't mean they wish to share it. They can hoard information just like they do gold.

This Wizard Myne is called Wynfola, which is derived, as you might expect, from our Arvyndase word for Leprechaun, which is Wynfol (win - foal).

What This Oracle Means:

It is quite possible in getting this Wizard Myne that there is someone you are interested in, someone who is quite attractive to you, whom you would like to get to know better but who is very reserved and cautious and perhaps a bit paranoid and sees your approach as a potential threat and an intrusion. If this is the case, proceed with care. Don't attempt to force things. It is better for you to hang back and give them a chance to get some sense of you at a distance, to become familiar with you before you approach them.

Even then, there is no guarantee they will ever open up and let you into their inner circle. Only time will tell. However, you need to realize that hanging back and waiting gives you some possibility, whereas trying to push things gives you none.

There is another possibility here as well and that is that someone has invaded your social circle and is now constantly seeking to hog the limelight, to be the knowing one, the self-appointed authority about everything and ever the center of attention. Again, the best thing to do is simply hang back and let them do what they do. In time, they will most likely make a fool of thems'elves and, at any rate, people will get tired of their routine in the course of time. There is almost nothing you can do but be confident in yours'elf and be patient and watch the show.

Enchantment Spell:

You need not fear

I'll bring no harm
I simply seek
To view your charm

This Spell in Arvyndase:
Le golt kon mak
El'yon cura kon gras
El unkala hed
Va sant le'na elfat

Pronunciation:
Lee goal-t cone make
Eel'yone cur - rah cone grace
Eel you'n - kay - lah heed
Vah saint lee'nah eel - fate

Chapter 66:

Lychee

KEYWORD: **THE LETTER K**

TREE NAME IN ARVYNDASE: **LICHE** (PRONOUNCED: LIE - CHEE)

ARVYNDASE NAME OF THE WIZARD MYNE: **KAFYRTH** (PRONOUNCED: KAY - FIRTH)

THIS TREE AND ITS MAGIC:

The Lychee is another member of the Soapberry family of trees, usually found in China, Southeast Asia, the Indian subcontinent and South Africa. It produces a fleshy fruit that is used often in desserts, however, it has been known to cause hypoglycemia (low blood sugar) and has been linked to outbreaks of encephalopathy especially in undernourished and malnourished children in India and Vietnam due to the fact that methylene cyclopropyl glycine is contained in the Lychee seeds.

Therefore, we Silver Elves relate these trees to the Letter K and the idea of Elf School or elven education, which is directed, rather like ancient Chinese Medicine, to the needs of the individual. Thus, the Wizard Myne Kafyrth comes from the Arvyndase word Kafir (kay - fire) that means School. When educating someone, helping someone to learn, one needs to consider the present level of the individual, not only their intelligence but what they have learned thus far, and also what their interests and desires may be. One needs to be able to connect what one wishes to impart with what the individual is motivated to learn as well as what they already know.

Knowledge is a type of food. It is food for the mind, the spirit and the soul. However, not everyone is ready to learn the same things and teaching the same thing in the same way to nearly everyone is like giving everyone one medicine as the cure for whatever ails them or feeding everyone the same food regardless of their tastes. It is like a restaurant that serves one thing and one thing only.

Many, if not most individuals, especially when they are young, find education boring and often oppressive, which it is. However, elven education is exciting. It is fun. Nearly everything is learned through games and taught in keeping with the individual student's interests. This is, of course, not possible when you have one teacher for 30 to 40 students. That's not education, that's mass babysitting, which is not a good idea either. Elven education has one or two instructors for every student. And we play, nearly all the time. Thus, do we learn.

What This Oracle Means:

First, you have to figure out where their heads are at. What do they really want from this situation and from you? And, ask yours'elf, what do you want, really? If you need to communicate certain things to others, you have to know how they think. Giving them ideas that they don't comprehend is like speaking to them in a foreign language that they don't understand. What good is that? Connect all that you wish them to know to what they already know. In many ways, communication is all about building bridges, networks and links between what is known and what needs to be known.

Second, if you make it enjoyable, they will be more inclined to listen rather than pretend they are listening while they are actually thinking about something else. S'elf interest is the key to nearly all influence and enchantment. It is about making education attractive.

Third, repeat it without repeating it. They often say that you should tell your audience what you are going to tell them, then tell them and then tell them what you have told them, which is fine as long as you are not too redundant. Change it up. Some of the great keys to remembering things are mneumonic devices, patterns of words, rhymes and symbolic associations to make recall easier and fun. That is why chants and spells are often rhymed. Make your instruction fun.

Enchantment Spell:

I learn all things quite easily
I love to learn it's fun for me

This Spell in Arvyndase:

El adu wyl jartli ven hamla
El rynt va adu ter'da zyl fro el

Pronunciation:

Eel a - due will jay-rt - lie veen hame - lah
Eel rent vah a - due tier'dah zill fro eel

Chapter 67:

Mexican Buckeye

KEYWORD: **THE NUMBER 3**

TREE NAME IN ARVYNDASE: **SARGLABRA** (PORNOUNCED: SAYR - GLAY - BRAH)

ARVYNDASE NAME OF THE WIZARD MYNE: **ZILAR** (PRONOUNCED: ZIE - LAIR)

THIS TREE AND ITS MAGIC:

Mexican Buckeye is very like the other buckeyes, the ones we associate with Trolls, but its leaves are different. The Mexican Buckeye is commonly used in xeriscaping, which is to say it needs little water or care and while it is usually a small tree, it tends to take care of itself and can function well in arid climates.

We relate these trees to the Number 3, and to the Duende or Little People, who are sometimes seen as elfin-like or goblin-like and other times described as dwarves or small trolls. It is also associated with the Wizard Myne Zilar that is derived from the Arvyndase word Zil (zile), which means 'little', and is associated with the Arvyndase word Zila (zie - lah) that is our word for 'viva' as in "Viva Zapata". For the Spanish word Duenda, besides meaning a spirit, sometimes a spiritus loci or spirit of a place or location, is also used to mean spirit as in a bit of art that is especially expressive and fills you with a depth of feeling. A performance filled with energy and passion that touches your soul.

Buckeyes are mildly toxic. The little folk may not be greatly powerful, but they can look out for thems'elves, are a hardy and enduring folk, and when they act collectively can be quite formidable. For them, depth of feeling is more important than ostentatious display. The genuine is what really moves them.

WHAT THIS ORACLE MEANS:

In getting this Wizard Myne in response to a question, the answer says to look to the little folk, which also means, check the details. Often, we are told to see the Big Picture, but in this case the solution is in the minutia. The little folk, as we pointed out, may not be greatly powerful as individuals, the Buckeyes are only mildly toxic and may only cause a bit of indigestion, however, if you are taking a hike and you get a tiny pebble in your boot, it won't be long before you will want to get it out because it will irritate you continually until it does, creating a sore with every step.

So, too, if something is bugging you about this situation, check it out. Look down to the smallest details. Read the fine print. See what is really going on.

Also, don't neglect the small things, don't ignore the little people, the ones who may seem insignificant. However little and unimportant they may appear, they can arouse a passion that is far beyond their supposed stature.

And, most of all, be genuine. Do what you do with real feeling. Relate to everyone involved sincerely. Treat everyone with respect, even those who don't seem like they are held in high regard socially. They are more important in this situation than they seem. And, more than likely, they are the ones who are going to deal with all the details that are so very important. Or screw them up either intentionally or through inattention if you don't show them some deference.

ENCHANTMENT SPELL:

The atoms that you cannot see
Create the world that is to be

This Spell in Arvyndase:
Tae dayåli dij le vekkon ten
Talys tae telth dij da va te

Pronunciation:
Tay day - yah - lie dye-j lee veek - cone teen
Tay - liss tay teal-th dye-j dah vah tea

Chapter 68:

Sapodilla family

KEYWORD: **THE LETTER I**

TREE GROUP NAME IN ARVYNDASE: **INADÅELPA** (PRONOUNCED: EYE - NAY - DAH - EEL - PAH)

ARVYNDASE NAME OF THE WIZARD MYNE: **INADÅR** (PRONOUNCED: EYE - NAY - DAR)

THIS TREE AND ITS MAGIC:

The Sapodilla or Sapotaceae family includes approximately 800 species of evergreen trees and shrubs whose habitat is mostly pantropical. These trees include the Star-apple or Golden leaf tree, the Shi or Shea that is the source shea butter, a substance that has many cosmetic and health benefits and is edible, the Gutta-Percha that produces a latex with a vast variety of uses including being a good electrical insulator and was used for making underwater telegraph cables in olden times while its wood was utilized for walking sticks. Also, the Dodo tree, once thought to depend upon the now extinct Dodo bird for its propagation and life, is part of this family. As is the plant Synsepalum dulcificum that produces the 'miracle fruit', whose berries cause sour foods that are eaten subsequently to consuming it, to taste sweet. This fruit is also called the miracle berry, miraculous berry, and the sweet berry. Many of these trees and shrubs bear edible fruits or, in some cases, white blood-sap that is used to cleanse dirt, thus there is a connection to the notion of purification both actual and symbolic.

All of this has led us Silver Elves to link these trees to the Letter I, the Wizard Myne Inadår that comes from our Arvyndase word Inada (eye - nay - dah), which is our elven word for Miracle and therefore to Elven Thaumaturgy or the magic of creating miracles (see our book *Creating Miracles In the Modern World: The Way Of the Elfin Thaumaturge*).

WHAT THIS ORACLE MEANS:

First, purify yours'elf. Miracles are created through contact with the Divine Magic so connect to the divine, both within and without ones'elf. One must become like unto the divine to create miracles, which is to say more perfected and pure. Clear your mind, cleanse your aura, open your heart, and do this while washing your body. While cleaning the body may seem to take place in the material realm, physical cleansing is, in fact, the most symbolic of these activities. If you purify yours'elf and your aura, there is an excellent possibility that you can transform a sour situation into a very sweet one. This may seem like it will take a miracle, but then, if you are being true to yours'elf and your own pure and genuine nature, then miracles are possible.

And our connection with the Divine Magic also offers us a certain amount of protection and of insulation so that we might channel these potent and powerful forces of the Divine without being harmed by doing so. This is the magic of high wizardry. This is Gandalf and Merlin level magic. You can transform your life for the better with this magic and potentially change the world around you as well. But first, purify yours'elf.

ENCHANTMENT SPELL:

Sweetly, I do change the world
A life of magic is unfurled

This Spell in Arvyndase:
Nemla, El ba dyls tae telth
Na ela u êldon da marturfin

Pronunciation:
Neem - lah, Eel bah dills tay teal-th
Nah e - lah you l - doan dah mare - two-rf - in

Chapter 69:

Tree of heaven

KEYWORD: **EARTH**

TREE GROUP NAME IN ARVYNDASE: **GLISDASALDA** (PRONOUNCED: GLICE - DACE - ALE - DAH)

ARVYNDASE NAME OF THE WIZARD MYNE: **ALTDYR** (PRONOUNCED: ALE-T - DER)

The Silver Elves. . . . 211

This Tree and Its Magic:

Ailanthus, also called the tree of the gods or the tree of heaven, belongs to the tree family Simaroubaceae, which can be found naturally from southeast Asia to northern Australasia, which includes Australia, New Zealand and some of Melanesia, or the islands north and northeast of Australia and New Zealand. The Ailanthus silkmoth, a silk spinning moth, lives on the leaves of these trees, and creates a silk that is more durable and less expensive than mulberry silk, but lacks its fineness and gloss. Still, we elves love silk of all sorts.

Because of these things, we see these trees as being connected to the Shining Ones, the angelic heavenly elfae, but not the refined and glossy Shining Ones that live primarily in other dimensions, but those Shining Ones who, like Bodhisattvas, have willingly returned to the Earth out of a sense of compassion and duty to assist we elven who are still struggling with our souls and spirits and our development and evolution upon the material plane. Therefore, we further relate this Myne to the Earth Elementals and to Earth Magic.

We also associate these trees to the Wizard Myne Altdyr that is derived from the Arvyndase word alt that means 'high'. These Earthy Shining Ones are often seen as High Elves; but not high elves in the sense of acting superior to others, for they are surely quite humble beings, but rather as highly evolved, giving and loving individuals who devote thems'elves to the evolution of our kindred out of compassion. They are the Volunteers for a Better World and devoted to the Realization of Elfin upon the Earth. They make Elfin real through the manifestation of their being and are a Shining example of real elfin beings manifest in the world that most people consider reality.

What This Oracle Means:

Be humble, be genuine, be yours'elf without making a big deal about it. If you are truly a high elf, you don't need to mention it to anyone. It will be evident to all who have the elf sight. They will see you for who you truly are. As to the rest, it is probably best that they don't see you clearly anyway. That is the value of the Mists of Faerie (see our book *Through the Mists of Faerie*).

And see the Divine in each and every one. Certainly, all elfae are high elves or high fae in potential. That is why you came to the Earth after all, to help them realize this fact. Lead by example, manifest Elfin on the Earth and invite others to join you. This is the Great Work (Play?), for elfae folk, yes? This is the Great Play, the Great Dance, the Great Maneuver. Whatever else is going on, whatever seems to be going on, the real deal is your personal development as a spirit and soul and the evolution of our kindred. All the rest is just window dressing.

It is possible that there is a high elf, unrecognized by most folks, in your social circle. Radiant but not obtrusive with their light. Honor this individual and good fortune will come from this.

ENCHANTMENT SPELL:
Your light shines with a quiet glow
Some may not see but I do know

This Spell in Arvyndase:
Le'na lun glislu ena na shosha lums
Ina me kon ten kana El ba ken

Pronunciation:
Lee'nah loon glice - lou e - nah nah show - shah looms
Eye - nah me cone teen kay - nah Eel bah keen

Chapter 70:

Camellia family

KEYWORD: **THE NUMBER 7**

TREE GROUP NAME IN ARVYNDASE: **ONICAELPA** (PRONOUNCED: OH - NIGH - CAH - EEL - PAH)

ARVYNDASE NAME OF THE WIZARD MYNE: **MÊLAR** (MELL - LAIR)

THIS TREE AND ITS MAGIC:

Camellia is a family of trees and shrubs that are mostly evergreen. However, the Stewartia and Franklinia genera are deciduous, which means they drop their leaves upon maturity. Most of the flowers in this family are pink or white and often large and showy, yielding a strong scent. Many are a bit unusual because of their pseudo-pollen, which fools insects into pollinating them. Some of their fruits can have loculicidal capsules, splitting along their length; others have indehiscent baccate fruits, small berries that don't split to release the seed; or sometimes they are pome-like, like the apple. The seeds tend to be few (we elves and faerie folk are less inclined toward large families). Some of the seeds are winged while others are surrounded by fleshy tissue and some un-winged and nude.

All of this calls to these elves' minds, the acute angled seven-pointed Elven Star that the Faeries call the Faerie Star, although it was we elven who first started using it. The pseudo-pollen of this family reminds us of the pixies, their showy flowers with potent scent makes us think of the faeries, also the fact that some of them are winged recalls the faeries as well, while others are covered in fleshy tissues or are un-winged and nude, which is quite elven really.

Therefore, we link these trees to the number Seven and the Wizard Myne Mêlar that comes from the Arvyndase word Mêl, which means Star. Faerie and Elfin, as well as the faeries and elves and pixies, are vast realms and myriad peoples and, while we are related, we are all incredibly diverse.

WHAT THIS ORACLE MEANS:

Appreciate the diversity of this situation and the people in it. Getting this Wizard Myne, not only indicates that it is likely that there are numerous and differing personalities involved but also that the solutions to any difficulties or challenges are various as well. As the old folks used to say: 'there is more than one way to skin a cat'. Of course, they were talking mostly of the large cats: the cougars, bobcats and mountain lions that would prey upon them, their children and their familiars, and not house cats, at least we hope that is the case.

If you are creating an elven vortex, faerie wicca coven or an eald or demesne for otherkin in general, remember that we are very individual folk and diversity, tolerance and acceptance of differences will probably work better in the long run than pressuring everyone to conform to your notions of what being elven or fae may be. This is especially true for we elven who are inclined to be eccentric and for the faeries who often flitter here and there going their own ways, filled with wild ideas, although they do coordinate fairly well together when they have a common goal. Look for the similarities among the people you draw to you while accepting and appreciating their various skills and qualities. This way you will get the best from everyone and with all these various talents and outlooks nearly every difficulty will be easily solved. This situation may seem to be a puzzle but if you put the right pieces, or right people together, you will see that it all fits nicely.

ENCHANTMENT SPELL:

Come be yours'elf for you are free
To be just whom you wish to be

This Spell in Arvyndase:
Koso te le'na'eln fro le da alo
Va te oda jae le felj va te

Pronunciation:
Co - so tea lee'nah'eel-n fro lee dah a - low
Vah tea o - dah jay lee feel-j vah tea

Chapter 71:
Thymelaea family

KEYWORD: **THE LETTER N**

TREE GROUP NAME IN ARVYNDASE: **ELFIELPA** (PRONOUNCED: EEL - FIE - EEL - PAH)

ARVYNDASE NAME OF THE WIZARD MYNE: **NIELDÂN** (PRONOUNCED: NIGH - EEL - DON)

THIS TREE AND ITS MAGIC:

The Thymelaea family of trees and shrubs are so diverse that they are hard to define, and while scientists often debate what tree or shrub should go with what family, this family is particularly contested. Its most notable trees are the Ramin trees that are used for their comparatively soft, easily worked and yellowish wood and like to live in swamp forests growing up to 80 feet, with 60 feet of that being free of branches; the Wikstroemia or the 'ākia, as it is known in Hawaii, is used as a component of paper; and the Lagetta species, that can be found in the Caribbean and is known commonly as the Lacebark or

Gauze tree, because its inner bark is formed like a fine netting or lace, has been used to make clothing as well as rope and other commonplace useful products. These trees, while related, are quite diverse from each other and the Wikstroemia has individual plants that frequently create anomalous flowers. Sometimes the nonfunctional organs are seen as being deformed and they seem to bear small resemblance to the parts that they are supposed to be.

All of this brings us Silver Elves to associate this tree family to the idea of elven androgyny, not only in a gender sort of way, where elves may seem to be both male and female and the males and females sometimes mistaken for each other, but in a wider sense we give to androgyny, in that we elves are simply so diverse that we are hard, in fact nearly impossible, to define. We are like the Mists of Faerie ever swirling. Also, we are so eccentric and unusual that it is difficult to pin down what exactly being elven is. And, of course, there are the various blendings of faerie beings, of elves who are also part pixie, or faerie or whatever, hybrids of many types and yet all accepted as completely elven by those of us who are elves.

Therefore, we connect these trees to the Letter N and the Wizard Myne Nieldån that comes from the Arvyndase word Nielda (nigh - eel - dah), which means 'individual', and is related as well to the word Nieldåna (nigh - eel - dah - nah), which is 'individualize'. We are ever unique and becoming ever more so.

WHAT THIS ORACLE MEANS:

There is something amorphous about this situation. It is hard to pin anything down or pin anyone involved down either. Everyone seems to be enthused about it but no one seems to wish to make any sort of commitment. And everyone seems to have different ideas about how to go about everything. It can all be a bit puzzling really.

The important thing here is to simply proceed as you see best and trust that others who are truly interested will join in, in time. Many may pay lip service to your ideas, but action is something different. You know the saying, if you want something done right, you have to do it yours'elf? Well, in this case, the saying might be: if you want something done at all, you will have to do it, or at least get it started yours'elf. And, you may be surprised at who comes to help you. Don't assume that you know one way or the other, and don't presume that this one will or that one won't. It is all a mist and a muddle, so muddle on.

ENCHANTMENT SPELL:

Things are not the way they seem
So, I'll proceed as I best deem

This Spell in Arvyndase:

Vessali da kon tae yer tam kacer
Re, El'yon murfan tat El rildor ot

Pronunciation:

Veece - sah - lie dah cone tay year kay - sir
Ree, Eel'yone muir - fane tate Eel rile - door oat

Chapter 72:

Elm family

KEYWORD: SHAMAN

TREE GROUP NAME IN ARVYNDASE: HELYNELPA
(PRONOUNCED: HE - LYNN - EEL - PAH)

Arvyndase Name of the Wizard Myne: **Aldarel**
(pronounced: ale - dare - real)

This tree and its magic:

Elm as a family of trees consists mainly of the Elms and the Zelkovas. The Elms have suffered greatly due to Dutch Elm disease, but also because of the two World Wars. It is not only humans who suffer due to war. The Zelkovas, on the other hand, have simply been exploited near to extinction. There is something about Man that makes him want to use something until it is all used up until it exists no more. In the end, it will be his own kind that perishes.

While the Elm tree is often associated with the elven folk, it does not figure directly into the Druid Ogham. However, the Elm has long been linked to the vines, especially by the ancient Romans who said the Elm was married to the vine because Elms where used to support growing vines. The vine is in the Ogham, and is linked with prophecy, therefore the Elms support prophecy. Because of this, we Silver Elves associate this tree with Shamanism and the Wizard Myne Aldarel that comes from the Arvyndase word Alda, meaning tree, and Aldare (ale - dare - ree) that means shaman.

Of course, when the Romans linked the Elm to the vine, it was to grape vines and thus to alcohol as an intoxicant, a spirit. But there are many spirits in nature that will speak to us, including the spirit of Ayahuasca that is made by brewing the Psychotria viridis shrub along with the stalks of the Banisteriopsis caapi vine. There are many roads to Elfin.

At the same time, the first three gods of the Norse Aesir, Odin, and his two brothers, Vili and Ve according to their myth, created the first woman Embla from an Elm tree and the first man, Askr, from an Ash tree, the world tree that connects all the worlds together and is represented by the Ogham Nuin. The Elm is married in this sense or assists the Ash, which connects the worlds or dimensions. We might think, therefore, that the Elm helps one to travel from one dimension to another, just in case one is thinking of taking a trip to other realms.

What This Oracle Means:

There are numerous ways to induce visions and prophecy. Different plants and alchemical concoctions have been used all over the world throughout history and prehistory. Some use meditation, as the yogis do. Others use pain to induce visions, from the Catholics to some of the First Nations peoples of the Americas to the ancient aboriginal peoples of Australia and elsewhere. The macho way to enlightenment. The Way of Men and Orcs and Grimlins or those who live in deserts and have no other way to get there. Sometimes, you take what you can get.

However, be cautious. Remember, if you become addicted to a substance then you have become enslaved to the very spirit from whom you sought illumination. This is true of alcohol or any other spirit with whom you commune. Don't become enslaved. Don't sell your soul to have a vision or receive powers that aren't really yours.

This is true of love as well. Romance can be enlightening, so can sex, but if you become enslaved to your passions, you lose control and direction of your life. Remember, you are a shaman, a wizard, a magic wielder, a visionary. Speak with the spirits, but don't pursue them with your tongue hanging out, slobbering all over yours'elf like a teenager gawking at a movie or rock star. Get a grip on yours'elf and then the way to visions, enlightenment and power will come. And remember, respect and courtesy are great and true powers, but mindless and unquestioning submission is not.

Enchantment Spell:

Speak to me, oh, spirit true
Show me the way and what to do

This Spell in Arvyndase:

Nor va el, tra, tari lod
Teke el tae yer nar wu va ba

Pronunciation:

Nor vah eel, trah, tay - rye load

Tea - key eel tay year nair woo vah bah

Chapter 73:

Cabbage tree

KEYWORD: **THE NUMBER 11**

TREE NAME IN ARVYNDASE: **DELFURALDA** (PRONOUNCED: DEAL - FEW-R - ALE - DAH)

ARVYNDASE NAME OF THE WIZARD MYNE: **NIVAE** (PRONOUNCED: NIGH - VAY)

THIS TREE AND ITS MAGIC:

The Cabbage tree is endemic to New Zealand. The heart of its leaves can be eaten and it is thought that many early settlers used these as a substitute for cabbage, thus the name. The indigenous Maori also ate the leaves, used the tree for making clothing, rope and many other products. Some tribes buried the placenta of a newborn at its roots to ensure a good life. Some northern tribes buried their dead beneath it to promote a prosperous afterlife and perhaps rebirth. These trees also have many medicinal uses and were seen as a sort of first aid kit for dealing with many common ailments.

To the Chinese, cabbages represent 100 types of prosperity and luck. The Cabbage is also considered, because of its shape, to represent stuffed packages or gifts, also symbolizing wealth and luck. Of course, this tree isn't a true cabbage and its leaves are spikey and spear-like. This is not the luck of man and woman, but elf luck and it is not merely associated with material wealth, but more importantly linked with a good life, and even more importantly a lucky reincarnation from life to life.

Therefore, we Silver Elves connect these trees to the Number 11 that is considered a Master Number that vibrates upon a higher vibration. We also connect it to the Wizard Myne Nivae that comes from the Arvyndase word Niv (rhymes with dive), which means luck and nivath (nigh - vayth) that means lucky. We elves are born lucky, and having a good rebirth, lifetime after lifetime, is certainly part of this luck. But the very best of this luck, the luckiest part of all, is the fact that we were lucky enough to be born elves.

WHAT THIS ORACLE MEANS:

Elves in many ways equate luck and magic. We are lucky folk for the most part, but most of our luck comes from living a good life, being decent human beings, as best we can, and helping all of our kindred. Perhaps, the greatest part of our luck really is the love our kindred have for us and we for them.

Therefore, if you receive this Wizard Myne as an oracle, do your best. Be the best elf, fae or other you can be. Help your others to do the same. Do your magic not so much to control or manipulate the world but simply to make it a better more beautiful place and if you do this consistently and sincerely, day by day, luck will come to you and all you really need to do is continue on manifesting Elfin in your life and upon the Earth (or wherever you may be) by everything you do.

We may not be the wealthiest people in terms of money or material possessions, but that is often because we place less value on those things than many other folks do. But, we nearly always have what we need and it often comes to us serendipitously and just when we need it. Most of all, we tend to be lucky in love and friendship, in time finding those who are really right for us and that is a great, maybe the greatest, blessing. We help each other from one life to the next and find each other again and again. Live the life elfin and let luck flow into your life and the lives of your others and you will find healing by doing so as well.

ENCHANTMENT SPELL:
Life after life, luck comes to me
Born of your smile and a love that is free

This Spell in Arvyndase:
Ela låka ela, niv kosolu va el
Daend u le'na fiso nar na kyêla dij da alo

Pronunciation:
E - lah lah - kay e - lah, co - so - lou vah eel
Day - eend you lee'nah fie - so nair nah key - l - lah dye-j dah a - low

Chapter 74:

Dragon tree

KEYWORD: **DRAGON**

TREE NAME IN ARVYNDASE: **DRÅKANALDA** (PRONOUNCED: DRAH - CANE - ALE - DAH)

Arvyndase Name of the Wizard Myne: **Dråkana** (Drah - cane - nah)

This tree and its magic:

The Dragon tree is of the genus Dracaena a name that comes from the Ancient Greek drakaina that means female dragon and includes about 120 species of trees and succulent shrubs. These trees are mostly found in Africa. Many of the shrubs of this genus are grown as ornamental plants, however, they are often toxic to pets, although not to humans. Some of these trees exude a bright red resin, which is called dragon's blood. However, modern dragon's blood, which is often used as an incense, is more likely to be from the Daemonorops Rattan palms, which are unrelated to these trees (Daemon is a divinity or supernatural being born of a cross between gods and humans and often seen as an inspiring spirit). Are you summoning dragons or the demi-god spirits?

In some African tribes, the red resin from the Dragon tree is used for marking graves and designating sacred sites or marking off other significant areas. Thus, these trees indicate a certain power, the power of the dragon, and of destiny, fate and the anointing of the special ones. We associate these trees naturally with dragons but particularly with female dragons, whose menstrual blood, the red resin, signifies the processes of life, not only the ability to give birth, but especially, in this case, to give birth to dragons, which is to say to give birth to the great and the powerful. Its Wizard Myne is Dråkana that comes from the Arvyndase word Dråkan or dragon.

What This Oracle Means:

Are you one of The Chosen Ones? Have you been selected by fate and/or destiny to gain wealth and/or power in the world? Are you special? Do you have influence with others? Do they look up to you? Seek your advice? Hang on your every word? Do you wield power over others? Have a position of authority? Are you stunningly beautiful or handsome and people defer to you and give you preference due to your great beauty?

And what do you do with that? Do you respect people or lord your power over them? If you are poor and then become wealthy, how will you act? Will you despise where you came from and disassociate yours'elf from those you previously knew in order to fit into this new society? Are you the sort of slave who becomes free only to oppress and enslave others?

Use your power well. Use it to help others as well as uplift yours'elf. Treat others with respect. Don't be haughty and arrogant or it may very well be that in your next lifetime you will probably come to regret it. Much of our elf luck comes from the blessings and well wishes of those to whom we've been kind. Be kind, be compassionate. Not naive and foolish, there are surely those who would take advantage of your position of power and influence, but even then, treat them with respect as you respectfully tell them no and delineate the limits and boundaries of your relationship. They are, after all, spirits struggling to rise and better themselves, as we all are.

We elves are often high beings. We are frequently more advanced and enlightened as spirits, sometimes better educated and often the recipients of wondrous good fortune, but we need ever remember that flaunting our superiority, of whatever kind, is an inferior thing to do. Be humble in your greatness and increase your magic and power thereby. And remember rudeness is weakness and courtesy is power.

ENCHANTMENT SPELL:
Though I'm great and mighty, true
Still I humbly bow to you

This Spell in Arvyndase:
Nåt El'da ralt nar jolvath, lod
Vila el corothla varse va le

Pronunciation:

Not Eel'dah rail-t nair joel - vayth, load

Vie - lah eel core - row-th - lah vair - see vah lee

Chapter 75:

Joshua tree

KEYWORD: **WARLOCK**

TREE GROUP NAME IN ARVYNDASE: **DARPALALMAE** (PRONOUNCED: DARE - PALE - ALE - MAE)

ARVYNDASE NAME OF THE WIZARD MYNE: **TERAVYN** (PRONOUNCED: TEA - RAY - VIN)

THIS TREE AND ITS MAGIC:

Yucca trees are also known as Joshua trees. The Spanish explorers of the South Western U.S., where these trees are mostly to be found, called them the Desert Daggers for their bayonet like leaves. They are tough and enduring in harsh conditions and while they seem to be top heavy, if they survive their early years in those difficult environments, they can live for hundreds of years, due in great part to a very deep root system that can grow down to at least 36 feet and spread widely.

We link these trees to the Elven Warlocks and to the Wizard Myne Teravyn that is derived from the Arvyndase word Terav (tea - rave) which means Warlock. Some use the word Warlock to mean a male witch or a sorcerer. Others say that traditionally a warlock was a traitor or betrayer of witches, someone who betrayed the coven. The Elven Warlock, however, is the being who does all sHe (she/he) can to prevent or stop war. It is the opinion of the elven that no one should send others to war who has not been to war thems'elves. Thus, warlocks are almost always veterans and know what war is like. If they can, they will always promote diplomacy and negotiation over conflict.

Some say that these trees represent the strength and beauty that comes from overcoming or experiencing dysfunction. Experience can age us but it can also define us and give us character. These trees, in that way, represent the beauty of age and experience. Some of the First Nations peoples of the Americas, believed that these trees symbolized transmutation, protection and purification. The Elven Warlock seeks to transmute war into peace in order to protect their people and the only way to do that, really, is to purify ours'elves and do what is right and just for everyone involved in the potential conflict.

What This Oracle Means:

There may be a conflict of interest incipient here, perhaps even a conflict already going on. Do what you can to compromise in this situation. But don't compromise your principles and ever keep in mind what is right and fair for everyone. This is not about seeking advantage over others. It is not about getting the most you can out of the situation, but of creating balance and equanimity and this is only possible if everyone feels they have been treated fairly.

It is possible that there is someone who just won't let this go, who simply won't come to an agreement and insists on pushing the issue. More fool they. Still, do what you can to be fair and to work things out to everyone's satisfaction. Not everyone will be satisfied, no matter what you do, but that is not as important as the fact that you have done what is right.

And if it does come to a conflict and you win, you still need to establish the new situation upon what is right and fair. It is only in this way that you can create a lasting peace, otherwise, the individual or individuals will come at you again and again. Work it out as best you may, and if you can, withdraw from the situation and them entirely. You don't need these sorts of people in your life.

ENCHANTMENT SPELL:
Stop before you even start
So friendly we can be or part

This Spell in Arvyndase:
Vird lokan le jåja altu
Re edarla eli vek te sa zårl

Pronunciation:
Vie-rd low - can lee jah - jah ale - two
Ree e - dare - lah e - lie veek tea sah zar-l

Chapter 76:

Palm family

KEYWORD: **THE LETTER R**

Tree Group Name in Arvyndase: Almaelpa (pronounced: ale - may - eel - pah)

Arvyndase Name of the Wizard Myne: Retonta (pronounced: re - tone - tah)

This Tree and its Magic:

This is the Palm family of trees, plants and shrubs that includes the Coconut, the Daemonorops Rattan palm, previously mentioned that produces dragon's blood, the Date palm and many others. It has been used as a symbol of victory by the Romans and other ancient peoples, also as being symbolic of peace and abundance in the Kabbalah and, in modern times, as a symbol of the 'fun in the sun' of vacation time, which is another indication of abundance and plenty.

The Palm surely provides as great deal of abundance, offering many things to humanity, such as palm oil, coconuts, palm wine and much else. It has been cultivated by humanity since way back before history began being written down, and these trees extend to at least to 80 million years ago. They are ancient beings and really quite generous, although they like to live in warm climates for the most part. They are great benefactors of humanity and other creatures. They love the tropics and subtropics, sunning by the beach and feeling the cooling ocean breezes, sipping coconut water from the shell.

We relate this tree family to the Letter R and to the Wizard Myne Retonta that comes from the Arvyndase word Reton (re - tone), which is our elven word for gift. We elves are noted for gifting certain individuals with greater power, increasing their talents as musicians and artists and much more, placing enchantments upon them that make them, and their art, more enchanting. We are patrons and benefactors of the Arts and of Artists and increase their individual abundance and prosperity as well as making the world a more beautiful place through them.

What This Oracle Means:

Give to those with talent. Help them to increase their skills and abilities. Buy their art, crafts or donate to the buskers on the street.

Promote art by giving to artists and musicians, for there are few things more inspiring to an artist than being loved, appreciated and, especially, financially rewarded for their creations.

And if you are the struggling artist, then it is likely that a mentor or patron will appear who will appreciate your skill and talent and will help you with a gift of energy or money. Perhaps you will have a big sale, a great weekend at the fair or other venue, a really good day upon the street playing for donations.

Mostly, realize that the Shining Ones and the higher spirits have taken notice of your abilities and are sending you enchantments to further you and improve your skill. So, keep at it. Don't give up your art and by all means encourage others to continue to improve their art and skills as well. This is the path to Elfin.

Enchantment Spell:
Wondrous the gifts that come to me
Better my art for all to see

This Spell in Arvyndase:
Tyltålsey tae retonli dij koso va el
Rilfa el'na lesse fro wyl va ten

Pronunciation:
Till - tahl - say tay re - tone - lie dye-j co - so vah eel
Rile - fah eel'nah lease - see fro will vah teen

Chapter 77:

Bamboo family

KEYWORD: **THE LETTER J**

TREE GROUP NAME IN ARVYNDASE: **MYTHYROELPA** (PRONOUNCED: MIT - HER - ROW - EEL - PAH)

ARVYNDASE NAME OF THE WIZARD MYNE: **JUSLARI** (PRONOUNCED: JUICE - LAIR - RYE)

THIS TREE AND ITS MAGIC:

Bamboo is not a tree, technically speaking it is a grass. However, it can grow so tall that it is called the Bamboo tree and we Silver Elves have no problem with this. Its uses are many, including being utilized for food, wood products and even martial arts weapons of various sorts. It is used as a writing pen and an art pen, particularly for calligraphy, you can still buy these bamboo pens in art supply stores. Bamboo has been used to make small bridges and scaffolding. It can be used in making rayon and for making paper. In fact, 'spirit money', burnt as offerings to the ancestors, is sometimes printed upon it. We sometimes get spirit money from China town and offer it to our beloved departed.

In Chinese culture, Bamboo is one of the Four Gentlemen or Four Princes, or Four Nobles that consist of bamboo, orchid, plum blossom and chrysanthemum. Bamboo is seen as representing uprightness, tenacity, and modesty, and as denoting integrity, elegance, and plainness. Though it is not generally regarded as being physically strong in this mode of thinking, in fact, Bamboo has a greater specific compressive strength than wood, brick or concrete and its tensile strength is close to steel. At the same time, its hollow center is seen as representing an open heart and an open mind, an essential aspect of elfin-ness.

Therefore, we Silver Elves link this tree to the Wizard Myne Juslari that comes from the Arvyndase word Juslar, which means modest. The elven noble is a person of integrity, of refinement and culture, often with a superior education and deportment, but most of all this is a being who is openminded, openhearted and modest in their greatness. Because bamboo is a grass and the grasses, to our elven minds, represent the mass of faerie being, bamboo symbolizes the fact that in elven society anyone can become noble. It is one's actions and behaviors, not one's birth, that determines nobility among the elven. It is nobility of character that counts among us.

What This Oracle Means:

Enhance your good qualities and make them greater. Do this consistently. Yet, be modest in your strength and your greatness, let your refinement be revealed indirectly through the genuineness of your character. It doesn't matter if you were born rich or poor, or somewhere in between. It doesn't matter if you were raised in high society or you were an outcast. Among the elven, it is your actions and character that count. Nothing can stop you from rising to the heights of elven society except yours'elf. So, accept yours'elf, at whatever level you are currently and make every aspect of your being better, stronger and more refined.

At the same time, recognize the nobility in others. Everyone has the inner potential for greatness. We are all a part of the Divine Magic and in perfecting ours'elves we express its being through our own. If you wish to be respected, treat others with respect. If you wish to be complimented, be modest and humble. If you don't laud your own qualities, others will, in time, do it for you. And that's what you really want, isn't it? That others shall appreciate you? There are those who were born into wealth and privilege who just waste it all away. Whatever you have, make the most of it and the Universe will send you more.

ENCHANTMENT SPELL:

I stand tall for all to see
In quiet elf nobility

This Spell in Arvyndase:

El lotz yath fro wyl va ten
Ver sosha êlda eldatu

Pronunciation:

Eel low-tz yeah-th fro will vah teen
Veer so - shah l - dah eel - day - two

Chapter 78:

Annona family

KEYWORD: **THE NUMBER 9**

TREE GROUP NAME IN ARVYNDASE: **CASTARJUFIELPA**
(PRONOUNCED: CAH - STARE - JEW - FIE - EEL - PAH)

ARVYNDASE NAME OF THE WIZARD MYNE: **ELOAR**
(PRONOUNCED: E - LOW - AIR)

THIS TREE AND ITS MAGIC:

This family of trees includes the Custard-apple or Cherimoya, the Soursop and the Ylang-ylang. The Ylang-ylang is noted for its scent and is used in aroma therapy. It is sometimes thought to be an aphrodisiac, as far as arousing one through scent, and thus it is linked to romance in its various manifestations. The Custard-apple, when its fruit is ripe, is said to taste like custard, thus suggesting the idea of dessert. Its leaves can produce a blue/black dye, sometimes used by the dark elves for their attire. The Soursop has a fruit that is said to smell similar to pineapple, while it tastes like a combination of strawberries and apple, with a slightly sour undernote, while at the same time having a creamy texture that reminds one somewhat of bananas.

We Silver Elves associate these trees to the Wizard Myne Eloar that is derived from our Arvyndase word Eloa (e - low - ah) which means beauty. Almost all elves and elfae and faerie folk are beautiful in their own way and we see beauty in nearly everyone and everything. But then, elven beauty has more to do with one's spirit and personality and the radiance of one's inner being than the outer physical manifestation that most people use to judge beauty. We even think the goblins and grimlins are quite beautiful when they aren't up to dark and wicked deeds. In fact, we find the dark elven and dark fae especially wondrous in their goth, emo, vampiric attire and fashion. They have style.

Our beauty not only lures people to us and makes them favorable toward us, it also serves, in its way, to draw good luck and good fortune to us, because the Shining Ones find us wondrous as well and shed their blessings upon us.

WHAT THIS ORACLE MEANS:

See the beauty in others. There is really beauty everywhere when you begin to see with elf sight. The Universe is wondrous, and magic and enchantment radiate from nearly all things. Use your beauty to attract others, but treat them well and they will pay you back many times over. Remember, your beauty is not born of your material being but arises from your spirit expressing itself through your life and your body. Beautify yours'elf. It is not wrong to be beautiful. And if you envy those who seem more beautiful than you, than you are failing to see your own true beauty. See your beauty as well.

If you get this Wizard Myne in response to a question put to the oracle, then know that creating beauty is the way to success. See beauty, but also strive to make yours'elf more beautiful, and help others to do the same without judging them. Sometimes, the most powerful way to help a person to change is to accept them for who they are so they can then be free to move on to something even better. See their beauty and they will become more beautiful and they will experience you as being more beautiful as well.

This is also the energy of dessert. Surely a gift will come to you. Probably something quite lovely. A bonus of some sort, as dessert is a bonus to the main meal. You have been blessed. Maybe even a bit of romance will come. Delight in it, for romance is another form of beauty. And those in love naturally create more beauty in the world.

ENCHANTMENT SPELL:
I look at you and I do see
The beauty that abides in thee

This Spell in Arvyndase:
El shi zan le nar El ba ten
Tae eloa dij rudenlu ver vele

Pronunciation:
Eel shy zane lee nair Eel bah teen
Tay e - low - ah dye-j rue - dean - lou veer vee - lee

Chapter 79:

American Pawpaw

KEYWORD: **THE LETTER Ê**

TREE NAME IN ARVYNDASE: **OPINÂTRE** (PRONOUNCED: OH - PINE - NAH - TREE)

ARVYNDASE NAME OF THE WIZARD MYNE: **ÊLKYN** (PRONOUNCED: L - KIN)

THIS TREE AND ITS MAGIC:

Pawpaw is used in Hoodoo to ward off dark magic. It is related to the Custard-apple, also called the Cherimoya, and to the Soursop and the Yang-ylang. It is an understory tree, which means it seldom penetrates to the crown of the forest and lives mostly in the shade and shadows of the larger trees. These trees are symbolic, not of the main characters in the story or the stars of the show, but of the character actors, the walk-ons and extras whose performance, none the less, adds or detracts from the ambience of the tale. They would not be Elrond, Haldir or Galadriel, but rather all those elves you see in the background. Often, they are the guards, guardians and protectors of the main characters.

These trees are related to the Wizard Myne Êlkyn that comes from our Arvyndase word Êlk (elk), which means wee, as in the wee folk, the supporting actors of your life. If you treat them well, they will help protect you. They will listen out for you and serve as your unofficial scouts, spies and assistants. Let them have a bit of light as well. Shine your light upon them and they will be grateful and do whatever is in their power to further you and shield you from dark magics. If they come to love you, they will even risk death for you.

WHAT THIS ORACLE MEANS:

If you receive this Wizard Myne then be careful of hogging the spotlight. Let others have a bit of recognition as well, and always, always, give credit where credit is due. Thank each one for their contribution, large or small, and appreciate every service that is done for you. This is your shield; this is your protection.

And remember, these seemingly minor characters may turn out to be stars in the future. You never know, or may not entirely be sure, who will rise toward the heights of success. It is true they may forget you when they do. But that has to do with their own spirit and progress as a spirit. However, if they do remember you, let them remember you for your kindness and for fostering their being, not for treating them as being beneath you.

Also, look around you. Something important may be going on. If you wish to know what it is, what is brewing, listen to the wee folk. They see and hear nearly everything and almost nobody notices them or pays attention. Most people see them as little more than furniture. Pay attention. There is much that you can learn by doing so.

ENCHANTMENT SPELL:

I note you there in the shade
And see the light of which you're made

This Spell in Arvyndase:
El doth le norn ver tae dasa
Nar ten tae lun u tild le'da kordïn

Pronunciation:
Eel doe-th lee norn veer tay day - sah
Nair teen tay loon you tile-d lee'dah cord - in

Chapter 80:

Cinnamon

KEYWORD: **THE NUMBER 30**

TREE NAME IN ARVYNDASE: **SORASYN** (PRONOUNCED: SOAR - RAY - SIN)

ARVYNDASE NAME OF THE WIZARD MYNE: **FOKENYT** (PRONOUNCED: FOE - KEY - NIT)

THIS TREE AND ITS MAGIC:

The Cinnamon tree is the source of true cinnamon, although commercially most cinnamon is derived from a related tree, the Cassia. These trees, the true Cinnamon or Cinnamomum produce this spice from their inner bark, which curls up into a tube-like structure when it is pealed from the tree. We love cinnamon toast. Elves surely must have invented it.

We Silver Elves connect these trees to the Number 30, which fosters the powers of self-expression, and promotes inspiration, enthusiasm, and creativity that the number three radiates and combines it with wholeness, the cycles of life and their connection to infinity, and therefore to the never-ending flow of life represented by the number zero. Continual and cyclic inspiration and creativity is born of this combination. We also connect these trees to the Wizard Myne Fokenyt, which is related to the Arvyndase word Fokenyta, which is our elven word for adventure.

Once upon a time, these elves were going through customs at the Sydney, Australia airport, having just flown in from Hobbiton in New Zealand, and Zardoa came upon two customs officials, in booths that were right next to each other, having a conversation in which one was urging the other to give up certain foods in his life and the other was resisting doing so. As Zardoa approached, they asked for his opinion, and being the elf that he is, he said that the one official was surely right in that it is important to limit the amount of desserts, liquor and other treats we have in our life, but that the other was correct as well, for if one didn't have anything to make life interesting, life wasn't really worth living. Therefore, he told them, the key was balance, to limit ones'elf most of the time and occasionally reward ones'elf for one's discipline, to give life a bit of spice.

What This Oracle Means:

If you have been doing almost nothing but partying, it's time you took a break and applied yours'elf toward something more productive. On the other hand, with this Wizard Myne, it is even more likely that you have been working steadily with almost no break or vacation and you really need an adventure. Life is dulling you down, grinding you into dust with its routines, and what is elven life if not a life of adventure?

Of course, we elves find adventure in nearly everything. We make every day, even when we seem to be stuck in the mundane and boring cycles of the world, into a challenge and a quest. Beneath the hum-drum of life is the beating heart of Elfin. It is all in the way we approach life. It is all about our attitude. Make life exciting for yours'elf and, in as much as possible, for those around you. This is the Great Quest, the Great Adventure, transforming the mundane world into the exciting and magical Realms of Elfin. You can do it.

This is true of education as well. If you want people to learn something, or you wish to learn something yours'elf, and retain the lessons learned, you have to make it enjoyable. Spice things up, but with limits. The cinnamon stick curls into a tube. It is enclosed in a sense and limited. Every adventure requires a bit of caution.

ENCHANTMENT SPELL:

Excitement rises from my soul
I breathe it in, it makes me whole

This Spell in Arvyndase:

Aronddir luftlu an el'na der
El rythor ter ver, ter kordlu el loj

Pronunciation:

A - roan-d - dire lou-ft. - lou ane eel'nah deer
Eel rith - thor tier veer, tier cord - lou eel low-j

Chapter 81:

Bay Laurel

KEYWORD: **THE LETTER Û**

TREE GROUP NAME IN ARVYNDASE: **REOLÅELDAE** (PRONOUNCED: REE - OH - LAH - EEL - DAY)

ARVYNDASE NAME OF THE WIZARD MYNE: **ÛLITENFAR** (PRONOUNCED: OO - LIE - TEEN - FAIR)

This Tree and Its Magic:

Laurel trees are associated with the Greek god Apollo, also to poetry and poets, to Daphne, who was a mountain nymph, which the Greeks called Oreads, and to visionary oracles and the possibility of Elven Far-sight and Far Seeing, since it is believed that certain ancient Greek prophetesses chewed the leaves of the Laurel or inhaled its burnt leaves to induce visions. You will note that the ancient prophecies of the Oracle of Delphi were usually given in poetic form.

This isn't, however, primarily about using substances such as Bay Laurel, or ivy or other intoxicants to induce visions. Nor is it about meditation, chanting, drumming, dancing or the various other ways to create trance and hypnogogic experience. Those are all technologies for doing these things. This is not about the technologies, that can be found elsewhere in this book, but about the farseeing that comes from direct communion and contact with the Divine Magic, with Magical Nature, the Earth and the Universe. (See the Netflix Spanish Language series from Columbia called *Frontera Verde* or *Green Frontier*).

The name of this Wizard Myne, Ûlitenfar is associated with the Arvyndase words Uli (you - lie) that means far and Tenfa (teen - fah), which is our elven word for seer. If you would see far, then connect to the world and universe about you. Particularly the living world, the world of the forest, the plants, the waters, air, earth and stars (fire). Open your heart, your mind and especially your soul, which is your link to all things.

What This Oracle Means:

Whatever is going on right now, whatever question you have posed to the oracle, wherever you happen to be, reach out right now and touch a tree, or touch the water, or touch the ground. Even if you are on concrete pavement, even if you are on the 17th floor of a building, touch the sidewalk or the floor and feel down to the Earth. Compared to the Earth, 17 floors are relatively nothing, a few sheets of paper, if that. The asphalt you may be standing on is less than a film of scum floating on the ocean surface.

Open your soul. Your soul is your link to all that exists. Feel the heartbeat of the Earth, of the trees, reach out to the stars, if you can see them or feel them. Let life permeate your being. Be one, at least for the moment, with the Universe. For this is the way to Ulitendas, or Farseeing. It is our connection to the Universe, our intimate connection to life that enables us to see, feel and understand things even if they are miles away or years in the future.

Then, wait for your dreams. For if you have been successful in uniting with Life, dreams will surely come to you.

ENCHANTMENT SPELL:
I feel the Earth beneath my feet
Connect with all that makes life sweet
I look beyond horizon's veil
As I into the future sail

This Spell in Arvyndase:
El self tae Eldanil usco el'na bondli
Madyn ena wyl dij kordlu ela nem
El shi hyrlon aferal'na fanj
Tat El verva tae lasel fasu

Pronunciation:
Eel seal-f tay Eel - day - nile youse - co eel'nah boned - lie
May - den e - nah will dye'j cord - lou e - lah neem
Eel shy her - lone a - fee - rail'nah fane-j
Tate Eel veer - vah tay lay - seal fay - sue

Chapter 82:

Avocado

KEYWORD: **THE NUMBER 100**

TREE NAME IN ARVYNDASE: **FRUORVE** (PRONOUNCED: FREW - OR - VEE)

ARVYNDASE NAME OF THE WIZARD MYNE: **FAERLAR** (PRONOUNCED: FAY - EAR - LAIR)

THIS TREE AND ITS MAGIC:

An avocado tree bear fruit that is technically a large berry. It is sometimes called the avocado pear or the alligator pear. The latter name due to the rough skin of some of the cultivated species. These trees and their fruits are thought to be an evolutionary anachronism, which is to say a fruit that had formed and evolved from a relationship with large mammals, as for instance, the giant ground sloths or gomphotheres, that are now extinct. These creatures were thought to swallow the berry whole and vacate it later when it was already sprouting. The word avocado comes from Nahuatl word āhuacatl, a word that was also used to mean testicle, since, well, that's what it looks like.

The Aztecs viewed the avocado as a symbol of love because an avocado tree can live for hundreds of years and when two grow together it is like a successful marriage, friendship or relationship. And from that they linked the avocado with fertility and lust and thought it acted as a natural aphrodisiac. Pass the guacamole.

This Wizard Myne Faerlar comes from the Arvyndase word Faerla, which is our elven word for romance. It is linked to the number 100, since it is hoped that our love and with it the romance that inspired it will last for at least one hundred years.

Romance is sometimes seen as being an evolutionary anachronism, but we elves don't view it as such. It is true that sometimes you have to develop a thick alligator skin concerning love and the pursuit of love. And you sometimes need to have a bit of daring or testicles or balls to engage in the romance game. But if you find the right person, your love and romance can last for over one hundred years, and that surely makes it all worthwhile.

WHAT THIS ORACLE MEANS:

If you get this Wizard Myne in response to a question put to the oracle then, more than likely, there is relationship or romance involved in this situation. For the elven, romance is one of our chief pastimes. It is one of the most fun things that we do and yet we are quite serious about our romance (also about other games we play), dedicated and devoted to those we love and friendly and respectful to all our lovers past and present, even while we're having a good time all the while.

Beneath this situation there lies the possibility of romance, even if it is merely flirting, for that's okay as well. As long as you don't violate the limits set up for you by the other, as long as you proceed only as invited and no further, then this can help the situation, whatever it is, immensely.

Others may view your chivalrous behaviors as quaint and out of date, but put on your alligator skin and don't let that bother you. Get out the flowers and the chocolates, romance is in the air and great things can come from it.

ENCHANTMENT SPELL:

I pluck romance from out the sky
The rush of love does make me fly

This Spell in Arvyndase:

El tälk faerla fro zes tae faln

Tae hars u kyela bâlu kord el fos

Pronunciation:

Eel talc fay - ear - lah fro zees tay fail-n

Tay hairs you key - l - lah bah - lou cord eel foe-ss

Chapter 83:

Sassafras

KEYWORD: **SORCERY**

TREE NAME IN ARVYNDASE: **DORYF** (PRONOUNCED: DOOR - RIFE)

ARVYNDASE NAME OF THE WIZARD MYNE: **TARJAR** (PRONOUNCED: TAIR - JAYR)

THIS TREE AND ITS MAGIC:

Sassafras root was once used for making root beer. Its name stems from a word that means stone or rock breaking. Sassafras root is still used in conjure and hoodoo for money-drawing, for prosperity, for general blessings, and for creating a happy home. Our old friend, Cat Yronwode says in her book *Hoodoo Herb and Root Magic* that sassafras attracts wealth, good fortune, and overall success in business. Our daughter, Elantari, used to work at Cat's shop, the Lucky Curio Mojo Company.

Steam distillation of the dried root bark creates an essential oil with high safrole content, and it was extensively used as a fragrance in perfumes and soaps, food and for aromatherapy. Safrole, however, is a precursor to the manufacture of the drugs MDA and MDMA, also known as Adam, Molly and Ecstasy, and therefore this oil and its purchase and importation are highly regulated. It is also thought that Safrole may be carcinogenic.

We Silver Elves associate this tree with Sorcery, the power to get to the root of things and by doing so attract love and success to ones'elf. This can be a dangerous enterprise at times and much frowned upon by the normal folk who relate sorcery to evil magics. But the exploration of the roots of the world and of magic and of one's own inner s'elf, can be greatly productive and lead to wondrous success in life.

WHAT THIS ORACLE MEANS:

Get to the root of things. Not simply the root of this situation, but the root of those who are involved in it. And here we don't mean just to the root of what they think, but more importantly to what they really feel. Behind the mind is a subtler awareness of sensory being. Delve to the depths of your feelings, if you dare, if you are willing to break the rock, to crack through what has been written in stone to what lies within the stone (see *Breaking Open the Head: A Psychedelic Journey into the Heart of Contemporary Shamanism* by Daniel Pinchbeck, also see *What's Behind Your Belly Button? A Psychological Perspective of the Intelligence of Human Nature and Gut Instinct* by Martha Char Love and Robert W. Sterling).

Deep within, the truth will be revealed and knowing the truth will, indeed, set you free, at least in this situation. It may not be a truth you wish to hear, or to feel, really, but in doing so and tracing it back to its source, you will be able to break down the prison walls that bind your being and your consciousness and step out into the light of a whole new world.

ENCHANTMENT SPELL:

To the very roots I dive
And come back feeling more alive

This Spell in Arvyndase:

Va tae lefa lamli El jun
Nar koso dyrn selfdas gilf alsaru

Pronunciation:

Vah tay lee - fah lame - lie Eel june
Nair co - so dern seal-f - dace gile-f ale - sair - rue

Chapter 84:

Tulip tree

KEYWORD: **THE LETTER Ô**

TREE NAME IN ARVYNDASE: **LORYNAL** (PRONOUNCED: LORE - REN - NAIL)

ARVYNDASE NAME OF THE WIZARD MYNE: **ÔNJORSI** (OON [AS IN SPOON] - JOUR - SIGH)

THIS TREE AND ITS MAGIC:

The Tulip trees are members of the Magnolia family of trees. They are sometimes known as Tulip Poplars or Yellow Poplars, although they are only distantly related to true Poplars. They are also sometimes called Saddle-leaf trees, White Wood trees and the Canoe-wood trees, the last because some of the First Nations People of Northeastern America used these trees for dugout canoes. The flowers of these trees are thought to resemble tulips, therefore their most common name.

We Silver Elves connect these trees to the Wizard Myne Ônjorsi, which comes from the Arvyndase words Onjors, which means traverse and Onjor that means travel. It is also related to the Arvyndase letter Ô that makes an oo sound, as in boo. We also associate it with the Gypsy Elves, the Travelers, the Trooping Faeries and the Faerie Rade, where the elfae people proceed on a long-term parade through the realms; a peregrination that is social both in the sense of being a social event and in the sense of going forth and observing people and how they live in order to get a more accurate idea of reality. It is, therefore, a sign of mobility, movement and travel and the experience and education that can come from travel.

WHAT THIS ORACLE MEANS:

This is a particularly good Wizard Myne to get if you are thinking of traveling, of venturing forth, of taking that first step into the unknown, of going out and seeing what is there. It is a sort of 'go for it' energy. Especially, if you will be traveling with others or going to meet up with others. It is great sign for attending a gathering of some sort.

At the same time, learn what you can. Challenge your assumptions by seeing what the reality of the situation really is. Go to where the truth is and discover it. Thus, there is an educational aspect to this and there is an energy for going to schools, classes or other places where people gather together to learn. Go out and see the world, it has something to reveal to you. Travel far and wide, if you can, the farther you go, the greater will be your reward.

Of course, if you can't travel, then remember, the Earth spins on its axis as it travels around the sun and the sun around the center of the galaxy. Feel the movement! We are elfin space gypsies.

ENCHANTMENT SPELL:

Out we go the truth to find
Of the world and elfin kind

This Spell in Arvyndase:

Zes eli tas tae lodver va lâc
U tae telth nar êldat faed

Pronunciation:

Zees e - lie tace tay load - veer vah lock
You tay teal-th nair l - date fay - eed

Chapter 85:

Magnolia

KEYWORD: **THE LETTER Y**

TREE NAME IN ARVYNDASE: **WONMALAR** (PRONOUNCED: WOE-N - MAY - LAIR)

Arvyndase Name of the Wizard Myne: **Yåtan** (pronounced: yah - tane)

This Tree and its Magic:

Magnolia trees are so old that it is believed they lived before the bees came into existence. Yeah, that's old. It is theorized by some that the Magnolia's lovely flowers developed after the bees evolved into their, more or less, current state as a strategy for encouraging them to spread these trees' pollen. Trees are clever. There are those who believe, and many elves are among them, that higher consciousness was gifted to us by the trees. It is the trees that woke us up to whom we really are and enlightened us.

Therefore, we Silver Elves, we elves of moonlight, starlight and the radiance of the trees, connect these trees with the Letter Y and the Wizard Myne Yåtan that is derived from the Arvyndase word Yåta (yeah - tah), which means olden. We further link these trees to the ancestors, the ancient and in many ways primal, preternatural and aboriginal elfin who passed on their lore to us through the trees and the illumination that they provide. Their ancient magic abides in the trees and in us and though we may live differently than our elfae ancestors did, due to the fate and circumstances of current times, in our hearts and minds we are still very much one people united across time and space.

What This Oracle Means:

In getting this Wizard Myne, you are called to look to the past, the ancient past, the deep past that exists mostly in your own subconscious that is contacted more easily by your feelings and imagination than your thinking and calculating mind.

Make an offering to the ancients. If you wish to speak to them, try talking to the trees. It is true that these ancients are no longer in the form that they once were. They have evolved as we have, have become Shining Ones or they are still struggling beside us to develop. For we are our ancestors reborn, over and over again, and yet, our experiences of those times that helped to shape who we are today still reside within us.

In honoring the ancestors, we are honoring ours'elves and all those around us for the efforts we have made in the past. We are in the process of forgiving, mostly by forgetting, past mistakes, while retaining the lessons we have learned and moving onward into the future knowing our ancient kindred live beside us on this plane or on some other dimension related to it.

It is true that we often see the past as being more advanced than it may actually have been. We mythologize the ancients but in doing so we are helping them, and us as well really, to advance to the higher, which is to say more expansive, realms of being. View the past in its reality as best you can but also see the potential that existed there that is still unfolding into the future. It is magic in motion and we are a part of it. We are who we are and where we are today because of it and we are still a part of Elfin Unfolding.

ENCHANTMENT SPELL:
Deep within the past lives still
A primal knowledge does me fill

This Spell in Arvyndase:
Dorae enaver tae log alsarlu vila
Na mastyn kenvu balu el ula

Pronunciation:
Door - ray e - nah - veer tay low-g ale - sair - lou vie - lah
Nah mace - tin keen - view bay - lou eel you - lah

Chapter 86:

Nutmeg family

KEYWORD: **THE LETTER B**

TREE GROUP NAME IN ARVYNDASE: **MYRISTÅELPA** (PRONOUNCED: MER - RYE - STAH - EEL - PAH)

ARVYNDASE NAME OF THE WIZARD MYNE: **BROSHYN** (PRONOUNCED: BRO - SHIN)

THIS TREE AND ITS MAGIC:

The Nutmeg family of trees are the source of both the spices nutmeg and mace. Mace is a word that is used not only for the spice, but also for a medieval weapon, like a spiked club, that was used for breaking open armor so one could attack the person underneath. It is also a word that represents a club that is sometimes carried by monarchs to symbolize their power and authority. These trees produce a red blood like sap. Nutmeg can be a hallucinogen as can the red resin of some of these species and may, in large quantities, cause delirium and even death. The oil of these trees, however, does have anti-fungal properties. Amazonian shamans are known to have made a hallucinogenic snuff from the bark of some of the varieties of these trees.

All this has led us Silver Elves to associate this Wizard Myne with elven psychology, which seeks to help people break open their armor, to know thems'elves better, instill them with confidence and therefore be better able to associate with others in a genuine and authentic way. The name for this Wizard Myne is Broshyn, which comes from the

Arvyndase word brosh (bro-sh) that is our elven word for mace (as a club or symbol of authority, not as a spice which would be piqu [pie-que]) and denotes our ability to open ours'elves up and become our own authorities, the rulers of our own lives.

In Hoodoo and Conjure, which are essentially hedgewitchery, nutmeg is often used to secure fidelity in one's mate. But it is really only once we have become whole and true to our own s'elves that we can possibly be true unto others.

What This Oracle Means:

Open yours'elf up. You may have been hurt in the past, but you need to gain confidence in yours'elf so much so that it doesn't matter what people think, say or feel about you. Let your scars make you stronger not weaker.

What is most important now is that you feel good about yours'elf in such a way that you also feel good about others. If you are raising yours'elf above them then you are really armoring yours'elf in order to hide your inner sense of inferiority and your fear of being vulnerable. In becoming confident in a positive way about yours'elf, you naturally instill confidence in others and lure them into feeling confident about you and attracted to you. Your true armor is your strength of character and your absolute fidelity to your elfae friends, family and kindred.

And it just so happens that when you are more open, you will take in more information from the Universe, rather than blocking it out. You will become more aware because you won't be spending your energy hiding and sealing yours'elf off from others and from life. Your life will naturally become more exciting and spicier, because of your openness and this new influx of energy. This is just the way it is. Ego is a bad thing when we use it as means of creating distance between ours'elves and others, but when we are truly confident in ours'elves, we have ego strength and experience s'elf validation and can live authentically, which will encourage others to open up and do the same.

ENCHANTMENT SPELL:
I open up my heart to you
So, you can see that I am true

This Spell in Arvyndase:
El caro rep el'na bom va le
Re, le vek ten dij El da lod

Pronunciation:
Eel car - row reap eel'nah bow'm vah lee
Re, lee veek teen dye-j Eel dah load

Chapter 87:

Araucaria family

KEYWORD: **THE NUMBER 18**

TREE GROUP NAME IN ARVYNDASE: **ELANATÅELPA** (PRONOUNCED: E - LANE - A - TAH - EEL - PAH)

ARVYNDASE NAME OF THE WIZARD MYNE: **ZESELTAR** (PRONOUNCED: ZEE - SEAL - TAIR)

THIS TREE AND ITS MAGIC:

These are an ancient family of trees that previously existed both in the northern and southern hemispheres but today are found mostly in the southern hemisphere. They can grow up over 200 feet tall and some are known in New Zealand as the Lords of the Forest. In Turkey, stones, which are called Black Amber, Jet and the Oltu-stone, are used in making jewelry from the fossilized remains of these trees. It is said that due to static electricity that when this stone is rubbed it attracts dust to it, like black hole sucking in the light around it.

There is something primal about these trees and we Silver Elves associate them with our animal instincts, our preternatural senses, to the number 18 that is the number for the Moon card in the Major Arcana of the tarot and to the Wizard Myne Zeseltar that is derived from the Arvyndase word Zesaltarvar that means preternatural. This Myne represents our Amygdala, our part of the brain that warns us of a sense of danger before anything even happens. It developed in our distant past and even though it seems somewhat fossilized in some folks, who are oblivious to everything going on around them, and unnecessarily active in others so that they are constantly paranoid, it is still an essential aspect of our inner consciousness and warns us when predators and parasites draw near wanting to suck the life out of us.

WHAT THIS ORACLE MEANS:

Sometimes you get that feeling, don't you? That something is impending, something wicked coming your way, a sense of danger in a place or situation that you can't quite explain except to know that you don't feel comfortable there and wish to move on before something happens. What do you feel now in the situation you are currently in? In the circumstances you are asking the oracle concerning? Is it safe? Do you feel something coming? Do you need to leave? Perhaps before you even realize what is going on, before it comes too close.

Sometimes this feeling passes, that is true. It comes and it goes again, as the dark passes by and keeps going on its way. You may think that you were just being paranoid because nothing happened, but you were right to be aware, to stand up and take notice, to be on your guard. If you stay very still, it may pass by, never even noticing you are there. But if the feeling continues to get stronger, you may seriously consider moving stealthily away from it. Getting to a place where you know you will be safe. Perhaps beneath the trees sheltered by the lords of the forest. What are you sensing in this situation? Trust your instincts. You may not be able to explain what you are feeling or know why you are having these feelings, but don't ignore them.

ENCHANTMENT SPELL:

I feel it coming deep within
Before it comes I'm gone again

This Spell in Arvyndase:

El self ter kosodas dorae enaver
Lokan ter koso El'da tasïn sasnana

Pronunciation:

Eel seal-f tier co - so - dace door - ray e - nah - veer
Low - cane tier co - so Eel'dah tace - in sayce - na - nah

Chapter 88:

Chamaecyparis

KEYWORD: THE LETTER Ä

Tree Group Name in Arvyndase: **Tonequathe**
(pronounced: toe - knee - q - a - thee)

Arvyndase Name of the Wizard Myne: **Älardyn**
(pronounced: al - laird - den)

This tree and its magic:

Chamaecyparis trees are also known as Cypress or False Cypress and are a genus of conifers in the Cypress family that are native to Japan and Taiwan and to the Western and Eastern coasts of the United States. The name is derived from the Greek words that mean 'on the earth' and 'cypress' thus we might say Earth Cypress or Cypress of the Earth. This may symbolically be explained by the fact that the wood, which has that wonderful cypress scent to it, is often used, especially in Japan, for the construction of temples.

Thus, we Silver Elves relate these trees to the Wizard Myne Älardyn that developed from the Arvyndase word Alard (a - laird) that means a 'grove', as in a grove of trees as a sacred space where the Druids, elves and others would gather. We elves don't have churches, mosques or temples really, but we do have sacred groves and sanctuaries, places in Nature where one can feel the sacredness of life, the potency of the Divine Magic and our connection to the Universe and the all of life. Our temples are the forests, Nature is our church, the sacred springs our mosques.

What This Oracle Means:

It is true that all of Life is sacred and all of Nature Holy and Magical as well, and yet, there are certain places that really arouse this sense in us. That's what churches and other 'holy places' are meant to evoke in their devotees. We elfae find this sense arising most profoundly in Nature, in the wilds and the woodlands, in the morning mists and the evening twilight, near the tides and waves breaking upon the shore.

Where is this feeling evoked for you? Get ye there. If you wish to know the true answer to the question you have asked of the oracle, go to your magic spot, your sacred sanctuary, your power spot. Go out into Nature if you can, or wherever you get a sense of the infinity of Life and the Universe and let that feeling wash over you. The sense that everything is sacred, everything is magical and everything is connected. Then, your answer will come. And if you don't have a power spot as yet, it is time to go find it.

ENCHANTMENT SPELL:

As above so here on Earth
Elfin magic given birth

This Spell in Arvyndase:

Tat usel re jän ton Eldanil
Êldat êldon luthta daen

Pronunciation:

Tate u - seal re jan tone Eel - dah - nile
L - date l - doan lou-th - tah day - een

Chapter 89:

Cryptomeria japonica, Sugi

KEYWORD: **THE LETTER Å**

Tree Name in Arvyndase: **Marynalda** (pronounced: may - ren - ale - dah)

Arvyndase Name of the Wizard Myne: **Åswyni** (pronounced: ahss - win - nigh)

This tree and its magic:

Cryptomeria japonica trees are generally call Sugi (Cedar) in Japan, where they seem to have originated. However, there are cultivated species of it in China and some of these are thought to be close to 1,000 years old. These trees are ancients. They are also known as Japanese Redwoods and Japanese Cedars. The name Cryptomeria literally means hidden parts so we associate these trees with the cryptic, the secret, the hidden, the occult and the esoteric. The Wizard Myne is called Åswyni and this comes from the Arvyndase word Åswyn (ahss - win) that means esoteric.

The Cryptomeria grows best in forests on deep, well-drained soils. where they may thrive on warm, moist conditions, and they grow quickly in this environment. So, too, esoteric and magical studies flourish best in the forests, which is to say, among one's kindred and others who tread the path, where the conditions are warm and loving and at the same time moist, which is to say filled with nourishment, energy and feeling and yet are well drained, which indicates that the bullshit detectors as active and what isn't true and valid is recognized and removed quickly. Deep soil denotes an ancient tradition such as the lore, mythology and legends of the faerie folk.

The reddish pink wood of these trees has a pleasant scent, is lightweight but also strong, and is fairly waterproof and resistant to decay. The true esoteric Masters, in their way, are like these trees. Reddish pink would symbolize that they are active without being aggressive. Lightweight but strong denotes confidence and being at ease and comfortable in ones'elf and having an enchanting disposition. Their aura is attractive like the scent of these trees, and they are impervious to being emotionally manipulated (waterproof) and they are resistant to decay on every level of their being.

WHAT THIS ORACLE MEANS:

There are secrets to be revealed. Secrets of esoteric knowledge, of Nature, of Life and the Universe. Your time has come for deeper initiation, and yet, this is only a beginning. There are vast realms still to explore. More to learn. Greater secrets still.

In getting this Wizard Myne, you are called to seek the inner side of life. To explore the realms of the unknown, which is to say look within yours'elf. For our link to the all of life resides in our unconscious being, which is to say our soul, which is our connection to all that is, has been and will be. It is seldom one can see this world directly. It is a world of shadows after all, but you can feel it if you put away your prejudices and preconceptions and simply let the world wash over you. Don't judge. Just feel.

And surely, if you are using this oracle then you are already upon the esoteric path, so continue on. This is a never-ending journey, but at this time, you will take a significant step that will grant you more profound understanding and a revelation that will yield to you more potent magical power. Use this power wisely.

ENCHANTMENT SPELL:

Secrets great revealed to me
Potent magic mine to be

This Spell in Arvyndase:
Marynli ralt sotosïn va el
Mamer êldon el'na va te

Pronunciation:
Mare - ren - lie rail-t so - toe-ss - in vah eel
May - mere l - doan eel'nah vah tea

Chapter 90:

Cupressus

KEYWORD: **THE LETTER G**

TREE GROUP NAME IN ARVYNDASE: **QUATHE** (PRONOUNCED: Q - A - THEE)

ARVYNDASE NAME OF THE WIZARD MYNE: **GILTAR** (PRONOUNCED: GUILE - TAIR)

THIS TREE AND ITS MAGIC:

These trees, the Cupressus, are one of several genera that bear the common name Cypress. These trees are conifers that can be found mostly in warm temperate regions in the Northern Hemisphere. This includes Western North America, Central America, the Himalayas, Southern China, Northern Vietnam, Northwestern Africa, and the Middle East. In the ancient Hellenic or Greek culture, these trees were seen as being sacred to the goddess Artemis, who was known as Diana to the Romans, and who was the twin of Apollo (so named by both Greeks and Romans). She is the goddess of the hunt, of the wild places, peoples and animals. She is related to the Moon, and its mystical aspects and to chastity, by which it was meant she was an independent woman not under the control of mankind or male gods.

Therefore, we Silver Elves connect this Wizard Myne Giltar, which comes from the Arvyndase word Gilta that means maiden, to feminism, lesbians, and to strong and independent women of whatever kind or kindred or esoteric race they may be. This is surely true of the elven and elfae folk, for our females are equal to our males in nearly every way and surely superior in some ways. However, among the elves we are always elven first and foremost and female or male second. Ours is not a gender based or gender discriminating society. All our people are strong, independent spirits.

WHAT THIS ORACLE MEANS:

In getting this Wizard Myne, you are called to make yours'elf stronger and to appreciate and foster the strength and independence of others no matter whom they may be. Act with confidence, explore the uncharted wilds where the normal folk fear to tread. But don't forget to take your bow and arrows. You are hunting for the truth, after all.

It is also likely when receiving this Wizard Myne in response to a question put to the oracle that the answer not only says to be strong and independent, to be fearless in your hunt for what you wish and the fulfillment of your vision and quest, but that the response to your question may very well come from an independent person, quite possibly female, who may seem somewhat wild or non-conformist but who is definitely strong, confident and more than likely seen as mysterious in some way by you and quite possibly by others.

Listen to the wild ones. Listen to those who are confident in their own s'elves, whatever others may say or think about them. They have something to tell you.

ENCHANTMENT SPELL:

You stand strong and I do see
This is the way for you and me

This Spell in Arvyndase:
Le lotz mylth nar El ba ten
Wyr da tae yer fro le nar el

Pronunciation:

Lee low-tz mill-th nair Eel bah teen

Were dah tay year fro lee nair eel

Chapter 91:

Fitzroya cupressoides

KEYWORD: **THE LETTER Q**

TREE GROUP NAME IN ARVYNDASE: **YATHDUCONELPA** (PRONOUNCED: YEAH-TH - DUE - CON - EEL - PAH)

ARVYNDASE NAME OF THE WIZARD MYNE: **QORTARI** (PRONOUNCED: QUAR [AS IN QUART] - TAIR - RYE)

THIS TREE AND ITS MAGIC:

These trees can grow to over 220 feet tall and are found in Andes mountains of Southern Chile and Argentina, although fossilized foliage of this species has been on the Lea River of northwest Tasmania, which is an island south of continental Australian. They have been known to live to over 3,500 years old. They often provide protection and cover for the Southern Beech, the Laurel and the Myrtle trees. Therefore, we Silver Elves link these trees to the Wizard Myne Qortari, which is an extension of the Arvyndase word Qortar that means fortress. For these trees are a protective fortress for other trees. Thus, we also associate them with elven parents, who are a fortress to their littles, to elven guards who protect our peoples and our borders and to elven guardians or teachers who protect our society by nurturing and educating our young. A liberal education is vital to a free society.

However, this is not just everyday education, but the education of the lore, the passing down of our myths, legends and culture to the young. Here we are protecting not only our young, our elven families but also our ancient elfae culture, for the lore of our peoples, passed through the ages, is a fortress for our society. It helps preserve us and nurture us in a world that is sometimes hostile and often incredulous and frequently scornful concerning our true natures.

WHAT THIS ORACLE MEANS:

While not all the legends and lore concerning our peoples are true, and it is important to understand these myths in the light of the reality of our own being and natures, it is good to pass these legends on to our littles. For in knowing them, they can learn much of our ancient peoples and our ways and can use them to insulate thems'elves from those who seek to enculturate them, pressure them to conform and to unquestioningly accept with faith their particular religion or ideology.

Also, it is quite possible that the answer to the inquiry you have posed to the oracle can be found in the ancient, or sometimes in the more modern, tales and stories of our people. Myths, legends and lore, after all, are meant to be educational. Fairy tales often have morals to them. They are instructional guides. A message that is designed to help one in one's life and the path through it. What elf story or faerie tale best fits the situation you are currently in and what does it advise you to do or warn you against doing? (See our book of short stories *Elven Silver* or our novel *The Elves of Lyndarys*.)

ENCHANTMENT SPELL:

In fairy tales, the way is shown
My magic powers by use I hone

This Spell in Arvyndase:

Ver fari dantli, tae yer da tekeïn

El'na êldon eldroli la nos El sherm

Pronunciation:

Veer fay - rye dane-t - lie tay year dah tea - key - in

Eel'nah l - doan eel - drow - lie lah knowce Eel sheer-m

Chapter 92:

Juniper

KEYWORD: **THE LETTER Ï**

TREE NAME IN ARVYNDASE: **ROMYNA** (PRONOUNCED: ROW - MEN - NAH)

ARVYNDASE NAME OF THE WIZARD MYNE: **ÏNELOSYN** (PRONOUNCED: IN - NEAL - LOW - SIN)

THIS TREE AND ITS MAGIC:

Junipers grow to different sizes in differing environments all over the world, including the high mountainous regions of Tibet. Some of them create berry looking seeds that can be ground up and used as a spice. The number of different species of these trees ranges from 50 to 67, depending on the opinion of the scientists involved and their particular method of distinguishing species. They can be a somewhat aggressive species (these trees, but also scientists) pushing out other types of trees but they can also be highly competitive among themselves.

In Scottish folklore and in the Gaelic Polytheism there is a practice of saining (cleansing and sanctifying) rites, such as those performed at Hogmanay, the New Year, in which the smoke of Juniper is wafted about to cleanse, bless, and protect the household and its inhabitants, just in the way that sage is often used.

So it is that we Silver Elves relate these trees to the Wizard Myne Ïnelosyn, which is formed from the Arvyndase word Inelos (eye - neal - lowce) that means heirloom. For we link these trees to the elven practice of shedding blessings upon people, of the ancient elven practice of wish granting and the fulfillment, thereby, of people's desires. In fairy tales, one must truly be careful what they wish for, how they delineate their wishes and how they use them, for often their own greed and ill intention serves to undo them.

To obtain the blessings of the elfin and have them last, as a sort of heirloom, one must purify ones'elf as an individual and strive toward fulfilling one's true and sacred nature that exists within one as an Heirloom of the Divine Magic. One must strive toward fulfillment as a spirit with devotion and yet one must give up one's tendency to unnecessarily vie with others. We are all in this together.

WHAT THIS ORACLE MEANS:

The blessing of the elves can last for lifetimes. How you use it, however, will determine whether this means good luck or misfortune. Blessings, by their nature, are something that are given, gifted, shared. Share your blessings with others and you will be carrying on the tradition of the elves, elfae and faerie folk of olde and potentially making the world a better place by doing so.

In receiving this Wizard Myne, you may wish to carry out a cleansing ritual in your home and personal environment or for your person or loved ones. See if there are places where you are being too aggressive, too competitive, where, in fact, your actions are causing you more difficulties than need be. Whenever possible make allies, not enemies. As we Silver Elves say (and chant): Together our magic is stronger by far. Join with your others and make magic. Spread your blessings, and the solution to your question will come as a gift from the Shining Ones and you may carry the blessing you receive as an heirloom of wisdom that you can pass down through the generations and for lifetimes to come.

ENCHANTMENT SPELL:

I clear the air and thus the way
And bless you on this sacred day

This Spell in Arvyndase:

El vyrn tae eron nar hern tae yer
Nar elsor le ton wyr elfro lea

Pronunciation:

Eel vern tay e - rone nair herne tay year
Nair eel - soar lee tone were eel - fro lee - ah

Chapter 93:

Dawn Redwood

KEYWORD: **THE NUMBER 60**

TREE NAME IN ARVYNDASE: **LAN SARÅMOFU** (PRONOUNCED: LANE SAYR - RAH - MOE - FEW)

Arvyndase Name of the Wizard Myne: **Êlfarlar** (pronounced: l - fair - lair)

This tree and its magic:

These are the Dawn Redwoods, which are fast growing trees, but are also the shortest in height of the redwoods. In China, local villagers call the original tree of this kind Shui-sa or the Water Fir. This tree is incorporated into a local shrine. These trees are sometimes referred to as living fossils because they had long been thought to be extinct when living varieties were discovered to be still existing, much to everyone's surprise.

We elves, and Elfin itself, have long been thought to be extinct, if in fact they believe we ever existed at all. Our lore, myths and legends are our fossilized versions of our culture. Therefore, we associate these trees with the number 60, which promises prosperity and security when one is in touch with the Divine Magic, and with the Wizard Myne Êlfarlar that comes from the Arvyndase word Êlfarla, which means utopia.

Elfin is a utopian or paradisiacal realm that some think once existed but is now extinct. Others believe it never was and cannot ever be, that creating a more perfect world is impossible. We elves know that we and Elfin are living fossils (just ask our friends) and that Elfin lives within us and is born into the world through us and is ever dawning, or coming into being, even as it lives in reality. It is an active, rather than stagnant, manifestation of living enchantment. A world and dimension that is ever growing and transforming.

What This Oracle Means:

Create Elfin in and through your life. Manifest elfin magic in all that you do. If you get this Wizard Myne then it says it is time to come out a little, at least to those you trust, and actively seek to bring Elfin into being through your actions and in your environment.

You may wish to start a vortex (elven coven) or other elfae group so that you can work in harmony with others. We know that this isn't always easy. It can be hard to find our kindred. We have been scattered all over the Earth and are often at great distances to each other. Fortunately, the internet helps unite us in near instant communication and we can find inspiration in what our distant kindred do and hopefully serve to inspire them as well.

Even if you are alone, and there are those that say they like it that way, even if you have become accustomed to being a loner in the world of the normal folk, you can still manifest your elfae magic through your own being. Make it real by living it. This will attract Elfin or Faerie to you and bring you luck in synchronous and serendipitous ways. Do you wish love? Do you desire success in the world? This is the way. Live your dreams as best you may. They may not manifest as exactly as you imagined, but they will have the advantage of being real.

ENCHANTMENT SPELL:
Elfin each day born anew
Deep in me and also you

This Spell in Arvyndase:
Êldat cha lea daend naves
Dorae ver el nar nawe le

Pronunciation:
L - date cha lee - ah day - eend nay - vees
Door - ray veer eel nair nay - we lee

Chapter 94:

Coast Redwood

KEYWORD: **GIANT**

TREE NAME IN ARVYNDASE: **JORNAR SARÂMOFU** (PRONOUNCED: JOUR - NAIR SAYR - RAH - MOE - FEW)

ARVYNDASE NAME OF THE WIZARD MYNE: **MOFUL** (PRONOUNCED: MOE - FUEL)

THIS TREE AND ITS MAGIC:

Coast Redwoods are also known as the California Redwoods. They are giants and can grow up to nearly 400 feet tall and live to over 2,000 years old. They are among the oldest living things upon the Earth. They are known for capturing fog and turning it into water drops. They are resistant to fire, insect attack, fungal infection, and rot, but unfortunately not to Man.

Therefore, we Silver Elves associate these trees with the Giants, who in many mythologies were some of the oldest beings upon the Earth. There are often portrayed as huge, often wicked beings, but that depiction comes from the new gods of Man who came and took over the Earth from them. The Norse called them the Jötnar (plural) or Jötunn (singular) and said they were in continual opposition to the Æsir and Vanir, although these groups sometimes intermarried with giants. The Greeks called these beings Titans.

This Wizard Myne is called Moful, which comes from the Arvyndase word Mofu (moe - few) that is our elven word for giant and Mofur (moe - few-r) that is our version of the prefix giga-.

WHAT THIS ORACLE MEANS:

You may be dealing with the old and powerful in this situation. They are probably ensconced in their power and privilege and look down upon everyone who is not of them and see all others as being naturally inferior. They are old money, old power and they are certain that they will always remain so. They are the aristocracy of old and feel they are designed by the gods for their privileged status. After all, they overthrew the even older ones, the forgotten ones, to get it. Did they not seize this world, wrest it by force from the Elder Gods?

You may need to tread carefully here. These are powers that are most likely too great to confront. Perhaps, the best you can do in this situation is try not to get stepped upon. Although, they do tend to get bored from time to time and if you can enchant them, entertain them, then perhaps you can draw their interest and the rewards they sometimes lavish on those who amuse them. But be careful. They can be vicious in their amusements. Best perhaps, if you just go your way and hope they don't notice you at all.

If you think you have the power, you can try to overthrow them, but that seldom ends well.

ENCHANTMENT SPELL:

You are great and powerful
But you see me not at all

This Spell in Arvyndase:

Le da ralt nar eldrofel
Kana le ten el kon zan wyl

Pronunciation:

Lee dah rail-t nair eel - dro - feel
Kay - nah lee teen eel cone zane will

Chapter 95:

Giant Sequoia

Keyword: **The Number 16**

Tree Name in Arvyndase: **Taldåalda** (pronounced: tale - dah - ale - dah)

Arvyndase Name of the Wizard Myne: **Eltori** (pronounced: eel - tour - rye)

This tree and its magic:

These trees are also called Giant Redwoods, Sierra Redwoods, Wellingtonia or simply the Big Tree, and due to this we surely could have associated them with the Giants, as we did the previous and related tree. However, their name Sequoia was given to them in honor of Sequoyah, who invented the Cherokee syllabary, so that the Cherokee language could be written down. Therefore, we Silver Elves associate these trees with the Wizard Myne Eltori that comes from the Arvyndase words Elto (eel - toe), which means language and Eltor that is our elven word for music. For the elven languages are musical languages, meant to float from one's tongue as though one is about to sing.

We also relate these trees to the Number 16 that indicates those who seek wisdom in order to learn and to teach and, in that way, to share with and help others. Our language is a link between us meant to uplift us and help us learn together, as well as distinguish our ancient elven culture.

WHAT THIS ORACLE MEANS:

The Elven languages are musical languages, languages of enchantment, languages of love. In getting this Wizard Myne, it is time to refine what you say, the way you say it and, especially, to refine your tone of voice. Not the words entirely and the content of what you say, but the sound you make when speaking them. This is the undertone, this is the secret message hidden in what you seek to communicate. It is not entirely what you say but how you express it. Did your parents ever say to you: don't take that tone with me? Have you ever heard others say this? If we say to you: you are really great, we might be praising you, or mocking you, being serious or facetious depending on our tone of voice. The tone is important, let your tone develop power and weight without forcing it. Don't be a ham. Don't overact. Let your tone be a genuine expression of your profound inner nature.

So, refine your tone. And listen carefully to the tone of voice of others around you in this situation. Although, remember as well, people may not be as developed as you are in their ability to express thems'elves with words or tones. Don't hold that against them. Try to understand and have some compassion for them as well. Not everyone is as advanced as you are. You have great power. Use it to uplift others so they also can stand tall and strong, like the sequoias, and endure for thousands of years just as your words and your wisdom may carry on for years to come, like a tune, haunting in its melody, that one can't forget.

ENCHANTMENT SPELL:

Let my words ring ever on
And greet the rising Elfin Dawn

This Spell in Arvyndase:

Lao el'na molli bre vari ton
Nar alos tae luftdas Êldat Lan

Pronunciation:
Lay - oh eel'nah mole - lie bree vay - rye tone
Nair a - lowce tay lou-ft - dace L - date Lane

Chapter 96:

Bald Cypress

Keyword: **The Letter P**

Tree Name in Arvyndase: **Nuel Quathe** (pronounced: New - eel Q - a - thee

Arvyndase Name of the Wizard Myne: **Paforcol** (pronounced: pay - for – cull

---

This Tree and its Magic:

Taxodium is a genus with three species in it: the Pond Cypress, the Bald Cypress and the Montezuma Cypress. Their heartwood is extremely rot and termite resistant, and this becomes even more so the older they get. They usually live in or near water (the world of feelings and psychic perception) and they often develop what are call cypress knees, although the exact function of these is not entirely known as yet.

We Silver Elves relate these trees to the wisdom of age, elven wisdom that grows stronger with time and experience, while at the same time we may go bald or, in some cases, grow more direct and bold as individuals as we age and have knees we are no longer sure quite what they are for. Knees are said to represent flexibility but also submission and surrender, since one is asked to go down to one's knees before gods, kings and conquerors. The older we get, the less inclined we elves are to do so. This Wizard Myne is called Paforcol, which comes from the Arvyndase word for Lyceum, (a place of education and study, a meeting place for discussions, lectures, and concerts) which is Paforco (pay - for - co).

What This Oracle Means:

We were once at a Renaissance Faire in Northern California and we encountered an elderly elven wizard and we noted how he seemed rather ancient and wise and we expressed how we hoped to be so wise as he one day. He advised us not to worry. It would all come naturally in time. There was no need or value in hurrying anything.

Let this situation have time to develop. There is no point in trying to rush things. Apply yours'elf to developing your own spirit, soul, body, mind and being. That is what is most important in the long run anyway. Still, take care of your body, especially your knees and your teeth. If you are going bald or have done so, already, don't worry about it. Construct your body of light with as much hair as you like. We also give ours pointed ears. We are creating ours'elves; and this incarnation is just a waystation on our journey to the eternal realms of Elfin. Still, here we are and it is best to do our best as best we may.

Enchantment Spell:

Time will tell and that is sure
But we're not saying any more

This Spell in Arvyndase:

Mern yon fram nar dij da vem
Kana eli'da kon desdas otir gilf

Pronunciation:

Mere'n yon frame nair dye-j dah veem

Kay - nah e - lie'dah cone dees - dace oh - tire gile-f

Chapter 97:

Western Red cedar

KEYWORD: **THE LETTER W**

TREE NAME IN ARVYNDASE: **THUJÅALDA** (PRONOUNCED: THEW - JAH - ALE - DAH)

ARVYNDASE NAME OF THE WIZARD MYNE: **WITANI** (PRONOUNCED: WHY - TANE - NIGH)

THIS TREE AND ITS MAGIC:

The Western Red Cedar is also known as the Pacific Red Cedar, the Giant Arborvitae or Western Arborvitae, the Giant Cedar and the Shinglewood tree (since it is used at times to make shingles). The species name, which is Plicata, is derived from a Latin word that means 'folded in plaits' or 'braided' due to the pattern of its small leaves. Therefore, we associate these trees with elf locks, also known in modern times as dreadlocks, the tangled and bunched hair that legend has it comes from the mischievous weavings in one's hair done by elves and other elfae folk while one sleeps at night. We further link these trees to

276 .... The Elfin Book of Trees for the Elven Druid

knot magic, for really that's what elf locks are, our wishes and enchantments tied in our hair.

The Wizard Myne comes from the Arvyndase word Witan (why - tane) that means knot in our elfin language. However, this form of the word is not the one we use for knots tied in strings, that would be Tarth (tair-th), but the knots one finds in trees, that come from branches that have reached out while the main growth of the tree has continued to grow on around it. These knots are like islands in a river or sea. And such is Elfin in these days, a series of knots in the tree of the world, islands of magic, mystery and sanity in the midst of the dull, mundane and often feverishly insane world around us.

Knot magic is usually done for binding something to one, or binding someone so they cannot do harm or, in some cases, unbinding to release something or someone from one's life. Knot magic is clearly related to Weaving magic, Spinning (the process of creating yarn or thread) magic, and Sewing magics of all sorts. These are often seen as the magics of women, of females, but we need to remember that there are male tailors as well and certainly among the elven this magic isn't exclusive to our female elves. In our society, our males often sew as well. In fact, in this elven eald, it is the male that does most of the sewing.

WHAT THIS ORACLE MEANS:

If you are having problems, encountering obstacles then, as you brush or comb your hair and undo any tangles that are in it, imagine undoing the tangles and difficulties of your life. Carefully, so as not to damage your hair.

If someone is giving you difficulties, unnecessarily creating obstacles for you, you can get a string and tie knots in it and bind them from doing any further harm. Our sisters often seal these bindings in glass jars and hide them away in the dark of their basement.

If you wish to draw someone to you, you can tie a knot in a string, or perhaps ribbon in this case, so they will be attached to you, but remember, if you are violating their free will, this is dark magic and you will regret it. Leave these knots a bit loose or use a slipknot, so they can get away if that is what they truly desire or fate or destiny demands. These knots are better as invitations rather than compulsions.

But mostly, go your own way. Branch out in the direction you wish to go in life, tie a knot, perhaps in a cord, linking you to your goals. For protection, knot a cord around your doorknob. If you wear an amulet, remember that if you are attaching it with a string you can formulate magic while tying the string.

And if you braid your hair, enchantments can be woven into the braids. Or draw Celtic knots, these are enchantments as well.

ENCHANTMENT SPELL:
I'm tied to the future and all that's good
So be you, too, as you know you should

This Spell in Arvyndase:
El'da sothïn va tae lasel nar wyl dij'da ril
Re te le, bil, tat le ken le jar

Pronunciation:
Eel'dah sew-th - in vah tay lay - seal nair will dye'j dah rile
Re tea lee, bile, tate lee keen lee jair

Chapter 98:

Fir

KEYWORD: THE NUMBER 13

TREE NAME IN ARVYNDASE: **TARLE** (PRONOUNCED: TAYR - LEE)

ARVYNDASE NAME OF THE WIZARD MYNE: **TÅLYN** (PRONOUNCED: TAHL - LYNN)

THIS TREE AND ITS MAGIC:

The Fir tree is associated with the traditional Ogham Ailim and with far sight. This is true especially of the Silver Firs, because of their great height. The Douglas Fir, by the way, is not considered a true Fir. Firs differ from other members of the Pine family due to the way in which their needle-like leaves. which together resemble a suction cup, are attached singly to their branches at a common base, and the fact that their cones stand erect on the branches reminiscent of candles being held upright (the origin of the lights or candles on the Yule tree?).

Due to this, we Silver Elves associate these trees to the Wizard Myne Tålyn that is an extension of the Arvyndase word Tål that means path, as in one's spiritual path, the path to which we elfae become attached like a suction cup, because it lights our way into the distant future like a candle, granting us far sight and the ability to see our Destiny. Like the leaves of these trees, we tread the Elven Way both singly and together, lighting the way for others who seek the path as well.

WHAT THIS ORACLE MEANS:

In getting this Wizard Myne, it is advised that you look into your future, your far future, your destiny and see how you can get there. Especially, join with others in a vortex or some other elfin band and work together toward your mutual and common spiritual goals. At the same time, always preserve your uniqueness as an elfae, your individuality, your sense of s'elf and the confidence and inner authority of your being. Often groups seek to break individuals down to make them conform to the group, but those are not truly elven groups. In elfin groups, we light the way for each other. We support each other's individuality and often each other's eccentricities and we tread the path together as strong individuals united.

Be strong, kindred. Look for yours'elf into the future and see what is there for you. Others may see something different, but hold true to your own sense of the path. People sometimes talk about the 'odd man out', but we elves are the 'odd that are in'. Individuality is a vital part of our culture and we are all different together, for our uniqueness is one of the things that we elfae share in common.

ENCHANTMENT SPELL:

I stand with you and you with me
Together we shall ever be free

This Spell in Arvyndase:

El lotz ena le nar le ena el
Eldan eli van vari te alo

Pronunciation:

Eel low-tz e - nah lee nair lee e - nah eel
Eel - dan e - lie vane vair - rye tea a - low

Chapter 99:

Cedar

KEYWORD: THE LETTER V

TREE NAME IN ARVYNDASE: **TARDEN** (PRONOUNCED: TAYR - DEAN)

ARVYNDASE NAME OF THE WIZARD MYNE: **VELTUR** (PRONOUNCED: VEAL - TOUR)

THIS TREE AND ITS MAGIC:

Cedrus or Cedar trees are coniferous trees in the plant family Pinaceae that are native to the mountains of the western Himalayas and the mountainous regions of the Mediterranean. They often get their water from snowfall. They are noted for the scented wood that has been used for ages to make cedar chests in order to preserve and store one's precious things especially those things one would protect from predatory moths. Their seeds contain two or three 'resin blisters' that are theorized to be a defense mechanism against squirrel predation due to their unpleasant-taste.

Thus, we Silver Elves associate these trees to the Wizard Myne Veltur that comes from the Arvyndase word Veltu (veal - two) that means treasure. Elven treasures, despite certain tales, are less inclined to be jewels or silver or gold (like the treasures of dragons), not that we entirely distain these things, but more likely to be things of beauty, things of the spirit, of poetry, song, and magical secrets and arcane wisdom. Love and friendship, perhaps most of all, are treasured by us. We treasure each other. We treasure our Elfin/Faerie culture, our legends and lore both ancient and modern and we seek to preserve them for the future by putting them in the scented chests of enchantment that are our very hearts and minds and protect them both from the moths of derision and the squirrel people or dragons of the world who would hide them away for themselves alone.

WHAT THIS ORACLE MEANS:

What do you treasure truly? What is most precious to you? And how may you preserve that which is so valuable to you? Protect yours'elf, protect your friends, but most of all in getting this Wizard Myne preserve your dignity, your values and what is good and true in your heart and soul. Without being naive, protect your innocence, for innocence is your true protection. The world seeks to corrupt you. To make you over in its own image. Turn you into a work robot slave that does its bidding without complaint and then tosses you away the moment it sees you as no longer being of use to it. So, treasure yours'elf and your elfae being. You are a gem shining in the darkness of the world.

And save a bit, as you can, if you can. Store for the future, like a squirrel, but store so that you and your kindred can thrive in the potentially difficult times to come. Most of all, protect your heart, your soul and your spirit. Make your true treasures those things that are truly priceless. Keep them in a sacred place within you, a place that exists mostly in the dimensions of light and magic in worlds that others can never enter without being transformed their own s'elves.

ENCHANTMENT SPELL:
My magic hides deep within
Until bright Elfin comes again

This Spell in Arvyndase:
El'na êldon rimlu dorae enaver
Murted ilu Êldat kosolu sasnana

Pronunciation:
Eel'nah l - doan rime - lou door - ray e - nah - veer
Muir-teed eye - lou L - date co - so - lou sayce - nay - nah

Chapter 100:

Larch

KEYWORD: **THE NUMBER 8**

TREE NAME IN ARVYNDASE: **DUCON** (PRONOUNCED: DUE - CON)

ARVYNDASE NAME OF THE WIZARD MYNE: **NESA** (PRONOUNCED: KNEE - SAH)

THIS TREE AND ITS MAGIC:

The Larch tree is another one of the many trees seen as the World Tree. Larches are among the dominant trees and plants in the boreal forests or snow forests. They are said to provide protection against dark enchantments and to serve as ladders that connect the material world to the higher realms of being. Because of this, they were sometimes used in funerary rites linking the material world to the more heavenly realms, the realms of pure spirit.

We Silver Elves link these trees to the Wizard Myne Nesa that comes from the Arvyndase word Nes (niece), which means thread. Unlike the Western Red Cedar that we associated with knot magic, this is the tread, the silver thread, that connects our astral bodies to our physical bodies and on the other end to our higher spirits. When we die this tread is cut from our material body, resulting in that thread, like a rubber band being released, drawing our body of light, our energetic body, onward toward our destiny.

We also associate these trees to the number 8, which is a symbol of infinity and represents a constant flow of energy and power in the Universe. At the same time, 8 can symbolize wealth and success in a material sense and a desire for things and pleasures of the flesh. Thus, 8 connects us to the infinite but also to reincarnation, bringing us, due to our own desires back into material manifestation over and over again from one life to another. As we become more attuned to our spiritual natures, we climb the ladder of the Larch toward the realization of our destinies on subtler dimensions.

What This Oracle Means:

Whatever challenge you are facing, first confront it with your imaginal body. See your way into the future, visualizing the thread that connects the present to future, and then, seeing it, use your energetic body, which is to say your actions and energy to move forward and enact the path you see.

Remember, in designing a building or planning a trip, we aren't always able to anticipate all the potential difficulties and detours we may encounter. We know we may encounter them, but don't always know when and where they will arise. If things don't go entirely as planned, then look again and plot a new course from where you are at that time and in that way you can slowly and surely make your way toward Elfin by the quickest and shortest paths available.

Enchantment Spell:

Direct the route betwixt now and then
I see the way and the future win

This Spell in Arvyndase:

Stran tae wat cata mat nar qut
El ten tae yer nar tae lasel bem

Pronunciation:

Strain tay wait cah - tah mate nair cute

Eel teen tay year nair tay lay - seal beam

Chapter 101:

Spruce

KEYWORD: **THE NUMBER 40**

TREE NAME IN ARVYNDASE: **PIF** (PRONOUNCED: PIE-F)

ARVYNDASE NAME OF THE WIZARD MYNE: **ÊLMLAR** (PRONOUNCED: ELM - LAIR)

THIS TREE AND ITS MAGIC:

The Spruce, when mature, has whirled branches and conical form. They can be identified from other members of the pine family by their needles, which are their leaves, for these are four-sided and each connected to small peg-like structures, that endure even after the leaves (needles) have been shed. In the mountains of western Sweden, there lives a Spruce tree that is nicknamed Old Tjikko, that is nearly 10,000 years old and may very well be the world's oldest living tree.

The name Spruce is derived from a Middle English adjective spruce which was used to mean 'from Prussia', since products were imported from Prussia in containers of spruce. From this comes the phrase, 'spucing ones'elf up', that refers to refreshing one's s'elf and becoming a bit trimmer and tidier since Prussia was seen as a stylish, orderly and tidy place.

This tree has many uses including the fact that its resin was utilized in the making of pitch (tar and asphalt) and its scientific name Picea comes from Latin picea for pitch pine and from piceus, an adjective meaning pix or "pitch". Pix is, of course, also the root of the word pixie; and pix or pyx is the name of the small box in which the consecrated bread of the Eucharist is kept, which is to say the trans-substantiated body of Christ in the Catholic religion. Further, in the UK, it is the name for a container at the Royal Mint in which specimens of gold and silver coins are kept to be tested annually at the 'trial of the pyx', which ensures that they are of the required standard of silver or gold content.

All of this leads us Silver Elves to associate these trees with the Wizard Myne Êlmlar that comes from the Arvyndase word Êlm that means 'flair'. When we elves think of sprucing ours'elves up, we are not talking necessarily about becoming neat and tidy and adhering to society's standards of fashion, but about finding one's own style or fashion, what we call one's 'flair' as a creative artist and as a life artist.

What This Oracle Means:

Find and develop your own style. Sometimes we do that by imitating others, but imitation alone cannot yield our flair. We need to copy what we like and then alter it to our own tastes and needs, eclectically putting together various things in our own unique way. There are people who can imitate Rembrandt or other great painters exactly, but they are not Rembrandt. There are people who can play music exactly like this or that great group or artist, but they are not that artist or group. What makes you special? What is your flair, your unique style? For when you find that, you will become a great success.

Deep within you there is a pix (pixie?), pyx, that contains your 'true name', which is to say your unique being and style and is sacred and holy and belongs only to you. People can imitate you, and if you develop your flair, they will surely try, but no one will ever be able to be you as well as you can be you. Everyone needs to find their own flair. Find yours.

ENCHANTMENT SPELL:

I am special as you see
Only I can truly be me

This Spell in Arvyndase:

El da doril tat le ten
Norae El vek lodla te el

Pronunciation:

Eel dah door - rile tate lee teen
Nor - ray Eel veek load - lah tea eel

Chapter 102:

Pine

KEYWORD: **THE NUMBER 90**

TREE NAME IN ARVYNDASE: **INU** (PRONOUNCED: EYE - KNEW)

ARVYNDASE NAME OF THE WIZARD MYNE: **OFORFAR** (PRONOUNCED: OH - FOR - FAIR)

THIS TREE AND ITS MAGIC:

The name Pine is theorized to be derived from an Indo-European root word pīt- which signifies resin and is the source of English word pituitary. In the past, most Pines were simply referred to as Firs and are still so called in some places today. The pituitary gland is sometimes called the Master gland, since it helps regulate the other glands. Therefore, we Silver Elves link these trees to the Wizard Myne Oforfar that is derived from the Arvyndase word Oforfa (oh - for - fah), which means leader and is associated with the number 90, a number whose vibration indicates a person whose energy serves as a higher spiritual example for others.

Leadership for the elven is not about being an authority or having arbitrary power over others but about being an initiate and therefore initiating or starting things. It is about being a pioneer and exploring the unknown. It is about sharing with others, fostering their unique being, and helping them to become initiate as well. Lead by example. Be the elfae you know yours'elf to be and let your fae light shine into the world for those with elfin sight to see so they may find their own way to the Initiate that is within them and they can lead their lives as they were ever meant to do.

WHAT THIS ORACLE MEANS:

Take charge, get things started. You don't need to order other people about. You just need to get things going and see who is inspired by your example. Are you waiting for someone to tell you what to do? It's time to stop waiting and simply do things as best you are able. Look to others who are on the path if you need some inspiration, and certainly we all need and seek inspiration at times. But do. Do your best. Help your kindred to do their best and take another step upon the path closer to Elfin and thus closer to your own true s'elf and then another step after that. Others seeing you do so will surely be inspired on their part to step a little closer to Elfin as well, to dare to be the elfae that they inwardly know thems'elves to truly be.

Perhaps it is time to start your own elven vortex, group or band. But remember, for the elven, leadership is always a fluctuating matter. Begin your project and see who takes things further and then who takes things a bit further still. When we walk together, we are all leaders.

ENCHANTMENT SPELL:

I am starting and you can come
Together we shall be as one

This Spell in Arvyndase:

El da altudas nar le vek koso
Eldan eli van te tat ata

Pronunciation:

Eel dah ale - two - dace nair lee veek co - so
Eel - dane e - lie vane tea tate a - tah

Chapter 103:

Douglas-fir

KEYWORD: **THE LETTERS Æ**

TREE NAME IN ARVYNDASE: **LAREQA** (PRONOUNCED: LAIR - REE - QWAH)

ARVYNDASE NAME OF THE WIZARD MYNE: **ROFETAE** (PRONOUNCED: ROW - FEE - TAY)

THIS TREE AND ITS MAGIC:

*D*ouglas firs are also known as the Douglas trees and the Oregon pines. There has been much debate about where these trees belong in relation to other trees but they were eventually (although such things are subject to change) grouped into a new genus Pseudotsuga, which is a word that means false, pseudo or perhaps fake Hemlock. The female cones hang downward, and unlike true Fir trees have persistent scales. These cones have a long three-pointed bract that can be seen protruding out of each scale and was thought to look like the rear half of a mouse, with its two feet and a longer tail sticking out. There is a myth arising from some of the First Nations Peoples of Northern California that mice once sought shelter in the scales of these trees' cones during a forest fire, and these trees, in their compassion, offered the mice enduring sanctuary.

Therefore, we Silver Elves link these trees to the Wizard Myne Rofetae, that comes from and is pronounced the same as the Arvyndase word Rofetey, which means sanctuary. It is also associated with the letters Æ, such as in Ægypt, or Ælf or Ælph, but which in Arvyndase nearly always appear as the last syllable in a word indicating that the word ends with a long A sound, unlike the 'e' sound it produces in Ænglish.

Unlike the Grove or Sanctuary of the Chamaecyparis trees found in Chapter 88, indicating a mystical, magical and holy space or spot, this is the sanctuary of refuge, safety and protection, a place where we can find respite from the world in an atmosphere that is strongly elfin or elfae or otherkin in nature.

We Silver Elves were once driving home from having spent a weekend with our sisters of the Elf Queen's Daughters and decided to loop through Muir woods in Marin county, California on our way. While we rode through these ancient woodlands, we had a vision of arriving at a large white Victorian style house in the middle of the night and being greeted by our elfin kindred at this elven sanctuary. Was it the past? A glimpse of the future? We know not, but the image and feeling of this vision has stayed with us ever since.

What This Oracle Means:

Some of our kindred think about creating an elven nation. That seems a bit ambitious to us, particularly when we are starting from a place where elves are scattered about the world here and there with but a few of us living or gathered together in any one region. Perhaps, we should start with something a bit more practical, which is creating elven vortexes (vortices), ealds, our own small elven and elfae homes in the world, our own little bits of Elfin manifest, our individual elven sanctuaries.

And if you have or can do that, perhaps it is time to consider offering a bit of sanctuary when you can to others of your kind. Sort of Air B&B for elfae. If you have the space. If you can afford to do so. We have had kindred come and stay with us over the years. We have lived with elves, fae, gnomes and other elfae for various periods, sometimes as much as year. At present, we do not have the room, living in a very small eald with only one bedroom, although it is in paradise, but we still hold this vision in our hearts.

Do what you can to aid and shelter your kindred. Whatever the question you have poised to the oracle, the reply is, do what you are able to create a safe place for yours'elf and others to be together.

Enchantment Spell:
You are safe within our eald
With sacred Elfin you may meld

This Spell in Arvyndase:
Le da del enaver le'na ald
Ena elfro Êldat le me futh

Pronunciation:
Lee dah deal e - nah - veer lee'nah ale-d
E - nah eel - fro L - date lee me few-th [rhymes with youth]

Chapter 104:

Yellowwood family

KEYWORD: **THE NUMBER 20**

TREE GROUP NAME IN ARVYNDASE: **OCARÅLTIELPA** (PRONOUNCED: OH - CAR - ALL - TIE - EEL - PAH)

ARVYNDASE NAME OF THE WIZARD MYNE: **EREPER** (PRONOUNCED: E - REE - PEER)

THIS TREE AND ITS MAGIC:

Yellowwood trees are native to the mountainous forests of Southern Africa and are also referred to as the Bastard Yellowwoods, the Outeniqua Yellowwoods, the African Fern Pine, and the Weeping Yews. Their size depends greatly upon their location, therefore, we Silver Elves link these trees to the Wizard Myne Ereper that is derived from the Arvyndase word Erepe, which is our elven word for adapt. However, this family of trees also includes the Totara, the Rimu, the Miro and the Kahikatea trees of New Zealand.

We also link these trees to the Number 20, which is a number of diplomacy; indicating our ability to use courtesy to ease our way through the world.

We elves are a very adaptable people. We fit ours'elves in various situations and circumstances and alter ours'elves and sometimes our habits and lifestyle to succeed. It is, after all, the survival of the fittest, which Men often think means the survival of those who are most physically fit or physically strong, but really means the survival of those best able to adapt to various environments and situations.

One possible explanation of the reason most modern elves don't have actual pointed ears, as much as we love them, is that natural selection favored those of us with less pointy ears when Men and others were killing our pointy eared ancestors indiscriminately. Our elven ancestors were able thus to fit in and adapt in the world of Man and pass our line on into the future. We expect that sometime further in the future, when it is safe to do so, we will grow our ears pointy again.

What This Oracle Means:

In this situation, you need to adapt. Don't insist on things being one way and one way only. Keep your goals and your visions in mind, but adapt yours'elf and the way you go about achieving those visions to the circumstances you are encountering. Sometimes, we just have to hide as elves. Sometimes, we feel so endangered in the world that we naturally evoke protective camouflage and mimicry to fool others into thinking we are just like them.

At the same time, some elfae are so affected by the past that they spend all their time hiding when they don't really have to do so. They are afraid to ever express their true natures and show their true elven s'elves. Look around you. Do you really have to hide in this situation? Fit yours'elf into the circumstances you are encountering but don't forget who you truly are otherwise you will become just like them, and what elfae would really want that? Be diplomatic while retaining what is essential to your needs and your nature.

Enchantment Spell:

You do see me but you don't
Perhaps you will but may'haps you won't

This Spell in Arvyndase:
Le ba ten el kana le ba'kon
Lajos le yon kana me'jos le yonik

Pronunciation:

Lee bah teen eel kay - nah lee bah'cone

Lay - joess lee yone kay - nah me'joess lee yo - nike

Chapter 105:

Yew family

KEYWORD: **NECROMAGERY**

TREE GROUP NAME IN ARVYNDASE: **WANDELPA** (PRONOUNCED: WANE-D - EEL - PAH)

ARVYNDASE NAME OF THE WIZARD MYNE: **SHYNAR** (PRONOUNCED: SHIN - NAIR)

THIS TREE AND ITS MAGIC:

The Yew family of trees are linked to the Druid and Celtic Ogham Ioho and to the idea of rebirth and reincarnation. We Silver Elves therefore associate these trees with the Wizard Myne Shynar that comes from the Arvyndase word Shyn (shin) that means dead and to Necromagery and Necromancy, which is our ability to connect with, communicate with and evoke the powers of the dead. When we read history to understand the wisdom of the ancients, we are using Necromancy. When we evoke the spirits of the Founding Fathers, or Mothers, of our particular country or people, we are using Necromagery.

In honoring Tolkien and learning from his wisdom, we are preforming Necromancy.

The dead have gone on. The spirits that once were, are now reborn in new bodies. Yet, their wisdom, their example, their writings may still inspire us, and this is the process of Necromancy and in honoring and making use of that spirit and bringing their wisdom to life in our own lives, we are doing Necromagery.

WHAT THIS ORACLE MEANS:

Look to the past to understand what is going on here and now and what you may do about it. This is not the first time this has occurred and if you look into the past you will see how it was solved previously and then may do so again. You may have to look far into the past. Tales, lore and history may be of help to you, but then, history is written by the victors, as it is often said, and it is also frequently idealized to soothe the vanity of the conquerors. So be careful. History is sometimes more fiction than fact.

Look deeper. Use your intuition, and understand that although the world has changed, it hasn't changed all that much. People tend to remain rather the same with the same drives and desires, temptations and foibles. Understand the past in terms of the present but understand as well that things do change, however slowly.

And if all else fails, evoke the ancestors and call for their help in this situation. They have been reborn, again and again surely, but they are out there somewhere and will instinctively sense your call and unconsciously send you energy to help you.

ENCHANTMENT SPELL:

From the past the truth revealed
The ancients will the future yield

This Spell in Arvyndase:

An tae log tae lodver sotosïn

Tae elanli yon tae lasel ped

Pronunciation:
Ane tay low-g tae load - veer so - toess - in
Tay e - lane - lie yone tae lay - seal peed

Chapter 106:

Ginkgo family

Keyword: **The Number 15**

Tree Group Name in Arvyndase: **Romydelpa** (pronounced: row - mid - eel - pah)

Arvyndase Name of the Wizard Myne: **Tynlasyn** (pronounced: tin - lace - in)

This tree and its magic:

Ginkgos have long been used in traditional Chinese medicine and there exist fossils of these trees dating back to 270 million years ago. It is sometimes reputed that their leaves help with brain function and memory. These are known to be enduring and tenacious trees, so much so, that six of these trees survived the atomic blast at Hiroshima, while all other trees and plants in the same area were

296 .... The Elfin Book of Trees for the Elven Druid

destroyed and while these Ginkgos were scorched, they revived, and, as of this writing, are still alive today.

Thus, it is that we Silver Elves relate these trees to the resilience of our elven culture and to the Wizard Myne Tynlasyn, which comes from the Arvyndase word for resilient. We also associate it with the number 15 that is a number signifying tenacity that leads to achievement and success.

Our elven culture has endured even though, in modern times, most people doubt that our ancient peoples ever really existed and that we are not really elves but merely fantasists. Well, we are fantasists, but we are also elves. We have been born again and again, picking up our culture as we have found it, lifetime after lifetime, enduring through the persecutions that our people have suffered, and rising again despite the fact that others think it their 'god given' right to ridicule and discount us out of hand, while most of these sceptics are those who believe in an invisible god based on faith or even those who believe in magic but find the idea of elfae folk somehow unacceptable.

What This Oracle Means:

Hang in there. The response to the question you put to the oracle is to endure. Don't give up. Keep trying. And if you seem to have failed, start again, from scratch if necessary. Pick up the pieces that are left and move on.

In the end, it is our culture that will be left standing, because our culture is linked to the reality of Nature and the unique manifestation of each person's being. We don't seek to pigeonhole reality and dumb everything down to simplistic terms and a black and white view of existence. We not only perceive the grays of life but the myriad spectrum of colors. We are the rainbow peoples and we accept all who accept and tolerate others.

Endure, beloved, be resilient. We are not done yet and, in fact, as ancient as we are, we are only just beginning.

ENCHANTMENT SPELL:
We'll endure and carry on
Long after you and yours are gone

This Spell in Arvyndase:
Eli'yon talos nar deca gos
Tiso låka le nar le'na da tasïn

Pronunciation:
E - lie'yone tay - lowce nair dee - cah goes-s
Tie - so lah - kay lee nair lee'nah dah tace - in

Chapter 107:

Cycad family

KEYWORD: **THE NUMBER 12**

TREE GROUP NAME IN ARVYNDASE: **SICÄDELPA** (PRONOUNCED: SIGH - CAD - EEL - PAH)

ARVYNDASE NAME OF THE WIZARD MYNE: **FRASÂDOR** (FRAY - SAH - DOOR)

THIS TREE AND ITS MAGIC:

The Cycas Angulata are a species of cycad that are native to Australia. The kernels of this Palm were consumed by aboriginal Australians for their high starch content and for the fact that these kernels ripen during the dry season, when nearly all other foods that were utilized by these hunter-gatherers were quite scarce. Alas, these kernels are quite toxic to mammals. However, realizing this, these ancient peoples leached the kernels with water and then baked the starch. In some cases, they fermented the kernels and then cooked them. However, in modern times we know these kernels contain carcinogens, and they are seldom eaten any more, even when using traditional methods of preparation.

These are the trees of innovation and the Wizard Myne Frasådor that comes from the Arvyndase word Frasådo that is our elven word for innovation. We must not only adapt to the times we live in, but we also need to innovate and alter what we do and how we do it to improve our abilities and techniques. It is not enough to merely accept the legends and lore of our ancient peoples. We must understand them in the light of current times and adapt them to make our life in this world and in the world of spirit ever more successful. These are the trees of the elven entrepreneur.

We also link these trees to the number 12, which is a number signifying completion. It denotes a cycle that has come full circle. However, once a cycle has been completed it is not enough to merely repeat it. We must tread the cycle again, but in a spiral, moving thus ever higher by doing what we do ever better.

WHAT THIS ORACLE MEANS:

Do it again. Do it better this time. Do it even better the next time, ever improving what you do and trying out and considering even better ways to do it. Some of these, perhaps most of these innovations may not work, but that in itself helps you improve your performance.

And it may happen that some things may work for a time, but still need to be changed and improved even more later. Just because it works doesn't mean it is the best way to do things. Constantly seek to refine your efforts and your activity. In this way, you get ever better.

Our elven culture does not need to be and, in fact, certainly shouldn't be forever defined by the past. We are the living embodiment of our culture and peoples and in bringing them alive in the modern world it is only natural that we should change things to make them better while continuing and retaining the essential principles of tolerance and individuality that help define who we are as a people.

ENCHANTMENT SPELL:
Every day in every way
I make it better and better

This Spell in Arvyndase:
Lotym lea ver lotym yer
El kord ter rilfa nar rilfa

Pronunciation:
Low - tim lee - ah veer low - tim year
Eel cord tier rile - fah nair rile - fah

Chapter 108:

Zamia family

KEYWORD: THE NUMBER 70

TREE GROUP NAME IN ARVYNDASE: **ZAMEÅELPA**
(PRONOUNCED: ZAY - ME - AH - EEL - PAH)

ARVYNDASE NAME OF THE WIZARD MYNE: **IPUWAR**
(PRONOUNCED: EYE - PEW - WEAR)

THIS TREE AND ITS MAGIC:

The Zamiaceae are cycads that on the surface seem to be Palm or Fern-like. They can be found in the tropical and subtropical regions of Australia, Africa, and North and South America. The roots of these tree plants form secondary roots, so their roots have roots.

Generally, when we think of the elven and elfae peoples, or any peoples for the matter, or Life itself or Creation, we think of it all coming from one source, despite the fact that we, each of us had two parents, four grandparents, eight great grandparents and so on, and if we mate, we will unite with another, forming more individuals. Perhaps we might consider that elves and Elfin, don't come from one source, but have more than one root, deeper and farther back than we realize. Certainly, as a people we continue to diversify, becoming ever more individual and unique, forming more and more tribes, clans and types of elfin and elfae born not of one source but many.

Therefore, we Silver Elves relate these tree beings to the Wizard Myne Ipuwar that is related to the Arvyndase words Ipuwa (eye - pew - wah) tolerate and Ipuwara (eye - pew - waer - rah) tolerance. If we are to continue as one people, we must be very tolerant and accepting of each other and our differences. We are many, and we came from many and we continue on as many, one in our tolerance for our individual and unique natures.

WHAT THIS ORACLE MEANS:

Be tolerant. Accept and foster others individuality and diversity. If we seek to define Elfin and what it means to be elfae too tightly, with too many restrictions, we will end up strangling and destroying what by Nature is meant to be free and ever evolving.

So, too, in this situation, see all the alternatives that you can. It is quite feasible things can work out to everyone's advantage. You can get what you want by helping others get what they want. This is not necessarily a zero-sum game. Consider all the win-win possibilities and move toward those.

And, however far you look back into this situation, the roots go deeper still. That is just the way it is. At some point, however, we all must accept, if we are wise, that all this has happened for a reason, that even if it all came about randomly that there is still an inherent destiny that draws us toward it, to the realization of our perfection as unique and special beings, each of us, shining beneath the light of the elven stars.

ENCHANTMENT SPELL:
I accept that you are free
To be yours'elf as I am me

This Spell in Arvyndase:
El tolo dij le da alo
Va te le'naeln tat El da el

Pronunciation:
Eel toe - low dye-j lee dah a - low
Vah tea lee'nah - eel-n tate Eel dah eel

Chapter 109:

Fern trees

Keyword: **The Number 50**

Tree Name in Arvyndase: **Ziltars** (pronounced: zile - tayrs)

Arvyndase Name of the Wizard Myne: **Mamera** (pronounced: may - mere - rah)

This Tree and Its Magic:

First, we love Ferns. There is just something magical, elfin and faerie-like about Ferns. Some Ferns grow so tall that they are called Fern trees. So it is that even the smallest person can have or develop great power in Elfin and Faerie. Size is not as important, or even social status, wealth, or any other outer means of judging a person, as the potency of their spirit and the depth of their soul. Therefore, we Silver Elves connect these Fern trees to the Wizard Myne Mamera that is derived from the Arvyndase word Mamer (may - mere) that is our elven word for potent, which is also the root word, in our elven language for mamervar (may - mere - vair) or potential, the inner potential for perfection that exists in all beings.

In Elfin, everyone has equal potential and opportunity to develop thems'elves as unique and powerful elfin beings. We are all individual and eccentric expressions of the Divine Magic that lives in potential in each and every one of us. And, as such, we are each and every one specially designed to perfect ours'elves in the light and radiance of Elfin.

We further connect these trees to the number fifty whose vibration urges each of us to become the best that we can be.

What This Oracle Means:

It doesn't matter how great or small you may seem to be in the world, you have the potential to become a great elfin wizard, witch, magician, magic wielder. A diamond may be small but if perfected it can be far more valuable than much larger gems and is harder than nearly anything. Size isn't everything.

Act with confidence. Whatever this situation or its challenges, you can master it with your magic. You are an elfae of some sort, after all, and magic is what you do. Relax yours'elf. Draw in your power and potency, and then, like a Fern leaf, let it unfold into the world, subtly transforming the circumstances you are encountering. Use the spell below and chant it into the ethers and let your magic do its work.

Enchantment Spell:

Fragile like a Fern I seem
But great the magic that I beam

This Spell in Arvyndase:
Anza sylar na Fril El kacer
Kana ralt tae êldon dij El dryn

Pronunciation:
Ane - zah sill - lair nah fry-l Eel kay - sir
Kay - nah rail-t tay l - doan dye'j Eel drin

Chapter 110:

Kusamaki

KEYWORD: **THE NUMBER 80**

TREE NAME IN ARVYNDASE: **KOYÅALDA** (PRONOUNCED: CO - YAH - ALE - DAH)

ARVYNDASE NAME OF THE WIZARD MYNE: **ZELTAR** (ZEAL - TAIR)

THIS TREE AND ITS MAGIC:

These trees are living fossils, once thought to have gone extinct but still existent in the world. They are sometimes called the Koyamaki or Japanese Umbrella Pines, and are conifer trees that are in a category all their own and are endemic to Japan. The fossil record puts them back to at least 230 million years. Its genus name Sciadopitys comes from the Greek prefix sciado- that

means shadow and the word pitys, indicating pine, with an addition of the name verticillata that indicates it has whirls. Thus, we Silver Elves call them the Whirling Shadow Pines.

They are seen as being one of the five sacred trees of Japan and it is thought that in the Kyoto area about a thousand or more years ago, these trees may have been honored or worshiped as part of Shinto belief, and later absorbed into Buddhist religious life in that area, often being located around temples that were converted to Buddhist practice.

We Silver Elves link these trees to the Wizard Myne Zeltar that is formed from the Arvyndase words zel, which means awe and the word tar, which means rod, thus the Awe Rod or the Rod or Wand of Awe, a great tool of magic.

Awe is often used with a positive connotation these days but originally it meant to evoke fear and trembling in one, as the word awful suggests. We also associate it with the number 80 and the introduction of the Divine into one's life with unexpected consequences but with eventual benefits to one's soul and spirit.

WHAT THIS ORACLE MEANS:

You can probably sense the swirling shadows and don't know whether this means rescue or destruction for you. Have your umbrella of protection ready and be as prepared as you can be under the circumstances, but don't try to interfere. There are ancient and powerful forces behind things and it would be best if you can be patient and just wait and see what really happens. It could turn out to be awful or it could be quite awesome. All that you know at this point is that you can feel it approaching in the shadows arousing your preternatural senses and setting your skin to tingling, giving you goosebumps and making your hair stand on edge.

However, sometimes those things that seemed disadvantageous at first, ultimately turn out to our advantage. Don't prejudge and don't get paranoid. Bide your time and wait for reality to reveal itself and in this case, a bit of faith in your own destiny and the benevolent nature of the Shining Ones would not be altogether amiss.

ENCHANTMENT SPELL:

I sense it in the darkness
Beyond the edge of what is known
I'll wait with steady purpose
As the truth of it is shown

This Spell in Arvyndase:

El faládar ter ver tae dastu

Hyrlon tae vag u wu da kenïn
El'yon ena virba ason
Tat tae lodver u ter da tekeïn

Pronunciation:
Eel fay - lah - dare tier veer tay dace - two
Her - lone tay vague u woo dah keen - in
Eel'yone e - nah vie-r - bah a - sewn
Tate tay load - veer you tier dah tea - key - in

Chapter 111:

Wattieza, fossil tree, the earliest known tree

KEYWORD: **THE NUMBER 14**

TREE NAME IN ARVYNDASE: **DORELDÅALDA** (PRONOUNCED: DOOR - EEL - DAH - ALE - DAH)

ARVYNDASE NAME OF THE WIZARD MYNE: **MYLIAR** (PRONOUNCED: MILL - LIE - AIR)

The Silver Elves.... 307

THIS TREE AND ITS MAGIC:

Wattieza fossils represent what are thought to have been the earliest trees known to have existed. They lived in the mid-Devonian period and are theorized to be related to modern ferns (plants not trees) and horsetails. More than likely they were Ferns or Fern-like plants that simply kept growing and developed into trees. They no longer exist, except in fossilized form, and in whatever transformed state their essential energy and spirit evolved into being in the modern world. This is to say, in the Eternal Now, for they may have become other types of trees, just as man is said to have evolved from the apes; or they may have evolved into the higher dimensions of manifestation. They may very well be the trees that shine and radiate in Elfin and Faerie shedding their light upon the Shining Ones and glowing upon we Fair Folk in those other realms and dimensions.

We Silver Elves connect these trees with the Wizard Myne Myliar that comes from the Arvyndase word Mylia, which is our elven word for memory. We also link it with the number 14 that represents our eternal love for and kindreth to Elfin. Many elves speak of memories they have of their past lives, often incarnations where they were kings or queens or were important in some way and this is all good and well, but those memories are fossils really. Tree fossils are the form of the tree, or their past, turned into stone by having become mineralized while the essence, the true energy of their being has moved on. Fossils are but statues of the past.

It is good to know and remember the past, but Elfin is an eternal realm, a Living Realm that is ever growing and changing. There is some benefit in sensing the past but it is more important to develop ours'elves and our powers in the Eternal Present. Living Elfin Now in our lives and seeing it all about us brought into manifestation by our own beings.

WHAT THIS ORACLE MEANS:

It can be important to know the past, remember the past, but you don't want the past to control you. Let its lessons make you stronger but don't allow your experiences to limit you and hold you down.

It is here at the end that we come to the beginning, for every ending really is the start of something new and that which once was passes on to other things, endlessly. Therefore, see your life and the present in terms of the destiny that is unfolding through you from the past toward the future that, like perfection itself, we are ever approaching and never completely obtaining. Still, it is the effort that counts, then, now and evermore.

Enchantment Spell:

From there to here and farther still
The Future yields to my bright will

This Spell in Arvyndase:

An norn va jän nar ulifa vila
Tae Lasel pedlu va el'na ilu yon

Pronunciation:

Ane norn vah jan nair you - lie - fah vie - lah
Tay Lay - seal peed - lou vah eel'nah eye - lou yone

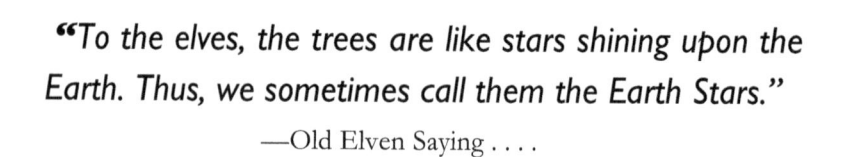

> "To the elves, the trees are like stars shining upon the Earth. Thus, we sometimes call them the Earth Stars."
>
> —Old Elven Saying . . . .

About the Authors

The Silver Elves, Zardoa and Silver Flame, are a family of elves who have been living and sharing the Elven Way since 1975. They are the authors of 50 books on magic and enchantment and the Elven Way, available on Amazon internationally, and your local bookstore, including:

The Book of Elven Runes: A Passage Into Faerie;

The Magical Elven Love Letters, volumes 1, 2, and 3;

An Elfin Book of Spirits: Evoking the Beneficent Powers of Faerie;

Caressed by an Elfin Breeze: The Poems of Zardoa Silverstar;

Eldafaryn: True Tales of Magic from the Lives of the Silver Elves;

Arvyndase (Silverspeech): A Short Course in the Magical Language of the Silver Elves;

The Elven Book of Dreams: A Magical Oracle of Faerie;

The Book of Elven Magick: The Philosophy and Enchantments of the Seelie Elves, Volume 1 & 2;

What An Elf Would Do: A Magical Guide to the Manners and Etiquette of the Faerie Folk;

The Elven Tree of Life Eternal: A Magical Quest for One's True S'Elf;

Magic Talks: On Being a Correspondence Between the Silver Elves and the Elf Queen's Daughters;

Sorcerers' Dialogues: A Further Correspondence Between the Silver Elves and the Founders of the Elf Queen's Daughters;

Discourses on High Sorcery: More Correspondence Between the Silver Elves and the Founders of the Elf Queen's Daughters;

Ruminations on Necromancy: Continuing Correspondence Between the Silver Elves and the Founders of the Elf Queen's Daughter;

The Elven Way: The Magical Path of the Shining Ones;

Through the Mists of Faerie: A Magical Guide to the Wisdome Teachings of the Ancient Elven;

The Book of Elf Names: 5,600 Elven Names to Use for Magic, Game Playing, Inspiration, Naming One's Self and One's Child, and as Words in the Elven Language of the Silver Elves;

Elven Silver: The Irreverent Faery Tales of Zardoa Silverstar;

An Elven Book of Ryhmes: Book Two of the Magical Poems of Zardoa Silverstar;

The Voice of Faerie: Making Any Tarot Deck Into an Elven Oracle;

Liber Aelph: Words of Guidance from the Silver Elves to our Magical Children;

The Shining Ones: The Elfin Spirits That Guide You According to Your Birth Date and the Evolutionary Lessons They Offer;

Living the Personal Myth: Making the Magic of Faerie Real in One's Own Personal Life;

Elf Magic Mail, The Original Letters of the Elf Queen's Daughters with Comentary by the Silver Elves, Book 1 and 2;

The Elves of Lyndarys: A Magical Tale of Modern Faerie Folk;

The Elf Folk's Book of Cookery: Recipes For a Delighted Tongue, a Healthy Body and a Magical Life;

Faerie Unfolding: The Cosmic Expression of the Divine Magic;

The Elements of Elven Magic: A New View of Calling the Elementals Based Upon the Periodic Table of Elements;

The Keys to Elfin Enchantment: Mastery of the Faerie Light Through the Portals of Manifestation;

Elf Quotes: A Collection of Over 1000 Ancient Elven Sayings and Wise Elfin Koans by The Silver Elves About Magic and The Elven Way;

The United States of Elfin Imagining A More Elven Style of Government;

Elven Geomancy: An Ancient Oracle of the Elfin Peoples for Divination and Spell Casting;

Creating Miracles In the Modern World: The Way Of the Elfin Thaumaturge;

The Magical Realms of Elfin: Answers to Questions About Being an Elf and Following the Elven Path, Volume 1;

Manifesting Elfin: Answers to Questions About Being an Elf and Following the Elven Path, Volume 2;

Elven Psychology: Understanding the Elfin Psyche and the Evolutionary and Esoteric Purpose of Mental Disorders;

The Elves Say: A Collection of Over 1000 Ancient Elven Sayings and Wise Elfin Koans by The Silver Elves About Magic and The Elven Way, Volume 2;

The Complete Dictionary of Arvyndase: The Elven Language of The Silver Elves;

Sticks and Stones, Feathers, Charms and Bones: An Original Oracle of the Elfin Peoples of the Ancient Future;

Elf Tribes: The Silver Elves' Guide for Finding Your Magical Kind and Kin; and it's companion book

Faerie, Fae and Otherkin: The Silver Elves' Guide for Finding Your Magical Kind and Kin; and

Elven Hedgewitchery and Found Magic: Using Art-Making for Evoking Elfin Magic and Living the Elven Way.

The Silver Elves have had various articles published in *Circle Network News Magazine* since 1986 and have given out over 6,000 elven names to interested individuals in the Arvyndase language, with each elf name having a unique meaning specifically for that person. They are also interviewed and mentioned numerous times in *Not In Kansas Anymore* by Christine Wicker (Harper San Francisco, 2005) and in *A Field Guide to Otherkin* by Lupa (Megalithica Books, 2007), and are discussed in Nikolay Lyapanenko's recent book *The Elves From Ancient Times To Our Days: The Magical Heritage of "Starry People" and their Continuation Into the Modern World* (2017) that gives a detailed account of their involvement in the Elven Movement since 1975. Also, an interview with The Silver Elves is included in Emily Carding's recent popular book *Faery Craft* (Llewellyn Publications, 2012). The Silver Elves understand the world as a magical or miraculous phenomena, and that all beings, by pursuing their own true path, will become whomever they truly desire to be.

You are welcome to explore The Silver Elves' website at http://silverelves.angelfire.com, visit their blog site at https://thesilverelves.blogspot.com on the Elven Way and also their blog site on Elven Lifestyle, Magic and Enchantment at https://silverelves.wordpress.com, and join them on Facebook with the names as "Michael J. Love (Zardoa of The SilverElves)" and "Martha Char Love (SilverFlame of The SilverElves)."

The Silver Elves also invite you to come join them in some of their elven and magical otherkin Facebook groups where you will find the elven-faerie-fae otherkin community interacting and sharing the Elven Way:

The Magical Books of the Silver Elves —
https://www.facebook.com/groups/539205916250397 — And if you would like to find out more about our Silver Elves books on The Elven Way, please do join us! We have discussions about our Silver Elves books as well as about Elven and Otherkin philosophy, elven lifestyle and the Elven Way and everything Elfin. If you have read our books and would like to discuss them with us, this is the place to come join in the discussions and share with us your reesponses.

Elf Witches of the Mystic Moon —
https://www.facebook.com/groups/806583242768352

The Elven Way and Friends —
https://www.facebook.com/groups/165938637423212 —A group for all our elven kin and friends to gather and share in discussions about The Elven Way and elvish life.

Elven Life and Magic
https://www.facebook.com/groups/629491797123886

Elvish Magical Chat —
https://www.facebook.com/groups/307775362744491

314 . . . . The Elfin Book of Trees for the Elven Druid

The Faerie Circle —
https://www.facebook.com/groups/1025483294180077

Faerie Craft —
https://www.facebook.com/groups/395403367195312 — This is a group to share and advertise your elven and fae artistic creations.

I Heart Elven Magic —
https://www.facebook.com/groups/2215672296

United Otherkin Alliance —
https://www.facebook.com/groups/328253710566869 This is an alliance for Otherkin/ Therians, where elves, faeries, dragons, kitsune, gnomes, hobbits, merkin, pixies, brownies, nymphs, driads, niaids, valkyrie, vampires, devas, fauns, unicorns, animal kin and all manner of Faerie Folk gather and come together! This group is open to anyone who wishes to be part of a congenial group of Otherkin.

Feasting With the Elves (come join us, we are just having some fun sharing elven recipes and healthy eating) — https://www.facebook.com/groups/597948240617006

Devayana: Buddhism, Vedic, & Asian Spirituality for Elves and Fae
https://www.facebook.com/groups/devayana
Nature & the Unseen Realms with the Elves & otherkin. A spiritual journey — https://www.facebook.com/groups/196916350335537

Have you always wanted to hear elves speak in Arvyndase, the magical language of The Silver Elves? Come listen! The Silver Elves just published their first You Tube video in their new The Silver Elves channel. And they would love it if you would please subscribe, like and comment! **https://youtu.be/unUkxT9QbNE**

Group 1 of the Wizard Myne:
Letters used in Arvyndase

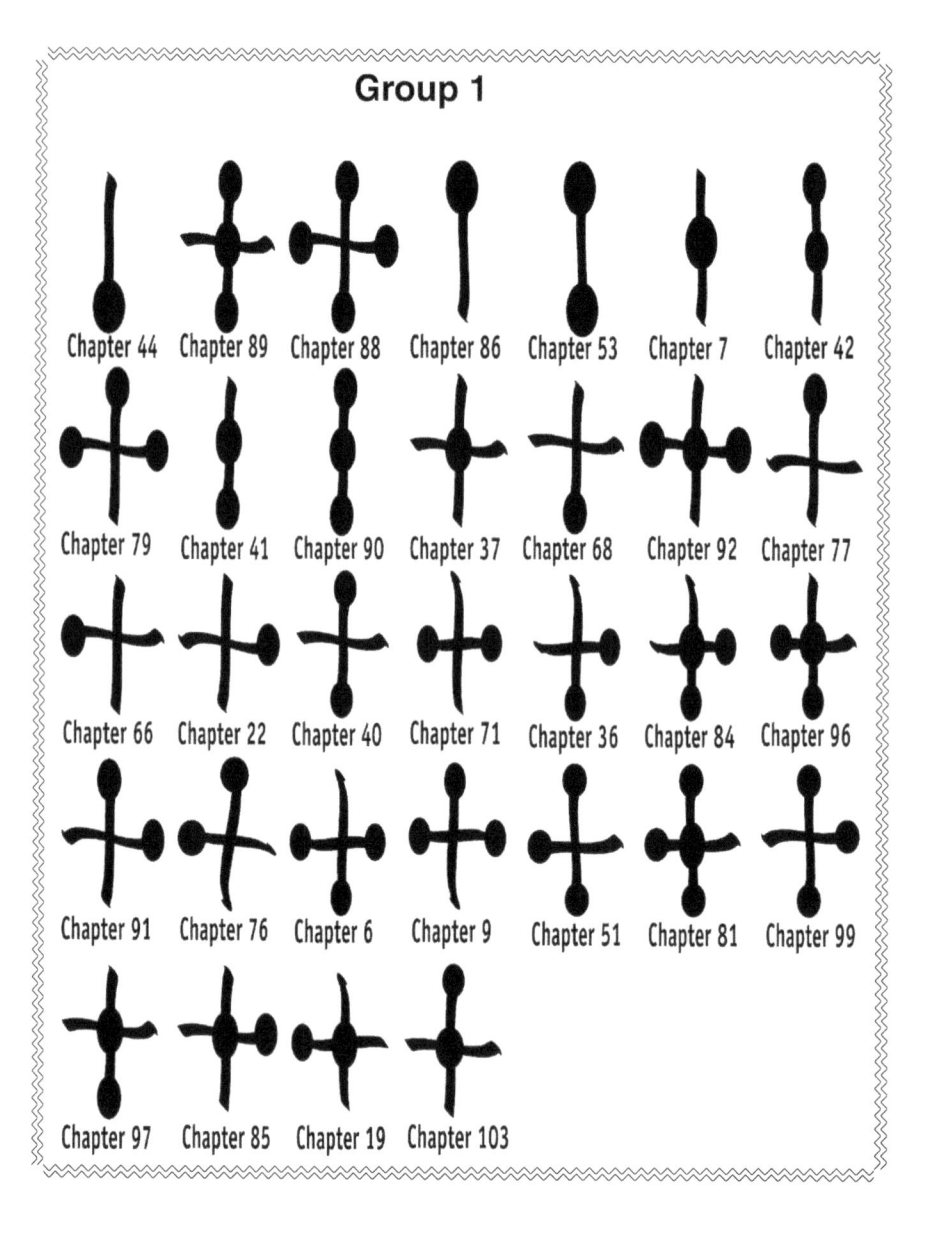

Group 1

Chapter 44	Chapter 89	Chapter 88	Chapter 86	Chapter 53	Chapter 7	Chapter 42	
Chapter 79	Chapter 41	Chapter 90	Chapter 37	Chapter 68	Chapter 92	Chapter 77	
Chapter 66	Chapter 22	Chapter 40	Chapter 71	Chapter 36	Chapter 84	Chapter 96	
Chapter 91	Chapter 76	Chapter 6	Chapter 9	Chapter 51	Chapter 81	Chapter 99	
Chapter 97	Chapter 85	Chapter 19	Chapter 103				

Group 2 of the Wizard Myne: Numbers

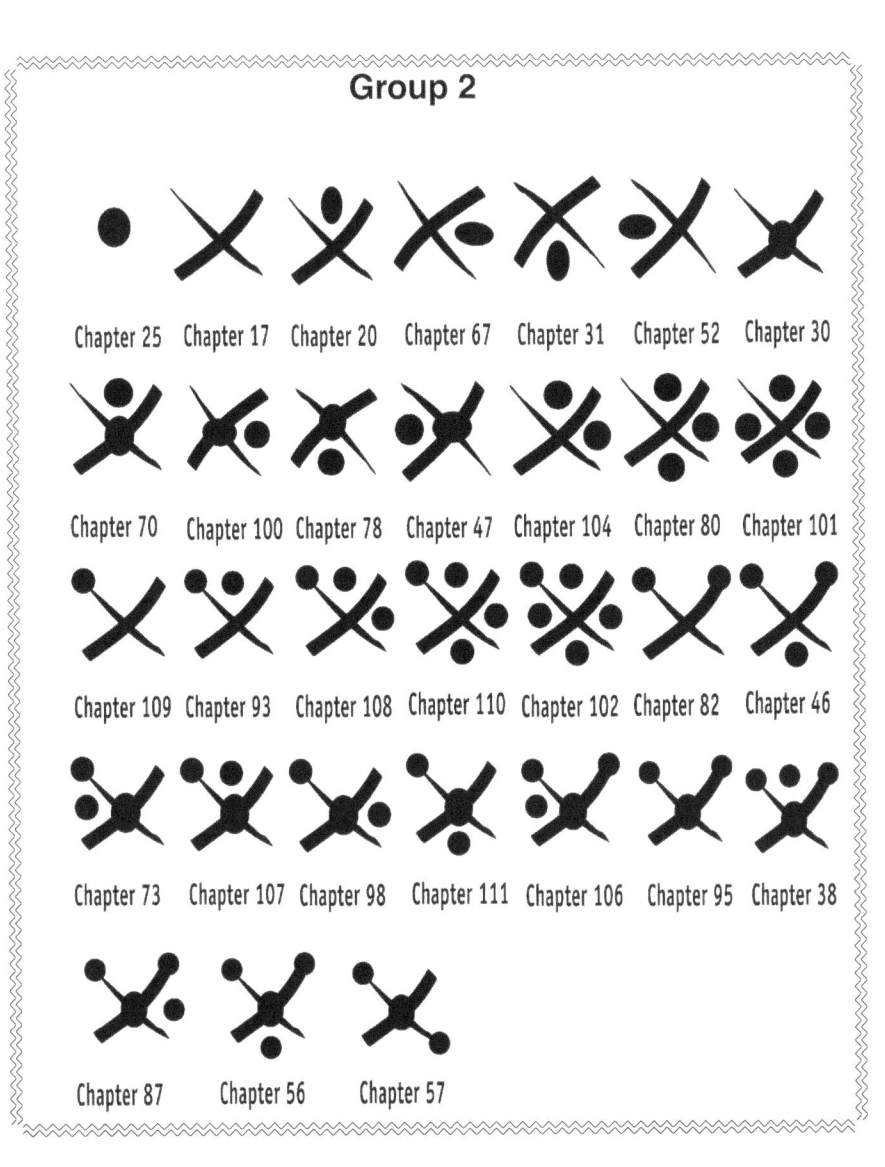

Group 2

Chapter 25	Chapter 17	Chapter 20	Chapter 67	Chapter 31	Chapter 52	Chapter 30
Chapter 70	Chapter 100	Chapter 78	Chapter 47	Chapter 104	Chapter 80	Chapter 101
Chapter 109	Chapter 93	Chapter 108	Chapter 110	Chapter 102	Chapter 82	Chapter 46
Chapter 73	Chapter 107	Chapter 98	Chapter 111	Chapter 106	Chapter 95	Chapter 38
Chapter 87	Chapter 56	Chapter 57				

Group 3 of the Wizard Myne:
Elfae Types

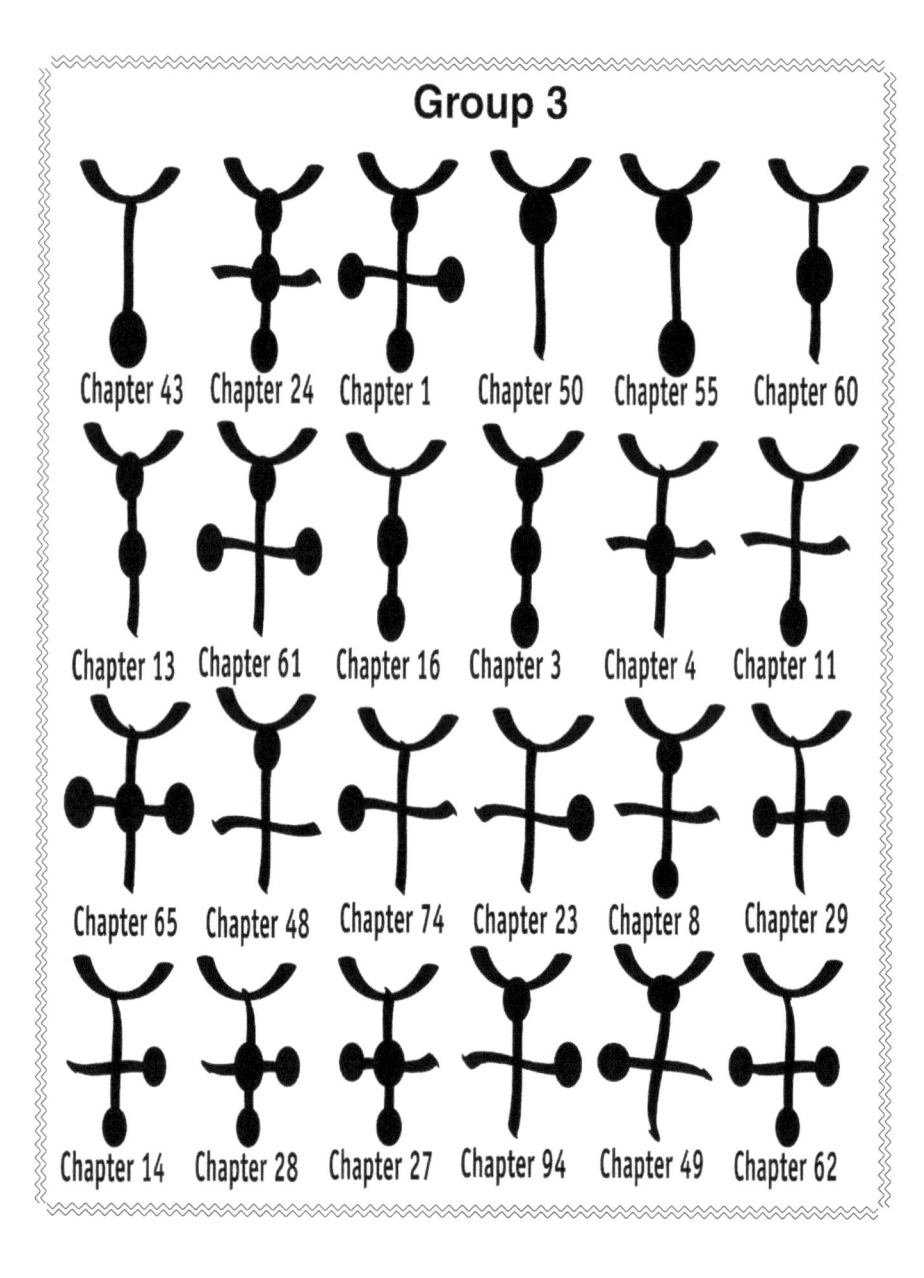

Group 3

Chapter 43	Chapter 24	Chapter 1	Chapter 50	Chapter 55	Chapter 60
Chapter 13	Chapter 61	Chapter 16	Chapter 3	Chapter 4	Chapter 11
Chapter 65	Chapter 48	Chapter 74	Chapter 23	Chapter 8	Chapter 29
Chapter 14	Chapter 28	Chapter 27	Chapter 94	Chapter 49	Chapter 62

Group 4 of the Wizard Myne: Miscelaneous Magics

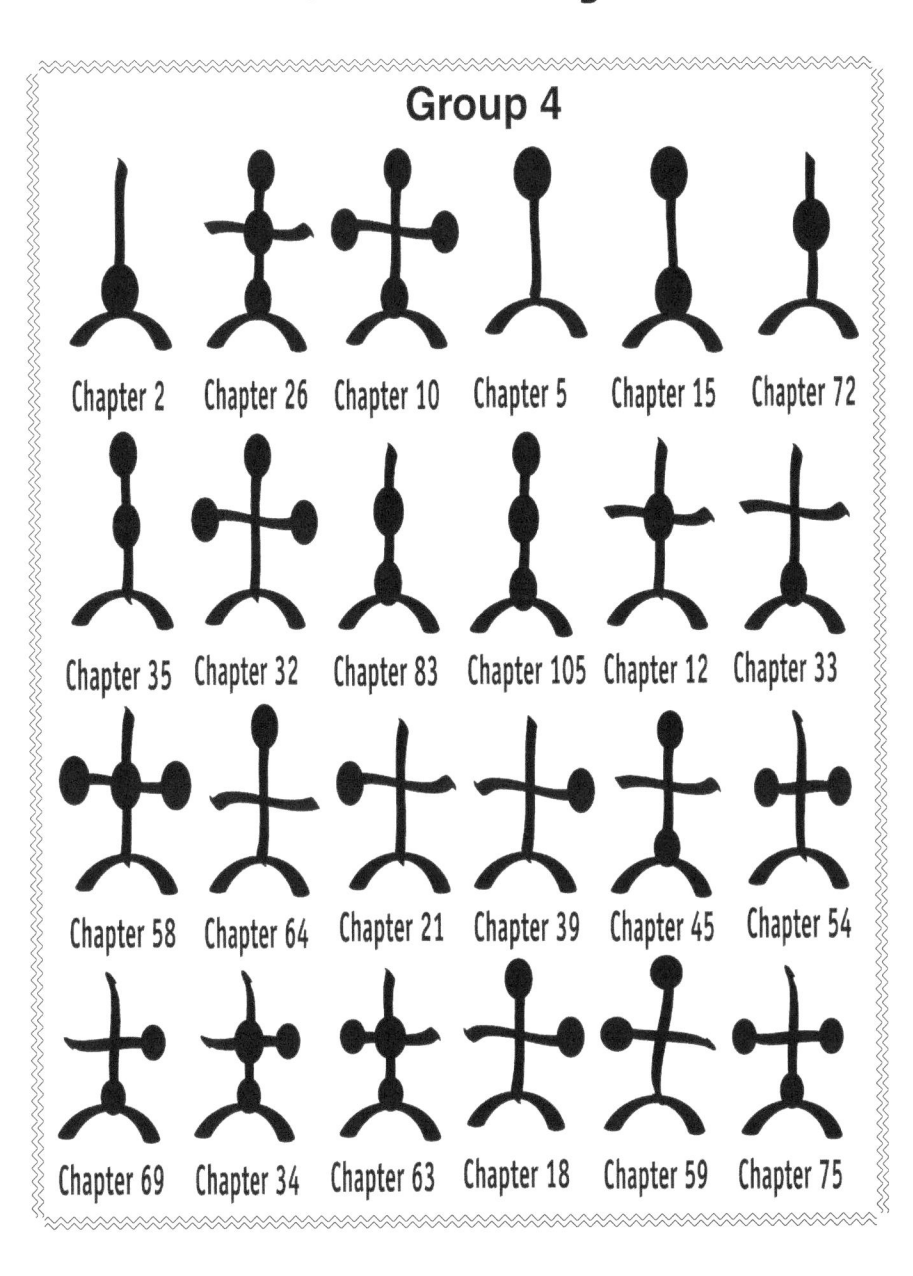

Group 4

Chapter 2	Chapter 26	Chapter 10	Chapter 5	Chapter 15	Chapter 72
Chapter 35	Chapter 32	Chapter 83	Chapter 105	Chapter 12	Chapter 33
Chapter 58	Chapter 64	Chapter 21	Chapter 39	Chapter 45	Chapter 54
Chapter 69	Chapter 34	Chapter 63	Chapter 18	Chapter 59	Chapter 75

"The woodland elves say that every leaf tells a story and every tree reveals the secrets of the Universe."
—The Silver Elves